THE FIRST PALESTINIAN INTIFADA REVISITED

ANDREW RIGBY

THE FIRST PALESTINIAN INTIFADA REVISITED

ANDREW RIGBY

IRENE PUBLISHING
Ω

Published 2015 by Irene Publishing
Sparsnäs 1010,
66891 Ed,
Sweden
www.irenepublishing.com
irene.publishing@gmail.com

This book is a revised and updated version of
Living the Intifada, published by Zed Books Ltd 1991

Cover design: J.Johansen
Image on front: Embassy of Palestine
Layout: Majken Jul Sørensen

ISBN 978-91-88061-05-8

e

Acknowledgements

The first edition of this book was published in 1991. At that time I recorded my thanks to all those people who had contributed in so many different ways to the process of researching and writing the study. Many of them displayed an amazing degree of trust and honesty as they responded to my questions and queries about all the different dimensions of the unarmed resistance that was at the heart of the first intifada.

In this second revised edition of the work I think it is important to record once again the debt I owed to so many people, without whose friendship and cooperation the work could not have been completed. So, once again I would like to thank in particular the following people: Kainat, Shareen and Sumer Abdul Hadi, Nayef and Naheel Abu-Khalaf, Abu Nadir, Dr Mamdouh al-Aker, Fayez Abu Rahmeh, Khalid Al-Qidreh, Sahar Al Malki, Nafez Assaily, Mubarak Awad, Dr Hisham Awartani and his family, Nadia Bilbassy, Antonia Caccia, Howard Clark, Margaret Dalgety, Dr Uri Davis, Dr Saeb Erekat, Khamis Afiz Eltwok, Dr Gordon Feldman, Amos Gvirtz, Dr Manual Hassassian, Hani Husseini, Joost Hiltermann, John Horton, Deena Hurvitz, Dr Jad Isaac, Mahmoud Hamdi El Jammali, Ali Jiddah, Dr Edy Kaufman, Adam Keller, Khalil Mahshi, Dr Ruchama Marton, Chris McConville and the staff at the British Council in East Jerusalem, Tikva Pamas, Alex Pollock, Roland Rance, Michael Randle, Charles Richards, Mohammed Salahat, Mayson Samor, Ibrahim Shaban, Alya Shawa, Randa Siniora-Atallah, and - of course - Thoma Schik, to whom I owe a special debt of gratitude along with Marwan Oarweish. Emma and Sean Rigby helped out on occasions. My partner, Carol Rank, was a key source of support and encouragement in addition to being a critical proof-reader.! would also like to acknowledge the financial assistance of the Barrow and Geraldine S Cadbury Trust and the Joseph Rowntree Charitable Trust. Finally I want to acknowledge my indebtedness to Dr Mahdi Abdul Hadi, without his support and encouragement, generosity and friendship, this research could never have been completed.

PREFACE

Twenty five years ago, in January 1990, a series of events were held in Jerusalem under the title of '1990 – Time for Peace' Below is the fragment of the bib I wore at one of the main events – the circling of the Old City walls of Jerusalem by Palestinian, Israeli and international peace activists. Looking at the photos now brings back the memories of what was then a time of hope as we looked forward to '1990 – Time for Peace'.

Unfortunately, in the months that followed the vitality of the Intifada started to fade, and by the end of the year the unarmed popular uprising was effectively over. By then I had completed my analysis of the Uprising as viewed through the lens of civilian-based resistance. It was published in 1991 under the title *Living the Intifada.*

Over the intervening years I have maintained my engagement with the Israeli-Palestinian conflict and nonviolent initiatives for some kind of peace and an end to the occupation. I wish I could claim that the research and study I have done around this conflict since that time has been a source of hope and optimism for peace in the Middle East – but I cannot. It has been a time of false hopes and disappointment. One of my dear friends, a Palestinian who I have known since the 1980s, used to amaze me with his optimism. I remember one evening during the Intifada we sat around discussing whether or not there would be prisons in the new Palestinian state that we both anticipated seeing come into existence. How naïve we were in those days of hope. Over 20 years later I was in conversation with a Palestinian coordinator of a network of non-governmental organisations and talk turned to my old friend. 'He used to be the most optimistic of people, but now he can only display his optimism out of a sense of political duty and obligation', I was told. Like others the sense of anticipation for a brighter future was no longer there, but as a public figure he had to work to produce a semblance of such positive emotion.

So, twenty five years on it seems an appropriate time to revisit the first Intifada, to remind ourselves of just how significant the Uprising was during those heady days of 1988-89 when there seemed to be genuine grounds for anticipating a break-through in the struggle to end the occupation and achieve freedom for the Palestinians in the West Bank and Gaza Strip, and help the Israelis liberate themselves from their role as occupiers and oppressors of another people.

I decided to leave the case study pretty much as it was. I have sub-edited the whole text and added a new chapter on the history of Palestinian unarmed resistance against occupation prior to the Intifada. In addition I have added a new postscript that explores the Palestinian narrative as it unfolded after the first Intifada, concluding with an analysis of the re-emergence of popular unarmed resistance which was occasioned by the construction of the Separation Wall which commenced in 2002.

Andrew Rigby

February 2015

1
THE HISTORICAL BACKGROUND

The outbreak of the Intifada took everyone by surprise. Yet it did not just happen. With the benefit of hindsight, it is possible to see the Uprising as a stage in the evolution and development of the Palestinian nationalist movement, one which can be understood as emerging out of the frustrations of the population in the occupied territories of the West Bank and Gaza Strip. The frustration and resentment that became the motor force behind the revolt were not just with the occupation itself, but also with the PLO and with the outside Arab world. In this regard there was a certain continuity between the factors that brought the Uprising about, and also contributed to its weaknesses, and earlier phases of resistance that characterised the history of the Palestinian national struggle during the decades prior to the outbreak of the Intifada. The aim of this chapter is to present a brief overview of this history – a history of a subject people whose attempts to achieve the full rights of citizenship were repeatedly thwarted by occupying powers and by their own internal conflicts, divisions and weaknesses.

Resistance to early waves of Zionist immigration

In the latter decades of the 19th century Zionist migration to Palestine began. The purchase of land from Arab landowners caused resentment amongst Palestinian peasants whose livelihood was threatened by the land acquisitions. So, by the end of the century a pattern of resistance had emerged of peasants clashing with the newcomers, whilst the Palestinian elite submitted petitions to the Ottoman authorities calling for action against the influx. In 1910 there was the first call for an Arab boycott of Jewish produce and businesses. The Palestinian historian A. S. Kayyali described the situation just prior to the collapse of Ottoman rule in 1917 and the establishment of British military control over the territory of Palestine in 1917.

> … within the ranks of the nationalist movement in Palestine, the notables performed the role of the diplomats; the educated middle classes that of the articulators of public opinion; and the peasants that of the actual fighters in the battle against the Zionist presence.[1]

Resistance during the 1920s

When news of the Balfour Declaration reached the Palestinians it led to a new awareness of the need to organise. A Muslim-Christian Association (MCA) was established as a counter to Jewish organisations, with branches around the country alongside new youth clubs and other organisations. A day of protest was organised to mark the first anniversary of the Declaration, but in February 1920 the British committed to implementing the Balfour Declaration. This provoked a wave of protest demonstrations, with businesses closing down and protest petitions handed in to the authorities by representatives of the various MCAs.[2] Porath noted,

> The organisation of these demonstrations revealed the degree to which the nationalist associations in Palestine had advanced. For the first time they showed an ability to organise a coordinated action on a nation-wide scale in which all the associations took part. The almost identical language of the protest notes strengthens this impression.[3]

A few weeks later the protests erupted again, and this time spilled over into violence, with attacks on Jewish passers-bye and stores, and open threats to use force as a means of preventing the realisation of the Zionist project.[4] The clashes reached their height early April 1920 – after four days of disturbances the toll was four Arabs and five Jews dead, 22 seriously wounded (including 18 Jewish victims) and 193 Jews slightly wounded.[5]

It was during this period that the weak and divided nature of the Palestinian political leadership became increasingly apparent. A younger and more dynamic strata of leadership was beginning to emerge, mainly middle-class professionals from the ranks of the Palestinian notable families. But their effectiveness was undermined by the rivalry that characterised the relationships between two of the Palestinian notable families, the Husseinis and the Nashashibis – a conflict that was to mark Palestinian politics throughout the British Mandate period.[6] The division permeated its way through the Palestinian social structure, insofar as each of the families could lay claim to the loyalty and the fealty of families and clans in the rural hinterland, on behalf of whom they had acted as patrons in representing their interests to the Ottoman authorities.

Examining the resistance during the first decade of British civilian rule in Palestine a number of features become apparent.

1. *Frequent clashes between peasantry and Jewish settlers*

For the peasantry who experienced eviction through Jewish land purchases, the immediate response was anger and resentment that could lead to clashes with those directly responsible for their dispossession. But these were localised for, as Rosemary Sayigh has explained, 'From time immemorial Palestinian peasants had found solutions to their problems in village-based collective action.'[7]

2. Lack of national leadership

The particularistic and localised world-view of the peasantry was one reason a national movement of resistance did not develop, but another cause was the dominant social and political elite within Palestinian society had no experience of leading large-scale political movements. In the words of Sayigh, 'Not only did the indigenous ruling class have no experience of mass leadership, but the individual notable would never attempt such a course since it would only jeopardise his access to government, and it was on this access that his influence and status depended.'[8]

3. Elite's commitment to negotiation

Throughout the Mandate period the main impulse of the Palestinian political elite was to continue their traditional role as interlocutors - representing their clients who owed them allegiance to the authorities. They were most at home as members of delegations to the British or the League of Nations, demanding the revocation of the Balfour Declaration and an end to Jewish migration and the establishment of representative self-government in Palestine.

4. Symbolic and polemical resistance

Regular items in the press urged people to oppose the Zionist project. Imams spread the message at Friday prayers in the mosques. Strike days were observed to mark the anniversary of the Balfour Declaration and commemorate other days of national historical significance.

5. From offensive resistance to violence

From time to time the political leadership would try to mobilise people for protest marches and demonstrations, usually as part of an effort to strengthen their hand in an upcoming round of negotiations with the British. However, large scale demonstrations would often spill over into violence, as happened in May 1921 when clashes that began in Jaffa spread to other parts of the country. After several days order was restored, leaving 48 Arabs and 47 Jews dead, and over 200 from both communities wounded.

6. *Accommodation to occupation*

There were no significant outbreaks of violence between 1922 and 1928. One reason for this relative calm was the decline in Jewish migration during this period. The second reason, according to Kayyali, was 'the over-riding predominance of factionalism, the ascendancy of personal rivalries and self-interest among the Palestinian political nobility' as the Husseinis and the Nashashibis fought for control of the SMC.[9] Moreover, as Porath noted:

> When at the end of 1923 it became clear to everyone that the political effort to effect a change in the pro-Zionist policy of the British government had failed, the reaction of many Palestinians was one of disappointment, despair, and sometimes a search for ways to get some good out of the situation by a policy of cooperation with the authorities. … . In this fashion Zionism gained seven years of undisturbed activity in Palestine, in the course of which it succeeded in nearly doubling the size of the Jewish *yishuv* and in enlarging the area of its map of settlement.[10]

7. *Religion as a driver of resistance*

The calm of those years was superficial, nothing had changed in terms of the basic dynamics and it did not take much to spark off another round of violence. Through 1928 religious tensions had been rising as the Jews sought to extend their rights to worship at the Western Wall, just adjacent to the *al-Haram ash-Sharif.* The perceived threat to one of their most sacred spaces enabled the Palestinian leadership to cast the struggle in a religious light, and thereby mobilise those who had remained untouched by secular appeals to nationalism, the right of self-determination and other phrases which meant very little to the mass of Palestinians who had virtually no exposure to such ideals nor any experience of self-determination in their own lives. In August 1929 violent clashes broke out in Jerusalem and spread quickly. Within 24 hours 67 Jews had been slaughtered in Hebron and a few days later 45 Jews were killed in Safed. The final death toll was 133 Jews and 116 Arabs, with over 500 wounded.[11] Most of the Jewish casualties were at the hands of Arabs, but the bulk of the Arab deaths and injuries were caused by the British as they sought to protect the Jews and restore order. The violence of 1929 marked a turning point. According to Kayyali,

> For the villagers and the masses of Palestinians two important facts were made clearer and sharper by the events of 1929. The first was that Zionism and the Jewish National Home depended, ultimately and inevitably, on British bayonets, and it was therefore necessary to fight Britain if the struggle against Zionism was to achieve its goals. The second concerned the cowardice of the Palestinian notables and their inadequacy to leads the Arabs in the struggle against Zionism and British policy in Palestine.[12]

Resistance in the 1930s – the Palestinian Revolt, 1936-39

The harsh measures meted out by the British who imposed collective punishments on whole villages and neighbourhoods caused added bitterness, strengthening the hand of those calling for violence. The tension continued to rise through the 1930s. It was a period when the economic situation deteriorated, and the suffering of the Palestinians was exacerbated by the rising tide of Jewish immigration, new land purchases and the Jewish boycott of Arab labour, all of which contributed to increased unemployment and indebtedness amongst the Palestinian people. The response was a rapid heightening of the tempo of events and developments running way beyond the control capacity of the established political leadership, whose influence consequently declined. Moreover, a new element had entered the mix with the activities of a para-military group called the Black Hand made up of recruits from the working-class neighbourhoods of Haifa and led by Izzadin al Qassem. During the early 1930s they started attacking Jewish targets and sabotaging government property, but in November 1935 Qassem was killed by the British military near Jenin. His funeral attracted thousands who saw him as a powerful symbol of self-sacrifice and as someone who pointed the way forward in the struggle.

In April 1936 two Palestinians were killed and Palestinian property destroyed in revenge attacks after the murder of two Jewish travellers. In response the Palestinians called for a general strike on April 20th. A few days later the Arab Higher Committee was established with with Haj Amin Husseini at its head –it became the central political organ of the Palestinians over the next few years. The strike was almost completely solid. Merchants shut up shop and transport came to a virtual halt. Efforts were also made to enforce a total boycott of Jewish products, but Husseini shied away from extending the strike call to Palestinian officials within the British administration, a failure that contributed to a weakening of the overall impact of the strike action. It was also weakened by the fact that the Jewish sector of the economy kept on functioning, providing goods and services, with Jewish workers replacing the striking Arab workforce in Jewish-owned enterprises. Moreover, the strike caused considerable suffering amongst the families of those on strike and who relied on their wage-packets for survival. The suffering was intensified by the draconian response of the British to the protests, with mass arrests, house demolitions, collective punishment and deportations. Such measures served to intensify the incendiary mood, with the result that after the first few weeks the Palestinian resistance took on an armed and violent dimension. Indeed, by the early summer of 1936 a British official was reporting,

> Armed bands which a fortnight previously consisted of 15-20 men were now encountered in large parties of 50-70. The bands were not out for loot. They were fighting what they believed to be a patriotic war in defence of their country against injustice and the threat of Jewish domination.[13]

The revolt spread over the succeeding months and by the summer of 1938 it was reported that,

> … the rebels were in control of most of the mountainous parts of the country. They were walking fully armed in the streets of Nablus without any hindrance ... By September 1938, the situation was such that civil administration and control of the country was, to all practical purposes, non-existent.[14]

It was during this period that Palestinians developed their own embryonic state structure, in the form of a country-wide network of 'committees'. Nourishment and Supply Committees had been formed in the early months of the strike as a way of meeting the basic needs of those who could not survive without such assistance. Women's Committees organised house to house collections of money and jewellery to provide funds for the movement, whilst a Central Relief Committee distributed funds received from overseas. National Guard Units were formed to enforce the strike and the associated boycott of Jewish products. Special 'Courts of Revolt' were also established to mete out rough justice to those accused of treachery.

The direction of the armed struggle was nominally in the hands of a Central Committee but in fact there was a chronic lack of coordination, with each regional commander jealous to maintain control over the armed bands within his domain against the intrusions of rival commanders. There were cases of commanders refusing to obey instructions from above because they considered their nominal superior to be socially inferior. Instances of extortion, corruption, intimidation, and betrayal for private ends became so common that some villages organised their own armed militia to defend themselves against the rebels. Underpinning the divisions that emerged lay the bitter rivalry between the faction around the Mufti al-Husseini and the supporters of the Nashashibi family. According to a British teacher in the village of Bir Zeit, by the winter of 1939,

> More and more the rebellion was tending to degenerate from a national movement into squabbles between rival rebel bands. Bir Zayt, like many other villages, was no little better than a hornets nest of long standing family feuds, stirred up afresh in the hope of getting some advantage through the help of this or that party of rebels.[15]

Such divisions in the rebel ranks made the task of the British in subjugating the revolt, assisted by the Jewish Haganah, somewhat easier than it might have been. As Porath commented:

> The British authorities used various means to weaken the revolt, including sowing dissension among the bands by disseminating rumours about information supplied by rebels of certain bands or areas or by sending extortionists who pretended to be true rebels. The authorities did not have to work too hard in this held in order to be successful. From the outset, but mainly since Autumn 1937, the rebel bands were torn by political, family and regional dissensions, personal jealousies and criminal abuse. The government's activity only marginally contributed to this state of affairs.[16]

By the spring of 1939 the revolt had virtually died out. It had failed as a nationalist struggle against the British and the Jewish inhabitants of Palestine, and it had failed as a social revolution, which at one stage it had threatened to become. A key factor was that Palestinians remained more divided by regional, village, clan, and family loyalties than they were united by the appeals of nationalism or class solidarity.

The failure of the revolt

The failure of the Palestinians to achieve their aims during the 1936-39 revolt can be attributed to a number of factors.

1. Theories of nonviolent resistance advise us that all oppressive regimes rely on different sources of support, and the challenge for nonviolent resisters is to erode those pillars upon which the regime relies. One key means by which this can be achieved is by getting key workers and personnel to withdraw their cooperation and deprive the regime of their essential services. But, as we have seen, the economic impact of the general strike was limited in part because there was a whole sector of society (the Jewish sector) that continued to work and provide for the basic needs of their population. In the Palestinian case, the real suffering was borne by the strikers themselves.
2. The British Mandate was dependent on its many Arab administrative officers and officials, from the level of the local municipality up to the office of the High Commissioner himself. If these officers had withdrawn their labour and cooperation the impact on the capacity of the British administration to function would have been significant. But the political leadership of the Palestinians refused to order the officials to withhold their services. In hindsight it would seem to have been a monumental error of judgement.
3. The main reason the strike call was not issued to the officials would seem to be that the Palestinian notables were too reluctant to risk their vested interests (property, wealth,

status and influence) which, to a significant degree, depended on maintaining good relations with the British administration. In effect they prioritised their personal and family interests above that of the nation and the common good.

4. The leadership refused to relinquish their reliance on diplomacy and negotiation as the means to achieving their ends. They failed to grasp the absolute commitment of the British to the Zionist project of establishing a Jewish national home in Palestine.[17]
5. The Palestinians suffered from a severe imbalance of power which they were unable to rectify. Their appeals to the Arab and Muslim worlds failed to produce significant interventions, in part because the targets of such appeals were themselves under foreign domination and had their own interests. An obvious example of this was Abdullah of Transjordan who had aspirations to absorb Palestine into his own kingdom.
6. The Palestinian leadership was weak and divided, reflecting in some way the fissured social structure from which they had emerged. They faced a Zionist society that was highly organised, well-financed, with a determined leadership and significant networks of support amongst the Jewish diaspora throughout the world.

Partition, the *Nakba* and establishment of state of Israel

Britain emerged from the Second World War exhausted and in February 1947 announced it was handing over responsibility for Palestine to the United Nations (UN). In August the UN announced its proposal for partition which was duly approved by the General Assembly on November 2 1947. On the ground violent clashes erupted almost immediately and by the end of the year a virtual civil war was underway, accompanied by large-scale ethnic cleansing. The aim of the Zionists was to cleanse the territory allotted to them by the UN and gain control of other areas where there was a significant Jewish population. In such a situation of escalating violence there was little space for nonviolent initiatives.[18]

On May 15 1948 the state of Israel was declared into existence, by which date more than a third of the Palestinian population had been driven from their homes.[19] Only at that point did the Arab states intervene militarily – an exercise notable for its lack of coordination and paucity of equipment. The motivation for such half-hearted intervention was suspect from the start, as Pappe has noted,

> That the Arab states succeeded in fielding any soldiers at all is remarkable. Only at the end of April 1948 did the politicians in the Arab world prepare a plan to save Palestine, which in practice was a scheme to annex as much of it as possible to the Arab countries participating in the war.[20]

The most significant illustration of this phenomenon concerned the machinations of Abdullah of Jordan who, with the connivance of the British, had reached an understanding with the Zionists to divide Palestine between them, with the territory apportioned to the Palestinians by the UN to come under the control of the Hashemite kingdom. As a consequence of this understanding Abdullah kept his well-trained Arab Legion in check during the war, restricting its advances to the control of the territory it was intended to annex.

By the end of October 1948 what had now become the Israeli army controlled over three quarters of the former Palestinian territory. The defeat for the Palestinians was total. Over 400 villages had been destroyed or rendered uninhabitable. Around 75 - 80% of the Palestinian population had been displaced and dispossessed. The Gaza Strip was under Egyptian military rule, whilst Jordan annexed the West Bank. In the new state of Israel all immigration restrictions were lifted for Jews, who flooded in and took over the abandoned properties of their previous Palestinian owners. Israel celebrated victory in its national liberation struggle, Palestinians mourned the catastrophe (*Nakba*) that had overcome them.

Battir – a small victory in the midst of tragedy[21]

Battir in 1948 was a small village of some 1000 inhabitants just a few miles south-west of Jerusalem abutting the Jerusalem-Jaffa railway line. It had been on the front-line during the fighting but had never been over-run. King Abdullah had come to an understanding with the Jewish Agency that his Arab Legion would not attack Jewish troops once they had reached the anticipated armistice line between the new state of Israel and what would be the Jordanian-controlled territory of the West Bank. The bilateral armistice agreement of March 1949 established the agreed border based largely on the front-line positions held at the time of the UN-sponsored ceasefire of June 1948. Where there was disagreement two boundary lines were drawn on the map, with the land in-between designated 'no-man's-land' (NML) whilst the matter was referred to a special bilateral armistice committee charged with reaching agreement over such disputes. Battir was one of the villages that fell within the strip of NML south of Jerusalem, which meant that the village should have been evacuated. That this did not happen was due largely to a civil resistance campaign orchestrated by one of the village leaders, Hasan Mustafa.

Mustafa had been active organising the defence of the village during the war and was determined that a village that had remained unoccupied during the hostilities should not be lost as a consequence of the peace. To defend the village he followed a two-pronged strategy: 1) Active and persistent lobbying of the members of the armistice committee, arguing that Battir had never been conquered and therefore should not be evacuated; 2) Creating the appearance of a village that was fully inhabited and ready to defend itself against attack in order to deter the Israelis from making any pre-emptive assault. He was helped in his lobbying by the fact that there were several Jordanian military officers involved in the deliberations who were unhappy with Abdullah's conduct of the war and were sympathetic to Battir's cause. In April 1949 his efforts bore fruit when the committee routed the armistice line such that the bulk of the village remained under Jordanian control, whilst allowing Israel to take control of the railway line running alongside the village. The decision was to come into force on May 1 1949. To deter any unilateral action by the Israelis to create more facts on the ground Mustafa organised young men to go and light lamps in the village houses at night, make as much noise as possible, and generally do all that they could to give the impression that the village was fully inhabited, when in fact most of the villagers spent their nights in a neighbouring village out of fear of an Israeli assault.

On the day the agreement was due to come into effect Mustafa went to meet the Israeli officer (Moshe Dayan) and it was agreed that the villagers would be allowed to cultivate their lands on the other side of the railway line, so long as they only used the access routes under the railway bridges and did not cross over the railway track itself. Once this agreement was reached Mustafa sent vehicles to collect those villagers who had been staying outside the village so they could get back to their homes as quickly as possible. In order to ensure that the villagers took advantage of the agreement he then accompanied them in accessing their land across the railway track. In this way the villagers of Battir succeeded in holding on to their land – one of the few 'Palestinian success stories' within the broader context of the overwhelming catastrophe experienced by the bulk of Palestinians during the partition period. As such various lessons can be drawn.

1. *The importance of strong leadership*

The resistance would not have taken place without the leadership of Hasan Mustafa. The fact that he was not only a 'son of the village' but also the son of the headman gave him the status and authority to influence and mobilise people. He also had the courage to lead by example, accompanying the villagers as they risked their lives in accessing their fields across the 'green line'. He also had the self-confidence and the status to negotiate with Moshe Dayan, the officer in charge of the Israeli troops facing the village on the day the new border was to come into force, asserting the villagers' right of access to their farm-land.

2. *Social solidarity and shared commitment to the cause*

Nothing is likely to mobilise people more than a perceivable and immediate threat to their homes and their means of livelihood, and this is what the villagers of Battir faced. The alternative they faced was dispossession and displacement.

3. *Recognition of the legitimacy of the struggle and good communication with third parties*

Hasan Mustafa was able to convince disgruntled Jordanian officers that the village had never been occupied, and as a consequence they were able to present his case to the Armistice Committee, which agreed on a re-routing of the border that took account of the Israeli interest in gaining control of the rail line whilst also accommodating the village interest in ensuring its own future existence.

The lost years of the 1950s

Between the disaster of 1947-48 and the establishment of the Palestine Liberation Organisation (PLO) in 1964 there was virtually no significant collective manifestation of Palestinian nationalism of any sort. The reasons for this are not hard to find.

1. *Dispersal, dispossession and division*

Palestinian society had been devastated. Over half the population had been dispersed to refugee camps in Lebanon, Syria, the Gaza Strip and the West Bank. Less than 200,000 remained in the territory that had become Israel. Not only were they divided geographically, they also confronted different host regimes. In the Jordanian-annexed West Bank they received Jordanian nationality. The Gaza Strip was under Egyptian military administration, whilst the Palestinians left in Israel received Israeli citizenship but lived under military rule until 1966. Conditions for the refugees in Lebanon and Syria varied over time and according to the political climate.

2. *The trauma of loss*

Scattered and separated from each other, Palestinians were also disempowered by the deep trauma and shock suffered by those with a deep attachment to place who found themselves uprooted, no longer a majority in their own homeland but relegated to minority and subordinate status in states that were not their own.

3. *Faith in pan-Arabism*

The quiescence of the Palestinians during the 1950s was also due in part to the popularity of the pan-Arab ideal as embodied above all in Nasser's rise to power in Egypt in 1952. As a dispossessed people the Palestinians could regain their strength and their agency through the resurgent power of the Arab nation, a single people sharing language, history and culture who had been divided by the machinations of imperialist powers. Palestine would be 'liberated' in the context of the renewal of the Arab nation and associated political unification

4. *The priority of economic survival*

For most Palestinians reduced to poverty and subordinate status in their new anomic conditions, the priority was survival – particularly economic survival. This was particularly challenging in the face of discriminatory regulations and practices that limited employment opportunities in Jordan, Lebanon and Israel.

1960s – The emergence of the Palestine Liberation Organisation

In 1950 a young engineering student at Cairo University who was later to be known as Yasser Arafat set up a 'Union of Palestinian Students' with some friends. A short while later in Beirut, George Habash, a medical student at the American University, set up another student group. Grassroots organisations were also being established in the Gaza Strip, and by the mid-1950s there was an embryonic network of nationalist organisations, all of them very small and very weak. Incursions into Israel from Gaza and the West Bank started in an ad hoc fashion, monitored closely by the Egyptian and Jordanian authorities who had no desire to provoke Israel. It was out of this network that the main resistance organisation, Fatah, emerged and in 1964 the Palestine Liberation Organisation (PLO) was formed. The 1967 'June War' between Israel and her Arab neighbours ended with Israel capturing the Gaza Strip from Egypt, the West Bank (including East Jerusalem) from Jordan, and the Golan Heights from Syria. This outcome rang the death-knell of popular faith in pan-Arabism and boosted the fortunes of Fatah which became the prime agency of the Palestinian national movement.

Looking back on this period prior to the first intifada through the lens of nonviolent or unarmed resistance, a number of observations come to mind.

1. The glorification of armed struggle

It was with the rise of Fatah and the PLO that the iconic figure of the Palestinian fighter with his Kalashnikov emerged and which was to become the symbol of Palestinian resistance in subsequent decades. Palestine was to be 'liberated' – i.e. a Palestinian state established - through 'armed struggle'. Indeed, resistance was synonymous with armed struggle - a belief that the PLO shared with other contemporary liberation movements who all adopted the rhetoric of third world nationalism and anti-imperialist struggle. Following the 1967 war the initial strategy of the PLO was the fanciful one of using the occupied territories as a base for a popular guerrilla struggle. After a few months this was abandoned and Jordan was identified as the most appropriate launch pad for guerrilla raids. This was complemented by a terrorist campaign characterised by plane hijackings intended to force a change in western policies towards the Palestinian-Israeli conflict.

2. Palestinians as victims

Rashid Khalidi has pointed to the fact that according to Palestinian perceptions they have experienced a series of crushing defeats throughout their recent history at the hands of an array of enemies so powerful as to have been virtually unassailable. Again and again Palestinian history is presented as one of heroic struggle against impossible odds betrayed by traditional leaders and perfidious Arab states. [22] One consequence of this world-view is that the Palestinians can be absolved from responsibility for their failures. As Khalidi remarked, 'From this perspective, if their enemies were so numerous and powerful, it is hardly surprising that they were defeated.' [23]

3. The portrayal of defeat as triumph

Khalidi has pointed to a related peculiarity of the Palestinian world-view - the way in which failures have been portrayed as victories, or at least as heroic perseverance against impossible odds. According to his analysis,

> This narrative of failure as triumph began during the Mandate, but reached its apogee in the years after 1948, when it was picked up and elaborated by the grassroots underground Palestinian nationalist organisations that would emerge and take over the PLO in the mid-1960s.[24]

Amongst the examples he cites is the martyrdom of Izzadin al Qassem, the 1936-39 revolt, the 1947-49 catastrophe, the battle of Karama on March 21 1968, Black September of 1970 when the PLO were expelled from Jordan by force of arms, and the subsequent expulsion from Beirut in 1982. A few months after the exodus from Lebanon there was a meeting of the Palestine National Council (PNC) in Algiers, when attempts were made to present the evacuation as a victory. Khalidi quotes the caustic comment of Issam Sartawi who observed, 'One more "victory" like this one, and we will have the next meeting of the PNC in the Seychelles Islands!'[25]

4. *Shifts in the Palestinian political centre of gravity*

As the PLO became the dominant agency within the Palestinian national struggle, the Palestinian political centre of gravity shifted. As the PLO was forced to relocate to Jordan after the 1967 occupation of the Gaza Strip and West Bank and after the subsequent expulsion from Jordan to Lebanon in 1970 it was the refugees who came to be seen as potential recruits for the armed liberation struggle. Moreover, it was amongst the refugee communities, especially in Lebanon, that the PLO pursued its own form of constructive resistance with the establishment of its own broad welfare infrastructure, which in turn enhanced its standing among the refugees. This focus distanced the PLO from the Palestinians in the occupied territories, a separation heightened by the problems of communication after the 1967 war and the ensuing Israeli occupation.

The situation of Palestinians in the occupied territories

The message for the Palestinians in the occupied territories embodied in all these developments became clear: stay steadfast, make babies, and eventually you will be liberated as a consequence of the pressure generated by the PLO and its allies outside. In essence their allotted role was a passive one. In truth, the space available for organising any form of collective resistance to the occupation was severely circumscribed. Any signs of opposition to the occupation met with severe repression.

This in turn made it difficult for any coherent leadership to emerge within the occupied Palestinian territories (OPT), a process that was also hampered by the suspicions of the the PLO leadership outside regarding potential rivals to its own leadership position. The grouping they were most wary of was the communists who were the most advanced underground political organisation. As early as 1968 the communists had established National Guidance Committees, but in 1973 it was the PLO that was instrumental in establishing the Palestinian National Front (PNF) as an attempt to coordinate nationalist activities in the occupied territories within a PLO framework. The Front was led by an eight member committee representing the communists and various PLO organisations. Although most of its activities were carried out clandestinely, its work was severely curtailed by the Israelis, and it was eventually outlawed in October 1979.

Denied the opportunity to express themselves openly in any overtly political organisation, the young nationalists within the OPT established other vehicles for education and mobilisation. Student and professional associations, trade unions, women's societies, social and cultural associations, and other grassroots organisations became the main agencies for promoting the struggle against the occupation. The activists received encouragement in this constructive resistance work from the outside leadership after the PLO had agreed in 1974 upon an intermediate goal of establishing a 'national authority' on any part of Palestine from which the Israelis might withdraw.

In anticipating the establishment of a Palestinian state alongside Israel, the leadership of the PLO was concerned to create the institutional infrastructure for such a state as early as possible. In fact, the grass-roots organisations that were established during the 1970s were seen as having a dual role. On the one hand, they were to serve as agencies for the political organisation and mobilisation of the people, seedbeds of offensive resistance. On the other hand, they also existed as forms of constructive resistance providing basic personal and community services that were not provided by the Israeli occupiers. Thus, in a somewhat paradoxical manner, the absence of certain state services created the institutional space for the development of alternative, Palestinian 'quasi-state' organisations and agencies. Through the provision of much-needed services and facilities, such grass-roots organisations gained the allegiance of the majority of the Palestinian population, and as such constituted the nucleus of an alternative structure of authority and power to rival that of Israeli military government. Indeed, according to Salim Tamari,

> This strategy of informal resistance ... or institutional resistance was actually far more successful than even its own designers envisioned. By the late 1970s, it had established the complete political hegemony of Palestinian nationalism and the PLO as the single articulator of Palestinian aspirations.[26]

This growth in nationalist sentiment and commitment amongst the inhabitants of the OPT was not due solely to the influence of the political activists amongst their number. It also reflected the enhanced prestige of the PLO following the October 1973 War and the 1974 Arab Summit at Rabat. Primarily, however, it was due to the growth in anti-Israeli sentiment aroused by the burgeoning settlements and the harsh treatment of protesters meted out by Israeli troops. The spread of nationalist feeling was illustrated most graphically in the 1976 municipal elections, which the Israelis allowed to be held. Most of the councillors and mayors elected openly identified with the PLO and their election marked the political ascendancy of a newer, more radical political generation.

Following the election of the Likud government in 1977 and the subsequent Camp David Accords, the new mayors were instrumental in establishing the National Guidance Committee in October 1978. Its composition reflected a very wide spectrum of Palestinian nationalist political orientations, including the nationalist mayors and representatives of trade unions, societies and associations. The aim was to organise and coordinate an open political struggle against the occupation in general and the autonomy proposals of Camp David in particular. However, its non-clandestine form and the fact that many of its members were public figures made the Committee particularly vulnerable to Israeli counter-measures. Its effectiveness was greatly reduced by the imposition of restriction orders, arrests and the deportation of leading figures in the Committee, whilst in June 1980 the mayors of Nablus and Rarnallah were severely maimed by car bombs. In March 1982, the remaining mayors were dismissed and the Committee outlawed by the Israeli Defence Minister, Ariel Sharon.

During the period following the destruction of the PLO's infrastructure in Beirut in 1982, morale within the occupied territories was low. The Arab world was in disarray as a consequence of the Iran-Iraq war, and the inhabitants of the occupied territories were left feeling isolated and alone. According to Sarah Graham-Brown, by 1983 Fatah had become the strongest political current in the OPT, followed by the Communist Party, the Democratic Front for the Liberation of Palestine (DFLP), and lastly the Popular Front for the Liberation of Palestine (PFLP).[27] Unable to organise openly, these different political factions had used the trade unions, professional associations, student union groups and the different grass-roots organisations as arenas for political competition. Even in the 1970s there had always been considerable rivalry between the different political organisations, with a consequent duplication of service-provision agencies in some areas, each affiliated with a different political faction. In the first half of the 1980s relationships between the different nationalist factions deteriorated, considerably, a process that to some degree reflected the disunity and factional rivalry within the PLO itself during the years after 1982. Arafat's courtship of Jordan's King Hussein and his seeming preparedness to consider some kind of Jordanian-Israeli condominium over the occupied territories, helped to provoke a rebellion from within the ranks of Fatah itself.

However, in February 1986, negotiations between King Hussein and Arafat finally broke down, whilst the pressure for the reunification of the PLO grew as Palestinian refugee camps in Lebanon were besieged by Syria's clients, the militia forces of Amal. Increasingly urgent demands were also coming from the inhabitants of the occupied territories, who were calling for some political initiative before it was too late and all their land was expropriated for the use of Israeli settlers. The USSR also played a key role as mediator helping to bring about a reconciliation between the different groupings. All this came to fruition at the 18th Palestine National Council (PNC) meeting of April 1987 in Algiers. It was at this meeting also that the Palestine Communist Party was welcomed as a full member of the PLO for the first time. This unprecedented display of unity provided a necessary basis for coordination and cooperation between the different nationalist factions within the occupied territories – which in turn was a necessary condition for the outbreak of the Intifada.

---

[1] A. S. Kayyali, *The Palestinian Arab reactions to Zionism and the British Mandate, 1917-1939*, University of London, doctoral thesis, February 1970, p. 61.

[2] According to Porath 1500 demonstrated in Jerusalem, 2000 in Jaffa and 250 in Haifa. Y. Porath, *The Palestinian-Arab national movement, 1918-1929* (vol. 1), London: Frank Cass, 1974, p. 96.

[3] Porath (1974), p. 96.

[4] Porath (1974), p. 97.

[5] Kayyali, p. 118.

[6] The occasion was the dismissal of Musa al-Husseini as Mayor of Jerusalem because of the role he was deemed to have played

inciting the crowd in the April disturbances, and the appointment of Raghib al-Nashashibi to replace him on the orders of the British Governor of Jerusalem District.

7 R. Sayigh, *Palestinians: From peasants to revolutionaries*, London: Zed Books, 1979, pp. 14-15.

8 Sayigh, p. 50.

9 Kayyali, p. 201.

10 Porath (1974), p. 135. It is also worth noting that at this stage Haj-Amin Husayni was amongst the most forceful opponents of any suggestion of resorting to violence, as he sought the support of the British in building up his power base within the SMC.

11 It is important to record that 19 local Arab families in Hebron saved 435 Jews by hiding them in their houses during the pogrom. See http://www.haaretz.com/hasen/spages/1106426.html (accessedApril 3, 2015))

12 Kayyali, p. 217.

13 Quoted in Kayyali, p. 292.

14 Y. Porath, *The Palestinian Arab National Movement 1929-1939; From riots to rebellion*, London: Frank Cass, 1977, p. 236.

15 H. M. Wilson, quoted in Porath (1977), p. 254.

16 Porath (1977), p. 249.

17 Whenever it seemed that the Palestinians might gain some concession from the British, the Zionists would arrange counter-lobbies in Jerusalem and London, mobilise constituencies of support in key locations, and get the concession reversed.

18 Nonviolence proved to be no defence whatsoever against the power of armed might. The villagers of Dir Yassin were raped and slaughtered despite having signed a non-aggression pact with their Jewish neighbours. Further north in the mixed-town of Tiberias the community leaders of both communities had also signed a non-aggression pact in March 1948. The following month the *Hagana* took control of the city and expelled the Arab residents.

---

[19] I. Pappe, A history of modern Palestine, Cambridge: Cambridge University Press, 2006, p. 130.
[20] Pappe, p. 131.
[21] This section is based on the unpublished MA dissertation of Jawad Botmeh, Civil resistance in Palestine: the village of Battir in 1948, Coventry University, September 2006. Accessible at http://wwwp.coventry.ac.uk/researchnet/peacestudies/a/1136
[22] R. Khalidi, Palestinian identity: The construction of modern national consciousness, New York: Columbia University Press, 1997, p. 196.
[23] Khalidi, p. 195.
[24] Khalidi, p. 195.
[25] Quoted in Khalidi, pp. 198-9. Satarwi was subsequently murdered in Lisbon. In 1983. The assassination was presumed to be the work of the dissident Abu Nidal group.
[26] S. Tamari, 'What the uprising means', *Middle East Report*, May-June 1988, p. 26.
[27] S. Graham-Brown, 'Report from the occupied territories', *MERIP Reports*, 115, June 1983, p. 5.

Andrew Rigby

2

THE ORGANISATION OF RESISTANCE

Introduction: the Palestinians as a subject people

At the heart of any successful resistance movement is a stubborn refusal to accept the status quo, and an equally determined struggle to change it. However, for as long as that stubbornness and determination is not crystalized into effective collective action, the character of resistance is prone to take the form of sporadic outbursts of anger and frustration, interspersed with sullen periods of resentment. The relative lack of success enjoyed by the Palestinians in their pursuit of some form of self-determination prior to the outbreak of the Intifada can be attributed, in part at least, to their failure to achieve the degree of social solidarity necessary for sustained mass struggle and to inadequacies of organisation and leadership. However, during the Intifada that erupted in December 1987 the Palestinians within the OPT managed to generate a degree of social solidarity sufficient to sustain a quite remarkable unarmed resistance struggle against occupation. The focus of this chapter is upon how the Palestinians, during the Intifada, attempted to organise themselves as a coordinated and effective force, with their own political authority; an authority that grew to rival and in many ways to supersede the power of the Israeli state.

The first months: the establishment of the Unified National Command

The outbreak of the Uprising in December 1987 was as great a surprise to the leadership of the PLO as it was to everyone else, although in the first few days there was little to set it apart from previous confrontations with the occupying power. However, as the weeks went by the insurrection took on a distinctive character. One aspect of this was its scale. Whereas previous outbursts had been dispersed in nature, which made them relatively containable, this time whole sectors of society became involved as the revolt spread from Gaza to the West Bank, from the camps to the towns and villages. The other key distinguishing feature was the emergence of an instrument of political unification for all the various political factions in the guise of the Unified National Command of the Uprising (UNC). Following the first announcement of its existence in a leaflet distributed in the first week of January, 1988, the UNC succeeded in establishing itself as the undisputed guiding force behind the Uprising, commanding the allegiance of the vast majority of the population in the struggle to end the occupation. Although it remained a completely clandestine body, with its existence most openly evidenced by the regular publication of its communiques and leaflets, the UNC soon acquired legitimacy as the main political authority in the West Bank and Gaza Strip. Along with the organisational infrastructure of popular committees that grew up alongside it, the UNC took on the character of an 'embryonic state': coordinating activities in civil society, administering the provision of certain basic services, and seeking to control the use of force within the boundaries of its own territory.

Following the spontaneous outbursts of rage and anger in the Gaza Strip, the key elements in maintaining the revolt during the early days were youthful street gangs and certain Islamic activists. It took local political cadres some time to grasp the significance of what was happening. It would appear that a group from Fatah were the first to issue a leaflet under the name of the

UNC, to be followed a few days later by one published by the Democratic Front for the Liberation of Palestine (DFLP).[1] Despite such inauspicious beginnings, by early January the basic structure of the UNC in the West Bank and the Gaza Strip had been established. In the West Bank the membership was made up of representatives from each of the four main nationalist organisations - Fatah, the Popular Front for the Liberation of Palestine (PFLP), the Democratic Front for the Liberation of Palestine (DFLP and the Palestine Communist Party (PCP). In the Gaza Strip Islamic Jihad was also represented. All parties, regardless of size, enjoyed the same status within the UNC. During the early weeks of the Intifada, as many as twelve to fifteen people would attend, but within a short while it was established that each party should appoint just one person as its representative. Each of the factions continued to run its own networks, with which their delegate on the UNC liaised, representing the network's views in the discussions of the UNC, and in turn reporting back to the party cadres, explaining and justifying particular decisions and platforms adopted by the UNC. The members of the UNC and its associated popular committees during the first months of the Intifada were predominantly activists who had been schooled in the disciplines of clandestine organisation during the time many of them had spent in Israeli prisons for security-related offences.[2]

Although the unity of the PLO had been proclaimed the previous April in Algiers, the rivalry between the factions represented in the UNC did not disappear overnight. There was an undercurrent of resentment against Fatah who, it was argued, had never invested the same amount of energy in grassroots organising as the other groups, except in its *Shabiba* (Youth) organisation. Fatah was accused of using its control of material and financial resources to 'muscle in'.[3] There was tension between the DFLP and the Communists, insofar as they shared similar political platforms and as such saw themselves competing for the same pool of potential recruits. The PCP also clashed with the

PFLP, criticising its representatives for repeatedly seeking to escalate the Uprising beyond a level that the Communists felt the population could withstand.[4] For instance, the PCP opposed the escalation of the violence entailed by the UNC's endorsement of the use of fire bombs in the Uprising and urged a 'taming' of the struggle, arguing that energies would be better directed to the strengthening of the social and political infrastructure of popular committees rather than in direct confrontations with the security forces.[5]

Another serious division came to light in March 1988 when at least two versions of Communique No. 10 were distributed. The first one called for the resignation of West Bank deputies to the Jordanian parliament. It had been issued by the PFLP, who had long held the slogan: 'The road to the liberation of Palestine goes through Amman'. The other groupings issued their own leaflet a few days later, again under the banner of the UNC, which omitted a demand that they felt to be premature and unnecessarily antagonistic towards the Jordanian regime at a time when its support might be crucial to the future of the Uprising.[6] Some months later, in May, the PFLP broke ranks once again with the publication of its own version of Communique No. 17. It urged a campaign of total civil disobedience, a demand which the other political groups once again considered premature and refused to endorse. There would also seem to have been breakdowns in communication between the West Bank and the Gaza Strip. In Communique No. 9, issued on March 1 1988, the leaders of the Gaza Strip called for a three-day strike on the occasion of George Schultz's visit to the region, whilst the leadership in the West Bank just called for a one day stoppage.

Despite such teething problems, the power of the UNC was revealed by the solidarity of response to its proclamations and instructions to the population. The response of shopkeepers and merchants to the strike calls and the order to restrict their opening hours on non-strike days, despite the efforts of the Israeli military to force them to remain open, was particularly impressive. Their unity and discipline was a forceful affirmation of the power and authority of the UNC. Any shopkeeper who dared to ignore the orders risked having his store firebombed as punishment for placing private interest above the national good.[7]

As part of its attempt to establish itself as the legitimate political authority through the de-legitimisation of the occupying regime, the UNC ordered all those Palestinians working for the civil administration of the occupied territories, the police and members of village and municipal committees appointed by the Israelis, to resign and 'stop betraying their people before it is too late'. This call went out in the ninth leaflet, and was repeated in ensuing communiques, each time with an implicit threat as to the consequences of defying the 'Palestinian will'. Communique No. 11, distributed on March 21 1988, advised that 'the people of the Uprising will be harsh with anyone who remains outside the national consensus and refuses to resign immediately', whilst the twelfth warned that the UNC could no longer be responsible for the safety of those mayors and officials who refused to heed the resignation call. By that time the majority of the police working for the occupying power had resigned, an emphatic statement of where the seat of power within the occupied territories lay. Those who challenged that power by refusing to heed its instructions faced the threat of sanctions. The mayor of El Bireh was assaulted with a knife, whilst the Israeli-appointed council head of Bureij refugee camp in the Gaza Strip only resigned after his car was set alight and his home fire-bombed.[8] As one activist remarked, 'It's a matter of getting rid of all the people appointed by Israel and Jordan; they are tools. We are cleaning out our cities. This is the real Intifada'.[9]

The Popular Committees

Accompanying this process of 'purification' and the assertion of the legitimate authority of the new Palestinian leadership, efforts were also made to establish an alternative organisational infrastructure to meet people's needs and provide some of the services previously administered by Israel and its appointees. Communique No. 11 called for the creation of popular committees in every city, village, camp and street. The Palestinian Centre for the Study of Non-violence examined the functioning of these alternative institutions that sprang up throughout the occupied territories, and listed eleven different types.[10]

1. Strike Forces

These acted as the 'front-line troops' of the Intifada in confrontations with Israeli troops and settlers. In addition to this 'external' function, they also exercised an 'internal' control function, enforcing the instructions of the UNC in their area. As such, their activities ranged from ensuring that merchants followed instructions regarding designated trading hours to the harassing and punishment of collaborators.

2. Women's Committees

Like the strike forces, the women's committees carried out a wide range of activities. In the early summer of 1989 I visited premises that acted as a women's centre in a small town in the central region of the West Bank. The ground floor was used as a cooperative shop, selling cost-price supplies, much of it produced by women in the surrounding villages. The women at the centre held a weekly discussion meeting, where they would discuss topics raised in the books they had set themselves to read. They also ran adult literacy classes. They arranged visits to outlying villages to give health-care classes and talk to the women of the village about developments in the Intifada. They performed a public relations function by providing interpreters to accompany visitors who wanted to visit villages in their area. They also arranged visits to sit with the bereaved, the injured, and those newly released from prison - expressions of concern and solidarity, letting people know that they were not alone in their struggles and sacrifices. In some areas the women organised themselves into 'snatch squads' to rescue children and youths from the clutches of Israeli soldiers. Here is one woman's account of how things proceed in a Gazan refugee camp:

> Women have been playing an active role in the Uprising, in the confrontations that you see ... How? For example, say the army arrives and there's a confrontation between the army and the youth. They'll chase them, there will be attacks with gas, shooting. They'll grab one youth, and so what will be the woman's role? She'll scream and shout. The army is affected by the screaming of women. It attracts their attention. It confuses them and they don't know what to do. She'll scream and follow them, attack them. She'll grab hold of the soldier who has got the boy. She'll do whatever she can. The women's methods sometimes work - the screaming and the attacking of the army. Some girls throw stones as well. So the soldier doesn't know whether to pay attention to the stones or the women screaming or the boys. So the confrontation will involve everybody. Sometimes the methods succeed and then the women just slip away.[11]

3. Guard Committees

Their task was to protect property from the security forces, settlers, and common criminals. They were formed to fill the gap left by the resignation of the police. In addition to this 'law and order' function, their most important role was to act as lookouts, providing advance warning of attacks from soldiers or settlers.

4. Popular Education Committees

The function of these committees was to organise community and home-based education for the young, as part of the attempt to fill the void created by the Israeli closure of schools and colleges.

5. Food and Supply Committees

Their responsibility was to survey the needs of the people in their area, and arrange the collection and distribution of food and other supplies locally and to neighbouring areas, villages and camps under curfew or closed off by the military.

6. Medical Committees

These committees were responsible for holding stocks of basic medicines, in addition to providing basic first aid instruction and medical treatment to those injured in confrontations.

7. Committees for Self-sufficiency

The members of these committees were at the heart of the movement to develop the 'home economy', showing people how to achieve greater self-sufficiency through growing their own produce, rearing chickens, rabbits, pigeons and other livestock.

8. Social Reform Committees

These committees were initiated as a community- based conflict resolution service designed to replace the Israeli courts by mediating in disputes between individuals and families.

9. Committees to Confront the Tax

The role of these committees was to engage with and expel Israeli tax collectors who invariably accompanied the soldiers on their incursions into villages and neighbourhoods.

10. Merchants' Committees

Their responsibility was to coordinate the efforts of the merchants in the conduct of strikes and other Intifada-related activities.

11. Information Committees

These were formed to compensate for the restrictions imposed on the work of journalists and other sources of information. Their task was to gather and disseminate information concerning the Uprising.

This list gives a good idea of the range of functions undertaken by the alternative institutions developed by the Palestinians during the Intifada. However, it is an overly schematic framework which implies a degree of consistency and standardisation which was never achieved on the ground. In practice there was an unevenness of development. The available evidence suggests that the alternative institutional network became most highly developed in areas where one or more of the political organisations were active prior to the Intifada, and where there was a pre-existing system of grassroots organisations and associations. In general, however, each neighbourhood or village created its own local coordinating committee, its composition loosely reflecting the balance of influence enjoyed by the different political organisations within the locality. Beyond and below this basic institution, each locality developed its own particular pattern of sub-committees in response to emergent needs in the area. Thus, villages adjacent to Israeli settlements gave priority to developing an efficient system of advance warning of attacks. Villages that spanned routes to settlements tended to develop highly organised strike forces, actively engaged in the harassment and intimidation of settlers travelling to and from their places of work inside Israel. In a similar manner, quarters of refugee camps that faced repeated incursions from the military, and sustained periods of curfew, tended to focus upon the efficient organisation of their guard committees and strike forces, along with an adequate medical relief system for the victims of the confrontations. Villages and neighbourhoods adjacent to such camps, on the other hand, tended to give greater priority to organising the supply of food and provisions to their neighbours, whose degree of suffering was so much greater than their own.[12]

Command, control and communication

The development of the popular committee structure took place in a relatively flexible and uneven manner, according to local circumstances and in response to local needs. It was an organic process, the network taking on its own shape and structure in response to its environment. Much the same can be said about the development of the UNC's own command, control and communication systems.

It took about four months, until the spring of 1988, before the basic organisational pattern was established. By then the composition of the key executive body, the UNC itself, had been reduced to a single representative from each of the four main nationalist parties. Each of these maintained its own organisational infrastructure in the occupied territories, as well as its links with its leadership outside.[13] The role of the UNC members, like party leaders in political systems elsewhere, was to represent the interests of their party members and constituents in the decision making process, and then to explain and justify to these same members the decisions that had actually been taken. Hence, each party maintained its own communications network and distributed its own leaflets and newsletters, in addition to the well-worn method of publicising its own slogans and position through political graffiti. In this manner the political party system continued to exist alongside, and to permeate through, the embryonic state system established by the Palestinians in the occupied territories.

Insofar as they had always needed to operate clandestinely, there was little new about the cellular organisational pattern of these parties. What was new was the compulsion they felt to remain within the 'national consensus'. There developed amongst Palestinians a real sense that they were laying the basis of a democratic and pluralist political system for the future - one within which people and parties could argue and disagree, each trying to promote their own particular point of view. Thus, at the end of the day, once a decision had been made, it was accepted as binding, even though some continued to disagree. It was as if the political rivalries that had always existed were still there, but they were being played out according to new rules, and within new parameters that acknowledged a basic unity and common interest underlying the factional differences.

The central decision making arena, of course, remained the UNC itself. Associated with it were a number of sub-committees, each responsible for a particular function such as finance, health, education, public relations. Included in the membership of these sub-committees were regional representatives to act as links between the national level and regional sub-committees. Below the regional level there were district level sub-committees, made up of representatives from the village and neighbourhood level sub-committees. There thus emerged a radically decentralised system of decision making and control, with its roots firmly embedded in the neighbourhood level committees. The whole variegated system could be compared to a bunch of grapes rather than a string of worry beads. The removal of one worry bead breaks the thread that holds them all together. In the organic structure of the grapes, the severing of one stem only affects the growth attached to that linkage, leaving unaffected the rest of the cluster.

Running throughout the whole network was a myriad of communication channels, and at their heart was the UNC itself. Its task was to guide the Palestinian population through the maelstrom of events, keeping people abreast of developments and trends, trying to maintain unity and morale in the struggle.

The key medium for the performance of this essential leadership function was the numbered communiques, issued at regular intervals by the UNC. In the early days of the Uprising the bulk of these were produced centrally at a printers in Issawiya, but following a number of security raids the process was decentralised. Thus, the earlier communiques were all professionally printed, including one glossy eight-page publication. Later issues were rather more low-tech. If one compared leaflets distributed in different areas, they would share the same wording but would be typed and reproduced on different machinery. However, whilst the technical quality deteriorated, the distribution network continued to operate with remarkable effectiveness. With only rare exceptions, perhaps due to a peculiarly heavy security clampdown in a particular area, the communiques were distributed at roughly the same time in every part of the occupied territories during the early years of the Intifada. It is difficult to convey the authority with which these came to be imbued by the majority of Palestinians, especially by the young members of the strike forces and popular committees. As one Palestinian expressed it, 'They are like the Koran to the people, to the youths. When they arrive in the villages they are studied, discussed ... they are our constitution'. Their continued regular appearance acted as a tremendous morale booster for the population at large. Here was the physical manifestation of the existence of their own political authority which, like themselves, continued to defy the occupying power. Of course their effect was more than psychological. The communiques performed an absolutely vital coordinating function, informing people of the timetable of actions and events due to take place over the forthcoming period, and thereby giving them the opportunity to plan their own activities accordingly.[14] Local committees also produced their own leaflets, listing their own timetable of events and actions. In addition, the different political organisations continued to issue their own communiques and literature as a way of keeping their membership abreast of developments and debates.

The communiques, leaflets and other literature were not the only means of communication nor the sole channel of political debate. The Palestinians continued to rely upon their 'wall newspapers', in the form of the political graffiti covering just about every wall in the occupied territories. Alongside the slogans and symbols of the different political currents, one could also find specific messages and instructions issued by the UNC giving details of strikes and other days of action.

The role of Palestinian 'personalities'

The communiques and leaflets issued by the UNC were read not just by Palestinians. As semi-clandestine documents that entered the public domain once they had been published and distributed, their contents were reported upon by the Israeli press and by media around the world. Consequently they were used by the UNC to outline their political position, not just to their own national constituency but also to the international community in general and to the Israelis in particular. Just prior to the Israeli general elections in November 1988 the UNC issued a leaflet in Arabic, English and Hebrew calling for a twin-state solution to the conflict, a call that was clearly intended to influence the Israeli voting public.

In the sphere of external affairs and public relations, a particularly significant role was also played by a network of Palestinian 'personalities', predominantly based in East Jerusalem. The grouping was made up of academics, intellectuals, journalists, publishers, lawyers, businessmen - many of them drawn from well-established and influential Palestinian families. As residents of East Jerusalem they enjoyed greater freedom of movement than residents of the rest of the West Bank and Gaza Strip. They also had access to better communication facilities, insofar as the Israelis never cut the international telephone links with East Jerusalem as they did throughout the rest of the occupied territories. All this facilitated one of their roles, acting as spokespersons for the Intifada at conferences, symposia and seminars around the world, including inside Israel itself. They had regular contacts with diplomats, foreign journalists, visiting dignitaries, statesmen and politicians. They were people whose command of English made them excellent sources for interviews and quotes by the media when a 'Palestinian perspective' on some current development was needed. Their relatively public profile, and their range of influential international contacts, also provided them with a certain degree of immunity from arrest and detention by the Israeli security forces. This meant that they could be used as spokespersons for the Intifada within the occupied territories and within Israel itself.

Thus, on January 14 1988 a press conference was held in East Jerusalem in which a set of demands were addressed to the Israelis in the name of 'Palestinian nationalist institutions and personalities from the West Bank and Gaza'. These fourteen demands became the political programme of the Intifada. They were presented by a group that included Sari Nusseibeh, a professor of philosophy at Bir Zeit University, Gabi Baramki, the president of that university, Mustafa al-Natshah, a former mayor of Hebron, and Mubarak Awad, the director of the Palestinian Centre for the Study of Non-violence. In similar fashion, in April 1989, 83 well-known Palestinians issued a signed public statement rejecting the proposal of Prime Minister Shamir for elections in the occupied territories, denouncing it as an attempt to divide Palestinians and 'ignore our political legitimacy and legitimate aspirations'. Once again, this was a clear political statement, made on behalf of the UNC concerning an issue that was causing some confusion within the Palestinian community. The degree of relative autonomy these personalities enjoyed also meant that they could float ideas and hypothetical scenarios. The reaction to such exercises from their fellow Palestinians inside and outside the occupied territories, from Israel and the international community in general, could then help the UNC shape their political strategy. As diplomats of the Intifada, representing the new political authority of the Palestinians to the outside world, these personalities were obviously in very close touch with the leadership of the Uprising. Indeed, insofar as their relative freedom to travel abroad provided them with the opportunity to meet with PLO officials and leaders outside, they performed an important bridging function between the two sets of leadership within the overall nationalist movement.

Relations with the 'outside'

The history of the underground resistance movements in the Second World War reveals that the amount of control that could be exercised over such movements by a nominal leadership based outside the occupied country was very limited. Resisters tended to resent instructions issued by a leadership ensconced in relative safety and comfort, far from the day-to-day dangers and hardships faced by those in the field.[15]

A similar sentiment was detectable amongst activists in the Uprising. At one level this manifested itself in a certain resentment of the lifestyle enjoyed by the PLO leadership and its entourage - travelling round the world in comfort and style, staying in luxury hotels, treated as VIPs wherever they went - a far cry from the daily confrontations with the Israeli security forces, the economic hardships, the threats of arrest and injury activists faced inside the occupied territories. But, beyond this all too understandable indignation, which was not without its element of self-righteousness, there was no serious or sustained questioning of the leadership role of 'the old man' and his associates in Tunis. The population of the occupied territories constituted only a third of the total Palestinian population scattered throughout the world. Consequently, the leaders of the Uprising remained very aware that whilst they might constitute the legitimate political authority within the West Bank and Gaza Strip, they had no remit whatsoever to speak for the Palestinian people as a whole.

Whilst acknowledging the sovereignty of the leadership outside, the Intifada indubitably wrought some profound changes in the style, the dynamics, and in the actual substance of Palestinian politics outside the occupied territories. Within the occupied territories during the Intifada politics took on a very participatory quality. It was a form of political practice which was intolerant of any factionalism that threatened the unity of the movement to end the occupation. It was also one which, because of the clandestine method of organising, did not focus upon individual personalities. This was in marked contrast to the style and practice that characterised the PLO over the length of its history – an alphabet soup of factions serving as vehicles for personal ambition, patronage, and the interests of various Arab regimes, with proud rhetoric masking organisational incompetence and inefficiency. Much of this appeared to change under the influence of the Intifada and the example set by its leadership. If the people on the inside, suffering and facing martyrdom, could sustain a unity of purpose and action, in spite of their political differences, then the least they could demand of their leaders outside was a similar display of national unity and 'Palestinian democracy'.

The influence of the Intifada on the political style of the PLO reflected to a significant degree the profound change in the balance of power that had taken place within the organisation. For the first time, the 'insiders' began to exercise the dominant sway in Palestinian politics. They were no longer spectators, observing their leaders outside decide on their fate. The feeling that they had achieved more than 20 years of armed struggle in promoting the Palestinian cause gave the 'insiders' an unprecedented degree of self-confidence and assertiveness. After all, it was the Intifada that forced King Hussein to relinquish his claim to the West Bank in August 1988, thereby consolidating the position of the PLO as the undisputed representative of the Palestinian people. Commenting on this mood towards the end of 1988, David Hirst wrote: 'they feel themselves to have earned the moral right to call the tune in Palestinian counsels in a way they have never done before'.[16] A major consequence of this shift in the centre of political gravity within the PLO was a strengthening of the mainstream 'moderate' trend within the organisation, which culminated in the November 1988 Declaration of Independence and the subsequent unequivocal recognition of the state of Israel. This major step revealed the way in which the leadership of the Intifada had begun to set the political agenda for the PLO.

The cadres of the Uprising were a younger generation than the leaders outside. Their formative influences had been post-1967. They had grown up under Israeli occupation, but with the example of the Israeli social and political system before them. They knew the Israelis in a way that their leaders outside could not hope to achieve. With this knowledge had come the recognition of the Israeli state and people as facts of life, and with this recognition came the reluctant acknowledgement that they could not be eliminated or wished away. As a consequence Palestinians had made it clear right from the start of the Intifada that the struggle was not aimed at the annihilation of Israel, but at ending the occupation and winning freedom for Palestinians. The political programme of the Uprising was for the establishment of a Palestinian state alongside that of Israel.

Hence, following King Hussein's relinquishment of his claim to the West Bank, local activists pressured the outside leadership to come up with a political initiative to fill the vacuum left by Jordan. Early in August 1988 a draft Declaration of Independence was discovered at the offices of Faisal Husseini's Arab Studies Society. This had in fact been written some months previously, and its contents had been the subject of discussion in certain Palestinian circles for some time. A couple of weeks after the 'leaking' of the contents of the Husseini document, the UNC issued a communique urging the Palestine National Council to 'adopt a comprehensive and clear political programme which will gain widespread international support for the national rights of our people and to do all it can to support and develop the Uprising'. The UNC leaflet addressed to Israeli voters just prior to the November 1988 Israeli general election proposed a two-state solution to the conflict. Thus, the pressure was sustained right up to the historic 19th meeting of the PNC in November 1988 at Algiers. Representatives from the occupied territories were prevented from attending but their influence remained paramount. The fact that the PLO remained united after what was, in effect, the formal relinquishing of their claim to over half their historic territory, was an even more powerful illustration of the dominant influence of the Intifada over the whole spectrum of Palestinian politics. Thus, whilst the PFLP in particular was critical of the concessions made by Arafat, and copies of George Habash's speeches were distributed in the occupied territories along with political graffiti denouncing Security Council Resolutions 242 and 338, none of the main political factions within the PLO were prepared to risk an open confrontation that would threaten the unity underpinning the Uprising.[17]

Their key 'front-line' role in the nationalist struggle enabled the leading activists in the Uprising to enjoy a degree of relative autonomy vis-a-vis the leadership outside. In the words of one of them, 'We are not employees'. When the occasion seemed to demand it they were not afraid to express their criticism of the outside organisation. Such an incident was the hijacking of an Israeli bus in early spring 1988 by a group of guerrillas who had infiltrated from Egypt, which resulted in the death of three Israeli civilians. It was argued that this action seriously undermined the international sympathy earned by the unarmed nature of the Palestinian resistance to Israeli oppression. Despite their relative autonomy, the leading figures within the occupied territories were always careful to emphasise their identification with, and ultimate accountability to, the outside leadership. That this commitment went beyond tokenism was evidenced by the fact that the general political statements that constituted the first section of the regular leaflets and communiques were always cleared with the leadership outside through the liaison committee that the PLO has established, with the approved draft being faxed back to the UNC. The communiques themselves were always issued in the name of the 'PLO/Unified Command of the Uprising'. Spokespeople repeatedly informed visiting diplomats, statesmen and others, including Israelis, that 'our address is Tunis'. Whatever feelings they may have entertained in private, they were careful to avoid giving any public hint of differences between the inside and outside, carefully scanning the

Arabic press and listening to Radio Monte Carlo and other sources to obtain signs of the mood and perspective in Tunis. They knew that in order to maintain morale during the struggle, unity throughout the movement had to be sustained. They were fully aware that the Israelis would try to exploit any hint of difference and discord as part of their attempt to promote divisions within the Palestinian community. In particular, Palestinians within the West Bank and Gaza Strip were fully cognisant of the Israeli counter-strategy to foment schisms between the Palestinians inside and the PLO leadership outside, in the hopes that a more 'accommodating' leadership might emerge with whom they might negotiate an end to the Uprising.

The Israeli response: Intimidation, repression and suppression

In facing up to the existence of a rival political authority within its own domain, the Israelis sought to undermine its strength in a variety of ways. At the most obvious and visible level, there were attempts to break the political will of the activists by arrest, detention, deportation, intimidation and even assassination. The Israelis also sought to undermine the power of the UNC by imposing sanctions on those who heeded its call. Hence, in the early weeks of the Intifada they made vain attempts to break the strike schedule by forcing merchants to remain open, welding shut the entrances of stores that refused to follow their countermands, closing wholesale markets and the like; warning head teachers not to open up their schools when the UNC urged students and staff to return to school and so on.

In addition, the Israeli state used a variety of administrative measures to impose its control on the Palestinian population, seeking to impress upon them just where the 'real power' lay in the land, forcing people to acknowledge the strength of Israeli state power and thereby impress upon them the futility of attempting to 'disengage' from the various state apparatuses in response to the promptings of the UNC. Thus, in May 1988 all adults in the Gaza Strip were required to re-register for new identification cards. The new card was only issued to those who could prove they had paid all their taxes, but a key purpose was to tighten up the control of the inhabitants. In response, the UNC called for a boycott of the ID changes in a supplement to Communique No. 15, reminding people that 'your national duty compels you not to change your ID card because this would harm the achievements of the Uprising'.[18] The Israelis came out victors in this particular clash of rival powers. They wisely commenced the re-registration scheme in the middle-class residential suburb of Rimal in Gaza City, before proceeding to the hot-beds of resistance in the refugee camps. The UNC, for its part, underestimated the strength of the cord that ties Palestinians in the occupied territories to their ID cards. As one young man explained to a British journalist, 'We need ID cards to work in Israel. I support five people, my friend here has twelve mouths to feed. Are the National Leadership going to pay for our families?'[19] Without a valid ID card normal travel was virtually impossible for Palestinians living under occupation. They could be arrested and detained at any of the innumerable road blocks and checkpoints. You never knew when you might be stopped by the security forces and asked to produce your ID. One Palestinian acquaintance wryly confessed that at one stage during the Intifada he had started going to bed with his ID safely lodged in his pyjama pocket, in order to reassure himself when he suffered one of his recurring nightmares - the loss of his identification documents. In a related move the Israeli administration also insisted that drivers re-license their vehicles. To obtain the new registration plates, people were once again required to prove they had paid their taxes and had 'good conduct' clearances from the security forces.

In June 1989 the Israelis commenced their most ambitious scheme to challenge the authority of the UNC. They issued an ordinance requiring all adult Gazan men to carry new computerised identification cards if they wished to travel into Israel for any purpose. Mindful of their relative lack of success the previous year, the local leadership of the Uprising organised the strike forces to confiscate the new cards from their holders before they had a chance to use them. Eventually, however, the UNC had to face the reality of Gazans' economic dependence upon work in Israel and acknowledge the bad feeling that was developing against West Bankers who were allegedly filling the jobs in Israel left vacant by the striking Gazans. They rescinded the instructions to ignore the new regulations. Although this could be seen as a defeat for the UNC, the very fact that it was prepared to acknowledge the mistakes and retreat from untenable positions reinforced its image as an authentic leadership that was willing to respond to the pressures from below.

Running in tandem with such attempts to intensify their control over Palestinians, the Israelis also pursued a sustained assault on what they considered to be the institutional foundations of the rival political authority: the grassroots organisations and popular committees. The Shabiba Youth Movement was banned in March 1988 as a 'front organisation of Fatah'. According to Joel Greenberg of the *Jerusalem Post*, 'Security officials considered it to be in fact a recruiting mechanism for Fatah, through which young Palestinians are mobilised for anti-Israel attacks and nationalist political activity'.[20] Trade unions were also among the early targets of the authorities' attempts to suppress Palestinian institutions that could serve as a base for collective organisation. Activists were detained and deported, premises were closed, and the organisations themselves outlawed for 'security' reasons.[21] By the summer of 1988 the attack had been extended to other organisations. In June the largest charitable association in the occupied territories, the Society of In'ash al-Usra (Family Rehabilitation Society) in Al-Bireh, was closed for a period of two years on the grounds that materials of an inflammatory nature were kept in the Society. The Arab Studies Society in East Jerusalem, the largest research and resource centre in the occupied territories, was closed at the end of July 1988 on the grounds that it was 'controlled and financed by the Fatah organisation and served as the organisation's tool to promote its aims and attain the objectives of the Uprising'.[22] Other voluntary associations and organisations were closed down, whilst many were threatened with closure if they persisted in trying to fulfil their normal pre-Intifada roles.[23]

Following King Hussein's announcement of July 31 1988, the main target for the Israelis became the popular committees, which they correctly considered to be the organisational and ideological backbone of the Uprising. On August 17 1988 Defence Minister Rabin announced that the security forces would use every legal means at their disposal to cope with the committees. They were declared illegal the next day, with membership punishable by up to ten years imprisonment. The *Jerusalem Post* then quoted a security source who promised that 'there will be no mass arrests, we do not intend to arrest popular committee members whose only activity is community service like aid to needy families or blood donations'.[24] There then followed a massive trawling operation to net in the activists. Deportation orders were served on 25 leading figures, and there were reports of between 200 and 300 members of the committees being placed under administrative detention within a few days of the banning order.[25] In the eyes of one Israeli commentator, this move was tantamount to declaring all Palestinian inhabitants of the West Bank and Gaza Strip illegal.[26]

> Let us do a little arithmetic: the Shabiba movement has been outlawed. All political organisations in the territories have long been illegal. Last week, the popular committees were outlawed, and alongside them their supporters, those who follow their instructions and those who do their work and aid them verbally, materially, actively or by default. There is a popular committee in every village and municipal district, and all residents accept its authority.

> We cannot, therefore, escape the pleasant conclusion that we have finally managed to outlaw all the inhabitants of the territories. There is no longer any need to prove that someone was involved in terrorist activity, that he tried to harm people, to plant explosives, set a tyre alight or threw a bottle in order to send him to a detention camp, confiscate his property, demolish his house or deport him. All that is required is proof that he is a resident of the territories.

All that happened as a consequence of the Israeli action was that the popular committee structure embedded itself a little deeper into the interstices of Palestinian society. As committee members were arrested, at whatever level of the structure from the UNC down to the local neighbourhood, their place was taken by the next in line. According to one well-informed Palestinian, the personnel of the UNC changed at least four times during the first year of the Uprising, due to arrests and rotation to protect activists at risk. At the provincial level, I was assured by an activist in a small town in the northern area of the West Bank that it took, on average, a period of only two to three weeks to re-establish a local network of committees following its complete dismemberment by the Israeli security forces. All this would seem to support the verdict of an Israeli security source, delivered at the time when the popular committees were outlawed: 'the new steps will slow the Intifada but will not stop it. It is too late to stop it now, despite the political echelon's wish. The Intifada will continue whether we want it or not.'[27]

The Israeli response: Divide and rule

A key factor affecting the commitment to struggle was the sense of unity within the Palestinian community. A major feature of the Israeli counter-strategy was to undermine that unity and to try and foment divisions in the Palestinian ranks. In the implementation of their divisive strategy, the Israelis adopted a range of tactics. A simple method of planting the seeds of distrust in a community would be to launch a security raid, arrest a number of suspected activists, and imprison them all - except one, who would be released after a few hours' interrogation. The invariable reaction of neighbours and acquaintances would be one of suspicion: 'Why was he released? Is it possible that he has struck a deal with the security forces? Has he promised to trade information for his liberty? Can he be trusted?'

The same approach could be adopted with any community, whether it be an isolated village in the West Bank or the community of intellectuals and 'personalities' in East Jerusalem. Thus, in May 1989 the Israelis announced that they had unearthed evidence to show that a number of prominent Palestinian spokespersons were, in fact, leaders of the Uprising - involved in drafting leaflets, distributing funds, liaising with PLO representatives in Amman and Paris, and other activities. Amongst those named were Sari Nusseibeh and Radwan Abu Ayyash, the head of the Arab Journalists Association in East Jerusalem. Despite the quite specific charges, these two were left at liberty and were not arrested, thus exposing them to criticism and suspicion in certain Palestinian circles. 'Why were they not arrested? They were even allowed to travel abroad, while others were imprisoned. Why? What kind of understanding had they reached with the Israelis? Had they agreed to participate in the Israeli attempts to promote an alternative leadership to the PLO within the occupied territories? If the Israelis had not arrested them, maybe this was because of the influence of the United States. Were they tools of the CIA?' These were the kinds of rumours and suspicions being whispered through various Palestinian networks during May 1989. As an attempt to counter the damage, a declaration was distributed around East Jerusalem on behalf of 'national figures and institutions in the State of Palestine', condemning the reports as fabricated, and denouncing the Israeli media for circulating 'lies and deceptions' with the aim of inciting public animosity against well-known Palestinian nationalists, and spreading discord amongst the inhabitants of Palestine.[28]

Another common tactic in the effort to create division involved the circulation of false and deceptive information. Daoud Kuttab described the misinformation campaign that was launched in the early spring of 1988.[29]

> Forged leaflets were distributed throughout the occupied territories outlining different protest schedules. One praised the policemen who had resigned, but called on those who hadn't resigned to stay in their jobs; another accused well-known Palestinian nationalists of appropriating money intended for the needy. In a forged document distributed in Gaza, Palestinians were told of huge sums that were to be given to striking shopkeepers and resigning tax collectors. ... The campaign climaxed with a statement by the Israeli police minister that the authors of the latest Unified Command leaflet had been captured ... The demoralisation campaign failed miserably. Palestinians had little trouble uncovering the forged leaflets and the misinformation campaign.

Undeterred, the Israelis launched another exercise in early July 1988. Two rival versions of Communique No. 21 were issued, both purportedly by the UNC. Once again, Palestinians knew from the differences in vocabulary and style which of them was a fake, produced by the Shin Bet to give the impression of divisions amongst the leadership, with the aim of spreading confusion and despondency amongst the wider Palestinian public.[30] Sometimes the same end of sowing discord and internal suspicion was pursued by facilitating the circulation of dissenting views within the Palestinian community, in the hope that the traditional rivalry between different political factions could thereby be heightened and intensified. Thus, in February 1989 Israel stopped jamming the broadcasts of the Al-Quds radio station based in Syria and run by the Syrian-backed Popular Front for the Liberation of Palestine - General Command (PFLP-GC). Its leader, Ahmed Jibril, had been one of the most virulent critics of Arafat's 'defeatist' policies. The station devoted much of its rhetoric to condemning the PLO for recognising Israel and accepting UN Resolution 242, and urging armed struggle to liberate the whole of Palestine, from the river to the sea. The purpose of the Israeli action was clear - to undermine Palestinian unity by the encouragement of sectarian extremists.

Islamic factions

In combating such efforts to create splits Palestinians had before them the example of the 1930s, when the revolt against the British and the Jewish settlers degenerated into bloody feuds and brigandage, fought out between rival groups and factions. It was just such a spectre that began to haunt them with the emergence of what appeared to be a rival to the leadership offered by the UNC, in the guise of the Islamic Resistance Movement, known by its Arabic acronym, Hamas (zeal). For most outside observers the first indication they had of the burgeoning power of this group came when Hamas called a strike throughout the occupied territories on August 21 1988, to mark the anniversary of the attempt to set fire to the al-Aqsa Mosque in 1969. The UNC had made a mistake in its twenty-third communique by merely calling for an intensification of the struggle on that day, thereby creating the opportunity for Hamas to make its move. Although Hamas had successfully organised a series of general strikes in the Gaza Strip, this was the first time it had flexed its organisational muscles in the West Bank. It was only partially successful, but for Palestinians there was the nightmare situation of supporters of rival organisations clashing in public as Hamas activists attempted to force reluctant shopkeepers to close their shops on a day when the UNC had instructed them to remain open.

The relationship between the secular Palestinian nationalist groups and the 'true believers' of Islam had always been strained. Political Islam was particularly strong in the Gaza Strip, where it was dominated by the Muslim Brotherhood, with its roots in Egypt and its base at the Islamic University in Gaza City. It was in Gaza City that the tension with the nationalists had peaked in 1981 when the Muslim Brotherhood burned down the Red Crescent library, claiming that it was a 'hot-bed of communism'.[31] During this period it received encouragement and support from the Israeli military government, who – it was reported - even supplied some of its activists with weapons to protect themselves.[32] At that time the Muslim Brotherhood believed that the raising of Islamic consciousness was its major task; liberation from occupation and the formation of an Islamic state would occur with Divine assistance once the Palestinians had become true Muslims. Consequently, it clearly served the interests of Israel to promote it as a counter-weight to the PLO. However, in the mid-1980s a change began to take place, particularly after the November 1985 prisoner exchange when a number of 'born-again' Muslims were released from Israeli jails. This new breed of believers accepted the importance of educating Muslims in the true ways of Islam, but also emphasised the need to actively oppose the Israeli occupation, arguing that the struggle could not wait until all Muslims had become committed believers. This group became known as Islamic Jihad and eventually forged working links with Fatah, which was far more acceptable as a partner than the non-believing socialists and Marxists of the other main nationalist parties. Since that time, and throughout the Intifada, Islamic Jihad adhered to the 'national consensus' and kept close contact with the UNC.

The importance of Islamic Jihad in the nationalist struggle within Gaza became apparent early in October 1987 when seven of its members were killed in ambushes set up by the Israeli security forces. This event helped to fuel the popular discontent that gave birth to the Uprising in Gaza a few weeks later. Concerned by its loss of support to Islamic Jihad, the Muslim Brotherhood decided to adopt a more activist stance against the occupation, and created the Islamic Resistance Movement as its 'fighting arm' shortly after the commencement of the Uprising. Up to that time it had been Islamic Jihad that had attracted the attentions of the security forces, and in many ways the emergence of Hamas as the dominant Islamic grouping in the Intifada can be attributed to the vacuum created by the arrest of so many members of Islamic Jihad, which Hamas was only too eager to fill, with the tacit support of the Israelis, who seemed remarkably reluctant to detain Hamas activists. The publication of its charter in August 1988 must have given fresh hope to the Israelis that the unity of the Palestinian Uprising was about to be riven asunder. In it Hamas expressed its opposition to PLO proposals for an international conference, and any settlement involving the partition of the land and a twin-state solution. Such initiatives, it was argued, 'run counter to the principles of the Islamic Resistance Movement, since giving up part of Palestine is like giving up part of our religion'. A Hamas sympathiser was quoted as saying, 'There can be no compromise about Islamic claims to Palestine; the Koran and history show that Jews are untrustworthy; and the PLO is a secular organisation full of communists and atheists'.[33]

Such pronouncements created a marvellous opportunity for the Israelis to taint the Uprising with the stain of 'Islamic Fundamentalism', setting off alarm bells in the international community. The fact that there was a strong element of anti-semitism in the Charter, and that Hamas looked forward to the establishment of an Islamic state between the river and the sea, was an added bonus for the Israeli authorities. Such a threat would help to seal over the divisions that had emerged within Israeli society concerning the suppression of the Intifada and the possibilities of a negotiated settlement with the Palestinians. It was also hoped that the emergence of Hamas would weaken the commitment to the Intifada of the Christians amongst the Palestinians, for whom the prospect of an Islamic state was a less than reassuring prospect.

Palestinian suspicion of Israeli connivance in the growth of Hamas was reinforced on September 9 1988, when members of the Israeli security forces stood by as Hamas activists forced shopkeepers to close their premises, contrary to the orders of the UNC which had called for a general strike the previous day.[34] In spite of such occurrences the UNC did all in its power to avoid the catastrophe of a split in the resistance movement. In Communique No. 25, issued on September 6 1988, it criticised the use of force by Hamas to impose its strike orders and warned of the 'free service to the enemy' that Hamas was providing by its divisive stance. However, the hand of solidarity was extended:

> We have stretched our arms in the past and we are extending them to every force that wants to contribute to the national effort. We do not exclude Hamas from our efforts to unify our positions ... we call for strengthening the national unity and for not breaking the national consensus by coordination with the unified leadership. We call on preachers at mosques to speak on unity, in order to guarantee the Uprising and assure its continuity.

In the succeeding months a series of intense meetings were held, inside and outside the occupied territories, in order to effect some kind of rapprochement. By January 1989 these negotiations appeared to have borne fruit. Hamas was beginning to observe the same strike days as the UNC, and whilst relationships could not be described as cordial, there was a mutual commitment that both sides should try to coordinate their activities in pursuit of their common goal of ending the occupation, accepting that their visions of the nature of the Palestinian state to which they ultimately aspired were markedly different. Subsequent cases of conflicting instructions being issued by Hamas and the UNC as regards strike days were often due to the inevitable problems of coordination between the leadership of two organisations, both operating clandestinely in the context of a military occupation, with all the problems of arranging and keeping meetings that such a situation entailed.[35]

In May 1989, the Israeli authorities finally seemed to realise that they had helped to create a monster they could no longer control. They arrested over 250 Hamas activists in the West Bank and Gaza, including their unofficial leader Sheikh Ahmad Yassin. Four months later they finally outlawed the movement. Informed sources suggested, however, that the reason for such a reversal in policy was related to Israel's proposal of elections in the occupied territories, and the consequent desire to promote a 'moderate' and pliant Palestinian leadership that would cooperate in such a scheme. Hamas clearly did not fit in with such a scenario.[36] Whatever the aims of Israel's policy, the simple fact was that during the first three years of the Intifada the influence of the Islamic movements grew, not just in their heartland of the Gaza Strip but throughout the occupied territories and indeed within Israel itself. One sign of their burgeoning presence was the political graffiti, with more and more walls covered with slogans like 'Through Jihad the country will be recovered!', 'Yes to resistance! No to political haggling!', 'Hamas is the true representative of our armed people!', 'The Koran is the sole and legitimate representative of the Palestinian people!'[37]

Promoting an alternative leadership

A key constituent of Israel's policy towards the Palestinians had been the refusal to recognise the PLO and hence a refusal to consider the organisation as a possible negotiating partner. Before the Intifada Israel could always produce internationally acceptable reasons for such a stance - after all you could not be expected to negotiate with terrorists. You did not negotiate with those who wanted to destroy the state of Israel and drive its people into the sea. After the PLO's historic concessions of late

1988 and early 1989 when, for the first time, it unequivocally recognised the state of Israel and accepted a two-state solution, and also renounced the use of lethal violence against civilian targets, the Israeli rationale for refusing to recognise the PLO was seriously weakened. Even its patron, the United States, began a formal dialogue with PLO officials. Israel came under considerable diplomatic pressure to follow suit, particularly since King Hussein had made it clear that he was no longer laying claim to represent the Palestinians. In an attempt to escape from his predicament Prime Minister Shamir proposed that elections be held in the occupied territories, excluding East Jerusalem, so that the Palestinians might choose who to represent them in negotiations with Israel over the terms of some Camp David-style autonomy for the future. This was Shamir's Peace initiative, launched in the spring of 1989.

As far as the Palestinians were concerned this was only the latest ploy in the familiar Israeli strategy of trying to drive a wedge between their leaders inside and those outside the occupied territories. In Communique No. 38, issued on April 10 1989, the UNC rejected the proposal out of hand, dismissing it as an attempt at 'undermining the Uprising' and 'finding an alternative leadership to the PLO'. In a further attempt to close ranks and counter reports from Israeli sources of local Palestinian interest in elections, a declaration affirming their rejection of Shamir's proposal was issued on behalf of 83 leading Palestinians. In case anyone still felt tempted to step outside the parameters established by the UNC, then more forceful means were at hand. A group of prominent personalities in Nablus were visited by local strike forces and warned in no uncertain terms to stop meeting with Israeli officials. Sometime later one of them had his store premises firebombed. Undeterred by such attempts to maintain a united front in opposition to their proposals, the Israelis continued to 'invite' Palestinians to meet with them. One exercise that caused considerable amusement in Palestinian circles was when the Military Governor of Tulkarm summoned the barbers and some other shopkeepers of the town to meet with the Military Adviser for Arab Affairs. Asked about their opinion concerning elections, they replied 'This is the authority of the responsible people of the PLO. We have nothing to do with political affairs'.[38] 'Is this what is intended by the search for an alternative leadership?' my Palestinian translator chortled.

In general, however, the Israelis targeted their invitations at representatives of the traditional, pro-Jordanian establishment: businessmen and political figures who could be considered to have most to lose by the continuation of the Intifada. Aware that they could not prevent such meetings taking place, the UNC declared that the contents of such meetings should be made public by those who were required to participate in them, in order to prevent the Israelis exploiting them for their own purposes. Thus, in July 1989 it emerged that Prime Minister Shamir had held meetings with some Palestinians, when one of their number, Jamil al-Tarifi, the ex-deputy mayor of Al Bireh, held a press conference in which he gave details of the encounter. Faisal Husseini later explained the thinking behind this new approach to the problem.[39]

> It is obvious that these meetings more often than not are a sort of monologue rather than a dialogue. What happens in such meetings is that Shamir tries to explain his plan and listens to some comments from the other party, nothing more than that. Shamir, at the same time, tries to make these meetings secret to convey the impression that there is something going on behind the curtain. This is meant to be a message to the West not to press Israel to talk to the PLO because there is something cooking which may lead to results. Shamir, however, knows very well that his attempt to create a new leadership will never be successful, so in fact what Shamir is after is to gain more time

> in his war against the Intifada and an excuse to cover his operations against it. Given that these meetings cannot be avoided, the Palestinian leadership should know about them before and after they take place, in order to avoid their negative effects.

Underlying the determination to defeat the Israeli attempts to create an alternative leadership was a persistent concern at the level of unease experienced by some representatives of the established pre-Intifada order in the occupied territories. As one Palestinian observed to me: 'There is a new mood, and a new style of leadership. There is a profoundly democratic social process taking place that is very threatening to the bourgeois leadership in Tunis and within Palestine.'

As the Intifada moved into its third year the temptation to risk a political initiative increased, especially amongst those Palestinians who felt their status and influence to be under threat. The reasoning was along the following lines: 'Everyone is suffering during the Uprising. The existing leadership, and the PLO in Tunis, are failing to make any political headway towards bringing the suffering to an end. No one would dispute that the elections proposals leave a lot to be desired, but maybe it is the best offer we can get. At least if we go along with it, we will have made some progress in the peace process, we will have started talking to each other ...' It was an indication of the strength and resilience of the political system established during the Intifada that people were not afraid to discuss and argue such points of view within their own circles. However, what kept such people within the bounds of the national consensus was the unity of Palestinian society during the Uprising, and the political solidarity behind the UNC. Only the followers of Hamas would publicly question the political authority of the UNC in its role as leader of the struggle against the Israeli occupation. In the words of one Palestinian, interviewed in 1989:

> You sense that the leadership is not separate from the Palestinian people, but that it is present everywhere... You feel a unity and an amazing solidarity which differs from anything else we've felt in the 20 or 21 years since the PLO was formed. One has never felt this unity between the Palestinian people and its leadership that one has felt during the Uprising. One feels about the Unified National Leadership, which is frankly the PLO inside, that its decisions and policies were issued in accordance with a sensitivity to the problems and suffering of the Palestinians people and to the directions of the legitimate leadership of the PLO outside. We feel one with them.[40]

Towards an organic state

If, by the term 'state', one refers to a set of institutional structures that command obedience from the inhabitants of a certain geographical territory, then the Palestinians succeeded during the early years of the Uprising in establishing their own state in the West Bank and Gaza Strip. In the UNC and the network of popular committees they created a body that commanded the loyalty and obedience of the vast majority of the population, and which fundamentally challenged the Israeli administration as the locus of power and authority in the occupied territories. The degree to which the Israelis lost whatever legitimacy their rule might once have enjoyed was evidenced by the extent to which they were forced to rely on coercion and other forms of domination in order to command obedience from the civilian population. By contrast with the Israeli administration, the embryonic Palestinian state structure was not seen as an imposed alien entity, but rather as an organic extension of civil society. A genuine sense of identification emerged between the population of the occupied territories and the UNC and its associated institutions. As one informant described this relationship: 'Our leadership express our ambitions and aspirations. They embody our ambitions, and respond to our aspirations'.

Such a close sense of identity between the state and civil society is a rare phenomenon. For most socialists, states appear as alienated social power, serving, in the final analysis, the interests of a minority in the name of the common good. By contrast the newly formed Palestinian 'semi-state' appeared as a natural expression of the political will of the population as a whole. Such an unusual phenomenon could be attributed to a number of factors: the nature of Palestinian society in the occupied territories during the Intifada, the form of organisational infrastructure developed, and the qualities of the leadership group itself.

For Marxists, the state, as a set of institutional structures serving the interest of the few in the name of society as a whole, will persist for as long as the society is riven by class divisions. A major characteristic of Palestinian society during the Uprising was that whilst class differences and social divisions persisted, they were overshadowed to a significant degree by a shared sense of purpose, and a common experience of oppression and suffering at the hands of the Israeli state. This was most vividly expressed to me during a conversation I had with the occupant of a refugee camp in the central area of the West Bank in 1989.

> Everyone helps each other ... all the people have the same way now, the same struggle against the occupation - from the children to the old men, all the same, they want to get rid of the occupation. One soul through many bodies, through many voices. It is not organised by the PLO, as they say. The PLO and the Palestinian people are the same. The PLO represents the aspirations, the ambitions for the future, of the Palestinian people .... The PLO is an output of the Palestinian people. The PLO without the Palestinian people means nothing ... The oppression is not against part of our so-

> ciety, it is against all of society. Every family in our society has suffered very much. People have come to feel that they are connected more together ... all the people are suffering, all segments suffer from the occupation.

The shared experience of oppression and suffering resulted in a narrowing of social divisions, with a corresponding increase in the level of reciprocity and mutual aid amongst all sectors of society. Underpinning this there emerged a common commitment to a body of values and beliefs, centred on the need to maintain the struggle in order to end the occupation. Such characteristics constitute some of the defining features of a 'community'.[41] Indeed, there is a sense in which Palestinian society at the height of the Intifada could be likened to a 'community of communities', a phenomenon to which the UNC and the popular committees gave organisational expression. Another characteristic of communities is their relatively small size - sufficiently small for most members to know each other. Socially, as well as geographically, the West Bank and Gaza Strip were small-scale societies. Particularly during the Intifada, with all the attendant problems of travel and communication, people tended to stay in their own neighbourhoods, quarters and villages. This meant that the popular committees at the base of the political system constituted *neighbourhood* committees. The members were friends, relatives, and neighbours - in addition to being local political leaders. As such, they never constituted any kind of separate political stratum, apart from civil society. Moreover, with the constant rotation and replacement of members due to the security situation, the level of political specialisation remained remarkably low. The division of political labour was not fixed and permanent, rather it was in a constant process of flux. This all worked to obstruct the emergence of any permanent political elite with interests separate from the rest of society. At every level of the organisational infrastructure, right up to the UNC itself, the occupants of political positions shared with the rest of the population the experience of oppression, the risk of arrest and injury, and consequently the likelihood of being replaced at some stage in the struggle by someone else.

Insofar as the political system that the Palestinians created was a radically decentralised one, with the devolution of powers to the local level, the role of the UNC became primarily one of establishing general political guide-lines and coordinating activities throughout the occupied territories. Thus, whilst it continued to issue authoritative instructions and commands, in a manner reminiscent of hierarchically organised state systems, the UNC had to be responsive to the promptings from below in order to sustain the commitment and unity essential to the struggle. A close observer of the Intifada commented on this aspect of the UNC's functioning during the first year of the Uprising.[42]

> The policy of the leadership to give authority and power to local committees, its willingness to listen and many times change or even reverse its own decisions, shows how close to the average person the leadership is. ... This quality meant that the command was seen as a communicator of ideas and suggestions of the population, rather than a leadership trying to impose its predetermined ideas.

This sense of an organic linkage between the political leadership and the population was brought home to me very strongly on one of my research trips to the occupied territories in 1989. I was given a lift by a young man who was in the final year of his 'underground' university degree course. As we drove through the West Bank he related to me how his original suspicions of the shadowy entity that called itself the UNC were dispelled. He had discovered that one of its members had been a fellow-student of his at university. He knew him to be honest, modest and, moreover, he was not from one of the well-known and established Palestinian families. He was not an opportunist politician, he was 'one of us!'

The symbiotic nature of this relationship meant that the unity of the leadership acted as an example to the rest of society, whilst the sense of solidarity amongst all sections of the population augmented the political alliance at the heart of the UNC and the embryonic state structures that grew up around it. Conversely, when stresses and tensions emerged within the wider society, they were reflected within the UNC itself. It was in the summer of 1989 that signs of such a 'negative' process began to emerge in the occupied territories. Its most obvious manifestation was in the mounting difficulty that the UNC encountered in maintaining 'law and order' - the core function of any state power. By the spring of 1990 more Palestinians were being killed by their fellow citizens than by the Israeli security forces. Most of the killings were of alleged collaborators. Tracing this thread of the collaborators and the treatment meted out to them through the wider fabric of the Intifada as a whole can throw some light on the process whereby the 'state power' of the UNC was eroded.

Collaborators

When Israel occupied the West Bank in 1967 it also captured the secret files containing the details of all the informers upon whom the Jordanian internal security forces had relied. Israel took over the management of many of these people to act as the eyes and the ears of the occupier. Their numbers were further augmented by means of blackmail, bribery and other forms of coercion and inducement.

Whilst the number of people who knowingly passed on information about their fellow citizens to the Israelis could be counted in their thousands, as 'collaborators' they fell into different categories. At a relatively innocuous level there were people like the traditional village leaders who acted as 'go-betweens' through whom fellow community members went to obtain licenses, permits and other necessary documentation from the occupying power. Such people provided a much-valued service. They were in a position to intervene with the authorities on behalf of their 'clients'. As 'brokers' they obtained services from their patrons, the Israelis, in return for information. However, their fellow citizens were generally well aware that the information that was passed on to the Israelis was of a fairly low-grade order. At the other extreme there were the out-and-out informers, the active collaborators who sought out sensitive information related to 'security matters' and passed it on to the Israeli security agenciest. On their shoulders lay the responsibility for the imprisonment of many Palestinians. They were readily identifiable in their local communities, not least because they carried Israeli-issued firearms for self-protection.

At the outbreak of the Intifada, the call went out for all informers to turn over a new leaf and re-enter the 'Palestinian house'. In Communique No. 11 March 29 1988 was named the 'Day of Repentance', when collaborators had the chance to confess their treachery and 'return to the national consensus on pain of the punishment due to them'. Whether through social pressures, genuine repentance, or fear of injury and death, many erstwhile informers responded to the call. Throughout the occupied territories those who had spied on their fellows attended special gatherings in their local mosques, where they publicly relinquished their weapons and vowed never again to work for the Israelis. They had before them the example of a collaborator from Qabatiya, who was killed by his fellow villagers on February 26 1988. Just ten days later the corpse of a Jericho policeman was discovered. According to some accounts, his fate had been sealed after an electronic listening device was discovered on his person as he was confessing the error of his past ways in the local mosque.

For those who had sunk too deep into the swamp of treachery to free themselves, life became increasingly difficult. In the most highly organised communities they faced a graduated scale of sanctions. They were treated as outcasts; people refused to have any social contact with them except to hurl verbal abuse. Their houses would be attacked with stones. They risked being beaten up and physically assaulted by the local strike forces. If these measures proved ineffective, then the next stage might be a fire-bomb attack on their house and premises. If the collaborator still refused to repent and give up his old ways, or failed to flee, then the death sentence would be passed, in consultation with the leadership outside, and would be carried out by special hit squads.

The apparent reluctance with which the leadership of the Uprising resorted to the ultimate sanction of the death penalty was due to a number of factors. At one level they were responding to the genuine sense of national solidarity that permeated the Palestinian community during the Uprising. There was a real desire to provide the collaborators with every reasonable opportunity to forsake their treachery and join the national struggle. The leadership was also keen to avoid damaging the image of the Intifada in the international community: that of a unified people pursuing an unarmed struggle against a brutal army of occupation. They were aware of the propaganda capital that the Israelis could make out of the killings, portraying them as part of a politically coordinated terror campaign orchestrated by the PLO to intimidate the inhabitants of the occupied territories. Behind such concerns lay the nightmare example of the revolt of the 1930s when false charges of collaboration were levelled against rivals as a means of exacting vengeance and the pursuit of private ends. This was the spectre that returned to haunt the leadership of the Palestinians during the latter half of 1989. Up until April 1989 the number of Palestinians killed for alleged collaboration was put in the region of 60 by the military authorities. At that time it was hard to find a Palestinian who did not believe that the collaborators had received their proper desserts, and that their sentence had been arrived at through a just process in which they had been given every opportunity to repent. However, as spring turned into summer there was a dramatic increase in the number of slayings. It became clear that the fate of suspected collaborators was no longer being referred up to the leadership, and that local strike forces were increasingly taking matters into their own hands as judges and executioners.

This development was a cause of great concern to the leadership, both inside and outside the territories. The UNC began to urge restraint, repeatedly reminding people that the utmost care should be taken when considering the evidence held against a suspect, that other forms of punishment should be considered apart from the death penalty, and demanding that no executions should be carried out without the approval of the Palestinian leadership. They were well aware that such killings would only serve to engender an atmosphere of suspicion and distrust amongst the Palestinian community, which could be readily exploited by the Israeli security forces. In October 1989 Arafat himself issued a special appeal calling for a halt to the slayings - seemingly to little effect. It became increasingly apparent that many of the so-called collaborators were in fact victims of old feuds and factional fighting. In a continuing effort to control the killings the UNC established reconciliation committees to mediate between the conflicting parties. Once again these had only a limited impact on the problem and by the spring of 1990 there was the awful statistic that more Palestinians were being slain by their fellow citizens than by the occupying forces. How had such a state of affairs come about?

The embryonic state - the threat of a miscarriage?

In the autumn of 1989 I travelled to Nablus to visit an old friend and his family. It had become a custom on such trips to spend a morning wandering through the old city, ending up at our favourite *kanafeh* stall. On this occasion, however, my friend dismissed the suggestion of a stroll. He confessed that he could not guarantee my safety. People might think I was an Israeli and, moreover, they might think he was a collaborator. If I needed a reminder of how tense the situation in Nablus had become after two years of the Intifada, this was it. My visit coincided with a period when two groups of armed young Nabulsis known as the Black Panthers and the Red Eagles had become the de facto power on the streets of the old city, executing those they suspected of collaboration or immoral behaviour such as prostitution and drug use. Although these two gangs caught the headlines, even posing for the media beside the body of one of their victims, they were in some ways merely the most public manifestation of a wider phenomenon - the erosion of the power of the UNC and its transfer to the young activists of the strike forces. To understand this process one has to take account of a number of inter-related developments. Throughout the latter months of 1989 and on through the spring of 1990 the PLO was engaged in laborious and protracted political manoeuvrings around Egyptian and American proposals concerning the modalities of a proposed Israeli-Palestinian meeting in Cairo to discuss the holding of elections in the occupied territories. For the Palestinians it was a time of growing frustration at the lack of political progress and mounting resentment against those suspected of collaboration with the Israeli authorities.

They had lived through the excitement of the declaration of an independent state of Palestine. They had invested hope in the US - PLO dialogue. They had waited for international censure to shame Israel to the negotiating table. Meantime they had spent nearly three years protesting, struggling and suffering. For what? The world seemed to have lost interest in the Intifada. The peace process had been still-born. In June 1990 the United States had broken off its dialogue with the PLO and an extreme right-wing government had been formed in Israel. Understandably tired after so many months of resistance, and increasingly frustrated by the lack of any significant breakthrough at the political and diplomatic level, the feeling grew amongst significant sections of the Palestinian community that what was necessary was an increase in the level of violence sufficient to shock the states of the world into action.

Within all political factions there was debate about whether or not the armed struggle should be resumed through an escalation in the level of violence. This went along with a growing concern that Arafat was prepared to concede far too much in exchange for far too little as part and parcel of his pragmatic diplomacy. The PFLP was loudest in its condemnation of the path of compromise and concession and there were a number of clashes between its supporters and members of Fatah, and with those activists of the DFLP who continued to align themselves with the mainstream of the nationalist camp, despite serious differences within their own ranks.[43] Indeed, at one stage during the spring of 1990 a rapprochement seemed to be emerging between the Marxist PFLP and the Islamic factions of Hamas and Islamic Jihad based on their shared opposition to Fatah's apparent readiness to accept James Baker's proposals for an Israeli-Palestinian dialogue.[44] A further manifestation of the growing political disarray within the occupied territories was a relative decline in the grass-roots activity of the popular committees as more of their functions were taken over by committees representing the different factions. These tensions and divisions within the occupied territories reflected the growing strains within the PLO outside, with radical factions becoming increasingly strident in their criticisms of Arafat's failure to produce political results.

The depth of resentment and frustration within the occupied territories was further evidenced by the widespread and passionate support voiced by Palestinians for Saddam Hussein after his invasion of Kuwait in August 1990. Here at last was an Arab capable of making the world take notice. The reaction of the United States and its allies only highlighted the hypocrisy of those states who were prepared to extend their sympathy to the Palestinians in their suffering, but were unprepared to act in any meaningful manner to force the Israelis to withdraw from the lands they had invaded and occupied in 1967. However cynical and opportunistic Saddam's efforts to link the issue of Kuwait to the question of Palestine, the majority of people in the occupied territories were so desperate that they were prepared to invest their hopes in any source that promised them relief from oppression. In the process, of course, they reversed the whole trend towards self-reliance in their struggle against Israeli occupation that had been the hallmark of the Intifada. Once again they were placing their faith in the rhetoric of an Arab leader. Few amongst their leaders had the political and physical courage to sound a discordant note about the fundamental inconsistency involved in a dispossessed people pledging their support for someone who was intent on annexing a people and their territory by means of force in another part of the Middle East region.

An unsought consequence of this burgeoning faith in an external saviour was that the Palestinians left untended the infrastructure of popular committees that had become the organisational backbone of the Uprising. This process of deterioration was in turn compounded by a number of other factors which contributed to a crisis of morale and discipline within the occupied territories. By the late summer of 1990, for the first time since the Uprising had begun, there were signs of a serious undermining of the authority of the UNC. Whilst seeking to replace the Israeli state as the locus of political authority within the occupied territories, the UNC was finding it increasingly difficult to perform that most fundamental of state functions - the maintenance of law and order. The unauthorised slaying of alleged collaborators continued unabated, family and clan feuds persisted, and theft and other forms of criminal activity increased.

A major reason why the UNC found it so difficult to counteract these forces of disorder was the simple fact that it could no longer rely on middle level cadres of experienced activists to control the young hot-heads of the streets. The Israeli policy of mass arrests had netted so many of them that many areas had been left in the hands of young leaders with little experience, political education or discipline. As one Palestinian remarked:

> Today there is no obedience any more. Every young thug organises a group of six or seven youths in his neighbourhood and gets them to throw stones or petrol bombs at Israeli cars. They are not connected with any central organisation; they do whatever they want. The real problem is that as new activists join the struggle, and as more activists are jailed, the level of street leadership deteriorates rapidly. Add this to the economic and other pressures applied by the Israelis, and you'll find there is a feeling of despair among many of us, who ask ourselves: where is all this leading to? [45]

The underlying fear of such people was that the Intifada would continue to degenerate into a cycle of escalating violence, not just between Israelis and Palestinians, but within the Palestinian community itself, a cycle borne of frustration and suffering.

In the weeks following the end of the Gulf War it seemed as if the worst fears about the deterioration of the Uprising were beginning to materialise. On a research trip to the region in April 1991 I was struck by the depths of depression displayed by once-confident friends and acquaintances. It was as if they were still in a state of shock following the total defeat of Iraq. One Palestinian friend told of how he was unable to summon the will even to step outside his house for two days following the Iraqi surrender. He, and others like him, had been shocked into immobility. Their hopes had been dashed, and what was left was a deep anger and disgust at what was perceived as the depths of hypocrisy displayed by the United States and its allies, so eager to pursue justice in the case of oil-rich Kuwait but so reluctant to exercise the slightest sanction against Israel. This shattering of self-confidence and morale was painful to witness. Equally disturbing was the sense of desperation and frustration which led people whom I counted amongst my dearest friends to admit to me that they were now prepared to countenance the extension of the liberation struggle along a new front - that of violence. If nothing else, this impressed upon me that the Gulf War had marked a watershed in the history of the Intifada. My research trip took place during the period of Secretary of State James Baker's series of visits to the region, in his efforts to capitalise on American post-Gulf War prestige and initiate some form of peace process involving Israel, the Arab states and the Palestinians. Opinion within the occupied territories as to the appropriate response to Baker was polarised, and this division was reflected within the UNC itself. One view was that the United States could never be trusted, that the real purpose of Baker's attempts to meet with Palestinians from the occupied territories was to marginalise even further the PLO leadership in Tunis. Hence, it was argued that the Palestinians should have nothing to do with the United States brokered peace initiative. As one informant expressed his version of this perspective:

> Maybe we can do nothing, and maybe we should do nothing. The Palestinian people exist. The PLO exists. It is a reality, and they will have to deal with it someday. We still exist and we have the power to wreck any peace settlement that denies us our fundamental rights. Maybe the Gulf Crisis will prove a blessing for the Palestinians, it will make us more realistic, rid us of the naive hopes we had, help us realise that civilian resistance on its own cannot bring independence ... Moreover, how long do you think the Arab regimes that supported America are going to survive?

This man was someone I had always considered to be a moderate, someone from the mainstream of Fatah. Yet, in his analysis and prescriptions he was aligning himself with the more radical factions within the PLO who urged that Baker be shunned, in the expectation that the balance of forces in the Arab world would eventually shift in favour of the Palestinians, and meantime the resistance to occupation should be intensified. Opposed to this standpoint was the mainstream of Fatah and the members of the DFLP who had aligned alongside them. From their perspective, the Gulf War had seriously undermined the substantial achievements of the Intifada. The suffering of the Palestinians during and since the war had reached new levels. People were in a parlous state, forced to concentrate on economic survival and without the will or the reserves to intensify the struggle. Furthermore, the influx of Russian Jews to Israel presaged an acceleration of settlement activity in the occupied territories. So, dreams of an intensification of the resistance struggle were misdirected, and any delay of a peace settlement would allow the Israelis to create more and more 'facts' on the land of Palestine. What was needed was a strategy of transition. The Palestinians should participate in the peace process, however gloomy the prospects, in the hope that out of it might emerge some form of home rule for the inhabitants of the occupied territories. This could then create the space necessary to rebuild the crippled economic and institutional infrastructure of Palestinian society, upon which could be based a new stage of the struggle for independence.

The advocates of such a politics of transition felt particularly vulnerable. They saw themselves treading a sensitive path, caught between an outside leadership that appeared to be out of touch with the realities in the occupied territories, and the street youths who were increasingly running out of control. Since the slaughter at the al-Aqsa Mosque of October 1990 there had been an increase in the number of stabbings and lethal knife attacks upon Israelis.[46] Moreover, the execution of alleged informers and collaborators had continued unabated. Despite all efforts of the UNC to curtail the actions of these vigilantes, by April 1991 it was estimated that somewhere in the region of 350 Palestinians had been killed by their fellow countrymen in the occupied territories.[47] Such was the concern that well-informed Palestinians were beginning to express their fears for the lives of people like Faisal Husseini who persisted in leading delegations to meet with James Baker, thereby incurring the wrath of a sizeable proportion of his compatriots. By mid-1991 a situation had arisen where the hot-heads dominated the streets whilst the political factions were split as to the best strategy to pursue in the post-Gulf War world. It was clear that the old days of political unity were disappearing. It seemed to more than a few observers that the political factions were once again manoeuvring and jockeying for political advantage, rather than seeking the basis for a new national consensus.

Despite the differences and rivalries, all factions were agreed that the Gulf Crisis and subsequent war heralded a new phase in the Palestinian struggle, and serious thought had to be devoted to the direction to be pursued. There was a growing awareness that many of the routine forms of resistance during the Intifada, such as general strike days and commercial strikes, constituted an additional burden upon an already pauperised population. Through such forms of resistance Palestinians were hurting themselves more than they were hurting the Israelis. From such a realisation two possible paths seemed to offer themselves. If one accepted that the Palestinian economy was far too weak to sustain any mass form of unarmed resistance for any meaningful length of time, then it followed that either one pursued a different form of resistance ('vertical escalation' in the direction of violence), or one adopted a strategy of creating the necessary base to sustain the 'horizontal escalation' of the struggle in the direction of mass disengagement from the Israeli economy upon which so many Palestinians remained dependent. For the second option to be achieved there would need to be some form of 'breathing space', a period during which economic growth and institutional development could be undertaken. This might be possible within the context of some form of home rule, hence the justification for some kind of 'compromise' that would facilitate such a strategy of transition.

The underlying fear of those who advocated such a strategy was that if they lost the debate, then the Intifada would continue to degenerate into a cycle of escalating violence - not just between Israelis and Palestinians, but within the Palestinian community itself. A cycle borne of frustration, suffering and desperation. If this were to happen it would mark a dreadful degeneration of the struggle. Far from being a people's movement of resistance, involving the mass of the inhabitants of the occupied territories in the struggle for their own national and human rights, it would be transformed into that old pattern of resistance in which the wielders of lethal weapons became the heroes, leaving the bulk of the Palestinian population as supporting actors in the drama. This in turn could have a profound impact on the nature and quality of political life, particularly with regard to the relationship between state and civil society in the occupied territories. Relegated to the role of auxiliaries while the professionals, the men of violence and the diplomats, resumed their trades wielding their guns and their olive branches, the mass of people would become increasingly marginal to the main decision-making centres of the resistance. After all, what can an amateur contribute to the strategic planning of an armed struggle? What can ordinary people contribute to the work of globe-trotting diplomats? They can supply material and ideological support, they can be loyal, they can follow instructions. Once again the flow of commands would be downwards and the mechanisms through which Palestinians during the Intifada had joined in dialogue with their political leadership would fall into disuse as the division of labour between expert and amateur, hero and auxiliary, leader and led was re-established.

---

[1] See Schiff & Ya'ari (1989), p. 195.

[2] In 1985 Israel had exchanged some 1000 political prisoners for six Israeli soldiers captured during the Lebanon War and held by the *Popular Front for the Liberation of Palestine – General Command.*

---

[3] See J. Stork, 'The significance of the stones', *Middle East Report*, Sept. - October, 1988, p. 7.

[4] See Schiff & Ya'ari, p. 199.

[5] D. Kuttab, *Middle East International*, March 19, 1988, p. 9.

[6] See L. Andoni, *Middle East International*, March 19, 1988, pp. 9-10.

[7] As early as January 18, 1988 a money changer's shop in East Jerusalem was fire-bombed for continuing to trade on strike days.

[8] *Independent*, July 14, 1988.

[9] Quoted in *Christian Science Monitor*, May 2 - 8, 1988.

[10] Palestinian Centre for the Study of Nonviolence, *Intifada: Palestinian nonviolent protest, part II*, East Jerusalem, May 1989.

[11] Transcript of interview carried out by Marwan Darweish for the film *Voices from Gaza*, directed by Antonia Caccia, 1989.

[12] These observations are based on information gathered during interviews and conversations with informed participants.

[13] In the early days of the Uprising leadership of the PCP was with people within the occupied territories. This gave them a greater degree of autonomy than that enjoyed by the other main groupings. See Schiff & Ya'ari, p. 198.

[14] This also involved an important educational function insofar as every special day of action usually commemorated an important event in Palestinian history.

[15] See M.R.D. Foot, *Resistance: An analysis of European resistance to Nazism, 1940-45*, London: Eyre Methuen, 1976, p. 8.

[16] D. Hirst, *The Guardian*, November 12, 1988.

[17] See M. Rabbani, 'The PLO and the Intifada – a complex relationship', *Middle East International*, March 31 1089, p. 20.

[18] Quoted in *Al Fajr* (English), May 15, 1988.

[19] Quoted in *Independent*, May 12, 1988.

[20] *Jerusalem Post*, March 20, 1988.

[21] See *Punishing a nation: Human rights violations during the Palestinian Uprising, December 1987 – December 1988*, Ramallah: Al Haq, 1988, chapter 9.

[22] Quoted in *Punishing a nation*, p. 320.
[23] The Economic Development Group and the Palestinian Association for the Study of International Affairs (PASSIA) were just two of the organisations prevented from operating normally following warnings from the Israeli authorities.
[24] *Jerusalem Post*, August 21, 1988
[25] B. Morris, *The Guardian*, August 20, 1988
[26] B. Michael, *Ha'aretz*, August 21, 1988
[27] *Jerusalem Post*, August 21, 1988.
[28] J. Greenberg, 'Salon activists feel the heat', *Jerusalem Post*, May 12, 1989.
[29] D. Kuttab, *Middle East International*, April 2 1988, p. 4.
[30] *The Guardian*, July 7, 1988. (Shin Bet is Israel's internal security agency.)
[31] D. Kuttab, *Middle East International*, October 24, 1987.
[32] M. Sela, *Jerusalem Post*, May 26, 1989.
[33] Quoted by C. Richards, *Independent*, September 26, 1988.
[34] Personal observation, East Jerusalem, September 9, 1988.
[35] This was not always the case. On occasion Hamas persisted in enforcing its own strike days in defiance of the UNC.
[36] See M. Seva, *Jerusalem Post*, May 26, 1989.
[37] A particularly provocative display of their power was in April 1990 when Islamic Jihad enforced a general strike in the predominantly Christian area of Bethlehem to mark opposition to the signing of the Camp David Accords. The UNC had instructed businesses to remain open that day in preparation for Ramadan. See *Jerusalem Post (International Edition)*, April 14 1990, p. 2.
[38] *An Nahar*, May 26, 1989.
[39] Faisal Husseini, *Al Fajr*, July 31, 1989, p. 16.
[40] Transcript, Voices from Gaza.
[41] For an elaboration of these ideas, see M. Taylor, *Community, anarchy and liberty*, Cambridge: Cambridge University Press, 1982, especially chapter one.
[42] D. Kuttab, *Washington Post*, September 4, 1988.

[43] See P. Lalor, 'DFLP differences reflect the debate within the PLO', *Middle East International*, April 27, 1990, pp. 17-19.
[44] In September 1990 an agreement was reached between Fatah and Hamas to regulate their relations as the basis for future cooperation and coordination of activities. See *Al Fajr*, September 24, 1990, p. 3.
[45] Quoted by Y. Litani, *Jerusalem Post (International Edition)*, September 16, 1989, p. 8.
[46] On October 8 1990, Israeli forces blocked worshipers from accessing the Temple Mount. The clash escalated. 20 Palestinian were killed and around 140 more were injured by Israeli fire.
[47] *Jerusalem Post*, April 9, 1991.

Andrew Rigby

3

REPRESSION AND THE THREAT TO LIFE AND LIMB

Introduction

States seek to obtain compliance from their subjects by a combination of methods. Antonio Gramsci identified two general types of political control: domination (the exercise of repression, physical coercion, and the threat of penalties and sanctions for non-compliance) and direction or hegemonic control (the exercise of control through the generation of popular consent within civil society). He assumed that no regime could sustain itself solely through coercive power. In the long run any state depended for its existence on engineering its acceptance as the locus of legitimate authority with the acknowledged right to rule over its subjects, through infusing civil society with a system of values, attitudes, beliefs and assumptions conducive to the perpetuation of the established order.[1]

The moulding of the consciousness of a people by a state in order to achieve hegemonic control obviously requires time for the various agencies of socialisation to exert their influence. When an alien state seeks to impose its will on a conquered people, it faces a serious problem of obtaining compliance from the newly subject population. Few are prepared to grant it legitimacy and accept the new regime with a whole heart. As a result, the occupiers are invariably obliged to exercise control through domination, and in particular through coercion - making credible threats about the penalties to be incurred for non-compliance. During the early years of occupation the power of the state is invariably exercised in a peculiarly open and violent manner. Those who dare to oppose the will of the occupier are made to suffer, until they lose the urge to resist and, however reluctantly, consent to submit.

According to advocates of civilian-based resistance, it is the refusal to obey and the preparedness to suffer the penalties of non-compliance and non-cooperation that erodes the social sources of an occupier's power - the subjects' willingness to obey. Gandhi maintained that 'all exploitation is based on cooperation, willing or forced, of the exploited ... there would be no exploitation if people refused to obey the exploiters.' Gene Sharp developed this argument, maintaining that:

> The power of governments derives from sources in society, such as legitimacy, economic resources, skills and knowledge, submission and obedience of the population, sanctions, and others. All of those sources in society depend on the cooperation and obedience of individuals and of institutions. When that cooperation and obedience are withdrawn, then that power is weakened in proportion to the degree that the sources are withdrawn.[2]

More than anything else the Intifada represented the withdrawal of the consent of the Palestinians of the West Bank and Gaza Strip to be ruled, and an active attempt to make the costs of continued occupation unbearable to Israel. Faced with the radical erosion of consent, the Israelis sought to impose their control by domination. The purpose of this chapter is to examine the predominant modes of domination that were attempted, particularly that of physical coercion.

Background: the Iron Fist

The authors of a Palestinian report on human rights violations during the Uprising observed:

> Few of the repressive measures undertaken by the military authorities since December 1987 were without precedent. These include beatings, opening fire at unarmed demonstrators, mass arrests, extra-judicial punishments like deportations, administrative detentions and house demolitions, collective sanctions like prolonged curfews, and other punishments which had been routinely meted out to the occupied population throughout the length of the occupation.[3]

Following the 1967 occupation of the Palestinian territories the Israelis relied disproportionately upon the 'stick' rather than the 'carrot' to impose their control. Any attempt by Palestinians to organise protest actions was quelled. Strikes by lawyers and teachers, protests against house demolitions and trade restrictions during the first year of the occupation were met by arrests and deportations, with 69 people being expelled during 1968.[4] In the Gaza Strip there was significant armed resistance against the occupation but in the West Bank those deported were generally opinion-leaders, activists in professional organisations, mayors, village elders and the like. The aim was clearly to forestall the emergence of any coherent political leadership in the territories. Palestinian sources estimated that at least 1156 people were deported between 1967 and 1978.[5] In general the Israelis justified their actions in terms of the suspects' alleged connections with 'terrorist organisations' such as the PLO. Thus, with regard to the demolition of houses, an Israeli official speaking in 1978 claimed their practice to be 'a very effective deterrent and to be a humane method ... there can be no doubt that the destruction of a few dozen houses of convicted terrorists ... has saved the lives of thousands of innocent people.'[6] Full use was also made of a measure introduced to Palestine by the British Defence (Emergency) Regulations of 1945: the detention of individuals without charge or trial for renewable periods of six months. In 1970 there were 1,131 administrative detainees.[7]

Soon after the Likud bloc came to power in 1977 the level of repression and intimidation grew as the rate of land confiscation increased and the settlement programme accelerated. Then, in 1984, the National Unity government was formed and Labour's Yitzhak Rabin became Minister of Defence. In August 1985 he launched his policy of the 'Iron Fist'. It was a clear attempt to force the Palestinians into submission by breaking their will to resist. The practices of deportation and administrative detention that had been allowed to lapse somewhat were revived. The effects could be seen in the statistics. According to Palestinian sources 43 Palestinians were deported between January 1985 and November 1987 and during the year immediately prior to the outbreak of the Intifada at least 20 people died as a direct result of actions of the occupying power. During this same twelve month period 180 suffered serious injury, 157 were imprisoned without trial under administrative detention, eight people were served with deportation orders, and 132 buildings were demolished or sealed.[8]

This tightening of the screw of repression, far from intimidating the population, served to feed their anger and frustration, their feeling that 'something must be done before it is too late'. In this way, Rabin's Iron Fist policy contributed to the emergence of the Uprising. Indeed, some would argue that it was the continuation and intensification of this policy during the Uprising that helped to sustain Palestinian resistance. As one Palestinian university student expressed it to me early in 1989:

> Economically we are suffering. Educationally we are suffering. Politically we are suffering, and in other aspects of life we are suffering. But the people have a strong will and trust in

> themselves - that they can defeat the Israelis at last, and that the Israelis should get out. We have one of two choices: either to the or to give in. This feeling is among all the people. The Israelis have taken many serious measures against the people. We are suffocated by the Israelis. But whatever measures they take, the Intifada will not end. The Palestinians have a strong will. The Israelis are very nervous, and sometimes they do not know what to do. All their measures, their killing, their arresting, deportations - they have no effect.

The Uprising as unarmed civilian-based resistance

The event that triggered off the Uprising was the death of four Gazans killed when an Israeli tank transporter crashed into a line of cars near the military checkpoint at the entrance to Gaza City. The funerals of the men were held later that day and were the occasion for demonstrations in Mughazi and Jabalya refugee camps. These continued the following day, and at Jabalya Israeli troops using live ammunition shot and killed a teenager. This precipitated further protest demonstrations throughout the refugee camps in the Gaza Strip and the West Bank. From the camps the demonstrations spread to the towns and to the villages. The pattern of large scale demonstrations and mass protest actions was soon widespread. People confronted the occupying force with slogans, flags and stones; roads were blocked with stone barricades and burning tyres, and primitive Molotov cocktails were sometimes hurled at the troops. Israeli property in the territories was targeted - banks and other premises, buses, and cars were attacked with stones and fire-bombs. This generalised form of mass protest is difficult to sustain for any lengthy period of time, and before too long spontaneous forms of mass protest gave way to more organised styles of confrontation, carried out by groups of resisters. Within different neighbourhoods and villages groups of predominantly young people developed their own tactics of harassment. I became familiar with the modus operandi adopted in one small town in the northern region of the West Bank during the summer of 1988. The youths divided themselves up into small groups, each with its own leader or commander. Some of the groups would lie in wait to ambush the settlers who drove through the town each day. Following a stoning incident the settlers would invariably stop their cars and fire after the retreating young men. The army would then hasten to the scene, along well-known routes where other groups lay in ambush armed with stones. Their aim was to entice the soldiers to pursue them into the back streets of the town where they would present a better target for other groups who awaited them there. It was all highly organised. Each squad of four to six members was supported by teenage girls supplied with cologne, lemons, and onions to counteract the effects of tear-gas. For the members of these strike forces the daily 'hit and run' confrontations had become an integral part of their life. Few of them slept in the same house every night, to minimise the risk of being arrested by the military. Of an evening one could observe many young men drifting off into the surrounding hills to sleep. In many ways theirs was the life of a guerrilla or outlaw - highly organised in small-groups, extremely mobile, completely integrated into the local society, and yet also separate from that society in terms of the type of resistance activity in which they participated. Although they did not use lethal weapons specifically designed to kill and injure, there could be no doubt that the immediate aim of their stone-throwing activity was to inflict physical injury on the potential victims.

For the young people that I came to know, stones and the occasional bottle filled with petrol was their armoury. According to Defence Minister Rabin, speaking in September 1988, 'Some 80 percent of the violence today is stone-linked - throwing and erecting barriers. The rest comprises incendiary bottles, assaults and violent demonstrations'.[9] It does not sound very threatening when compared with the weaponry available to the Israeli military (IDF). However, as one village leader reminded an interviewer:

> Don't underestimate our stones. Most of us here were brought up as shepherds, throwing stones at sheep to keep them from straying, and we learned to be very accurate. Some of us are good at using the *miqlaya* (a kind of slingshot) and can hit a sheep's rump at well over 100 metres.[10]

Stones and petrol bombs can cause serious injury and even death. At the end of October 1988 a young Israeli mother and two of her children were burnt to death after an arson attack on an Israeli bus near Jericho. In February 1989 a soldier was killed in Nablus when a concrete block was dropped on his head from a roof. Settlers and their families have been injured by stones and car accidents caused by stone-throwing attacks. Such incidents lent some much-needed credibility to Israeli attempts to label the stone-throwers as little better than terrorists, engaged in violent forms of assault with weapons almost as dangerous as guns or bombs.

One Israeli commander claimed that 'they (the Palestinians') use stones to kill, because they don't have grenades or something else'.[11] The truth is that grenades, knives and guns were used by Palestinians during the Intifada. The first soldier to be killed was shot in the head whilst he was on reserve duty in Bethlehem in March 1988. In May 1989 one soldier was killed and a number of others seriously injured in a shoot-out with three Palestinians armed with automatic weapons, grenades and small arms. A few months later, in November 1989, another was killed in an ambush on an army jeep in Gaza City. By mid-1990 a total of ten soldiers and nine Israeli civilians had been killed by Palestinians in the occupied territories. Within the borders of Israel proper 25 civilians and four soldiers had been killed by Palestinians over the same period. More often than not such killings were the result of individual anger and resentment that had welled up beyond control. For example, in November 1988 a Palestinian labourer stabbed a soldier to death outside a settlement, after he had become enraged over a dispute concerning unpaid wages. Early in May 1989 a Palestinian brandishing a kitchen knife stabbed two Israelis to death and wounded three more in Jaffa Street, West Jerusalem. Two months later, on July 6 1989, a Palestinian from Nusairat refugee camp in the Gaza Strip grabbed the wheel of a public transport bus on the Tel Aviv-Jerusalem highway, sending it toppling down a ravine and causing the deaths of 16 passengers. It was an individual act of vengeance, committed by a lone individual determined to avenge the crippling injuries inflicted upon a friend by Israeli troops in Gaza. The killing of three Israelis in a suburb of West Jerusalem in October 1990 seems to have been a similar act of vengeance committed by a Palestinian teenager in response to the slaughter of some of his fellow countrymen and the wounding of 150 others by Israeli border police in the confrontation at the Temple Mount on October 8 1990.

Whilst such lethal acts were primarily the responsibility of isolated individuals acting alone, the vast majority of the Palestinian community bore witness to their resistance by less drastic means. It is particularly worth mentioning at this juncture the various forms of 'semi-resistance' that Palestinians incorporated into their daily lives. This entailed such things as wearing clothes in the Palestinian national colours, wearing pendants and jewellery incorporating the shape of Palestine, wearing the *keffiya* head-dress or perhaps a t-shirt with a silk-screened pattern of the *keffiya* printed on it, following 'Palestinian time' by switching to summer time or winter time a week earlier than the Israelis. Such forms of symbolic, 'non-heroic' resistance were crucially important insofar as they enabled those who did not court martyrdom or imprisonment to affirm their solidarity with the Uprising. As such these forms of 'semi-resistance' were far more in keeping with the overall tenor of the Intifada as an unarmed 'people's Uprising' than the acts of murder and carnage committed by individual Palestinians.[12]

The decision to refrain from using arms was taken by the leadership of the Uprising for pragmatic reasons rather than any moral revulsion against the taking of lives as such. At one level, Palestinians knew that any resort to armed revolt on their part would invite massive retaliation with truly horrendous consequences. They knew they could not match Israel when it came to armed force. Therefore they sought to erode Israel's capacity to wield her might, and to impose political and moral costs upon Israel through the pursuit of unarmed struggle. There was a belief that so long as they refrained from using arms they could continue to appeal to the sympathy of the international community and sections of the Israeli public who would be appalled by the brutal repression of 'civilians' by military force, with Israel increasingly cast as the brutal giant waging an unequal battle against the brave 'children of the stones'.[13]

Force, might and beatings

Confronted by displays of mass defiance from broad sections of the Palestinian population, the Israelis reacted with force. The aim was clearly to restore law and order through physical intimidation and repression. If people chose to participate in protest actions, however symbolic these might be, then they must be prepared to suffer the consequences. The result was injury and death for many Palestinians. Within the first five weeks of the Uprising, some 47 Palestinians had been killed, the majority dying from bullet wounds. According to Yitzhak Shamir 'the barrier of fear of the IDF among the Arabs of Judea, Samaria and Gaza' had been broken, the task was therefore 'to recreate that barrier and once again put the fear of death into the Arabs of the areas so as to deter them from attacking us anymore.'[14]

In fact the harshness of the Israeli response became a crucial factor contributing to the intensification of the conflict, adding impetus to the Intifada during that early period. The Israelis found themselves locked into that familiar spiral where an initial act of protest is met by repression, which shocks and angers the protesters and thereby provokes a heightening of the protest, which in turn leads to an escalation of the repressive measures and so on. The cycle continued, with mounting costs to both sides. In an attempt to defuse the mounting international criticism of the use of live ammunition against unarmed civilian protesters Defence Minister Rabin announced on 19 January 1988 a policy of intimidation by non-lethal means - that of systematic beatings. Ironically, this attempt to assuage international opinion back-fired completely, particularly after footage taken by an American film-crew in late February was seen in Israel and around the world: it showed Israeli soldiers wielding rocks and clubs to break the limbs of four Palestinian youths on a hillside outside Nablus. The subsequent international and domestic pressure led the Israeli Attorney-General to insist that the illegality of beating demonstrators be made clear to the soldiers. A few weeks later the Chief of General Staff, Dan Shomron, reiterated the guide-lines under which force could be used:

> ... under no circumstances should force be used as a means of punishment. The use of force is permitted during a violent incident in order to break up a riot, to overcome resistance to legal arrest, and during pursuit after rioters or suspects ... Force is not to be used once the objective has been attained ... In every instance the use of force must be reasonable ...[15]

From the official Israeli perspective then, it was clear that any incidents of brutality were exceptions to the general rule and practice. For the soldiers in the field the situation seemed rather different. Shomron was forced to admit a year later, in March 1989, that the IDF's orders concerning the use of physical force against rioters left a 'grey area' within which each soldier had to use his own judgement. The occasion was the trial of four soldiers from the Givati Brigade accused of beating to death a resident of Jabaliya Refugee Camp on August 22 1988. Their defence was that they had 'followed orders' - these being 'to break the legs of people who violate orders' and to beat suspects in order to deter them, even when they were not resisting arrest.[16] The four were eventually found guilty of causing grievous bodily harm, but acquitted of charges of manslaughter on the grounds that so many soldiers beat and kicked the dead man that it was impossible to determine who had struck the fatal blow. The court concluded:

> It seems that every unit that arrived in Gaza received guide-lines that during the arrest of a suspected rioter, soldiers were to use their batons on limbs as a deterrent ... We learned that breaking hands was not exceptional. The court accepts the testimony that the accused were complying with the orders of their commanders, but upon investigation it appears that the written orders were completely different...[17]

In March 1988, the same month that plastic and fibreglass truncheons were introduced to replace the wooden ones that kept breaking and splintering, an Israeli army reservist attempted to map out the nature of this 'grey area' that created the space within which such shameful deeds could be committed.

> Every battalion works out its own set of norms, in accordance with its battle experience and the character of its soldiers. Every battalion commander is the sovereign of the area (under his command). Every company commander is the *mukhtar* of a village or two, and every soldier manning a road-block is a little god. He decides what to do: who will be allowed through and who won't be. Try to understand that every person there has considerable leeway when it comes to making decisions

> ... The best description I can find for what's going on there is total chaos. Our role has remained undefined. There are simply no rules governing the implementation of orders, behavioural norms, and methods of punishment. They don't exist.[18]

Reflecting on the evidence of systematic brutality committed by members of the IDF, Dr Jack Geiger of the City University of New York, suggested:

> There are two or three things going on: first there is a small community of sadists; second, soldiers find it becomes progressively easier to implement these harsh policies. The initial step is always the hardest. For all this you have to dehumanise yourself. If you convince yourself the other side is less than human, you can get away with anything.[19]

In many ways it was the practice of beating that shocked outside observers as much as anything else that the Israelis resorted to in their efforts to suppress the Intifada. Perhaps it has something to do with the paradoxical nature of beatings. At one level it is so 'human' and 'low-tech' - real people injuring others with their own hands, assisted by a few simple tools like rocks and clubs. Somehow, the use of more sophisticated weapons that allow death and injury to be inflicted 'at a distance' seems more 'civilised' - perhaps because it is so far removed from our everyday lives, beyond our comprehension. 'Face-to-face' violence is of a different order. Most of us have had some experience of it. We find it easier to identify with the perpetrator and the victim. We can recognise ourselves in them. The horror is therefore all the more when we witness the inhumane level to which 'someone like us' can be reduced; for the systematic breaking of another's limbs is not only a denial of the humanity of the victim, but by their actions the bone-breakers deny their own humanity. I quote from a newspaper report of a disciplinary hearing in which an Israeli officer was dismissed for occurrences that took place in January 1988:

> In Hawwarah, four officers and about 40 soldiers arrested twelve villagers, tied their hands and feet, shoved rags into their mouths and broke their arms and legs with clubs. They left the wounded Arabs in an orchard, witnesses said.[20]

'Non-lethal' methods of repression: gas, rubber, and plastic

Of course, beatings were not the only 'non-lethal' method adopted by the Israelis to deter and physically intimidate the protesters. Tear-gas is a common method resorted to by the forces of law and order throughout the world for dealing with riots and disturbances. Its safe use depends upon it being deployed according to the appropriate instructions. The IDF used gas canisters bearing the manufacturer's warning that the gas could cause death should it be used in confined areas. Whilst Israeli forces used tear-gas to disperse crowds and other public demonstrations, there is incontrovertible evidence that they also fired gas canisters into crowded neighbourhoods and refugee camps, into family homes and hospitals, and directly at individuals. The elderly, the very young, pregnant women, the bedridden, the chronically ill and those with respiratory problems are particularly at risk from the effects of the gas. Whilst from a medical viewpoint it is difficult to determine when tear-gas has been the sole and direct cause of death, Palestinian sources claimed that 66 deaths were caused by tear-gas during the first year of the Uprising, including 31 children - the majority of them aged under six months.[21] Many cases of miscarriage were also attributed to the effects of tear-gas.

In May 1988 Federal Laboratories of Pennsylvania announced that they were refusing to deliver any more gas to Israel until they received 'some confirmation that their [Israel's] intent [was] not to use it as a weapon'.[22] The following month a report was issued by a team of Israeli doctors who warned of the fatal consequences of using gas in closed areas. In September the IDF General Staff responded to the pressure by issuing a directive prohibiting its use in confined spaces. This resulted in a significant reduction in the number of deaths attributable to the effects of tear-gas, such that the US State Department felt able to report in the spring of 1990 that Israel 'has occasionally used tear-gas improperly and carelessly by employing it in closed areas, but this practice does not appear to be widespread'.[23] Be that as it may, after three years of the Intifada, the Palestinian Human Rights Information Centre estimated that 88 people had died as a result of tear-gas related causes.[24]

A variety of different kinds of rubber bullets were used throughout the Intifada. In fact the collection of the different types of bullet became one of the favourite past-times of Palestinian children. Whatever the type used, when fired at short-range they caused serious injuries and loss of life amongst Palestinians. A spokesman from Maqassed Hospital in East Jerusalem estimated that during the first two years of the Uprising twelve deaths had occurred at the hospital due to the metal from the rubber bullets entering the brain and that the majority of eye losses were attributable to rubber bullets shot at short range.[25] In August 1988, just prior to the issue of the new directive on the use of tear-gas, plastic bullets were introduced into the armoury of the occupation force, allegedly because rubber bullets had proved ineffective beyond a range of 50 yards. Defence Minister Rabin explained that the purpose of the plastic bullets was 'to increase the number [of wounded] among those who take part in violent activities but not to kill them.'[26] Capable of shattering bones at anything up to 70 metres, an Israeli military spokesman acknowledged in January 1989 that in the five months that plastic bullets had been in use they had caused about half the fatalities of that period, with 47 Palestinians dying from wounds inflicted by them and 288 suffering injury.

This period also saw a dramatic increase in the number of gunshot wounds suffered, with an average of 500 wounds per month. Palestinians and others explained this phenomenon by claiming that by permitting soldiers to fire plastic bullets even in non-life-threatening situations, the IDF had seriously relaxed the restrictions concerning 'open-fire situations', and contributed to an erosion of the threshold between 'lethal' and 'non-lethal' arms. Indeed, in September 1988 the army finally admitted for the first time that rubber bullets, tear-gas and plastic bullets could kill, when Chief of Staff Shomron acknowledged that 'In very isolated incidents it happens that people died of plastic bullets, but that happened also, by the way, from rubber bullets and even by those who inhaled gas.'

The rate of Palestinian deaths caused by gunshot wounds increased during the summer months of 1989 following the issuing of new open-fire orders by the IDF, which defined unarmed Palestinians who covered their faces with *keffiyas* as suspects who could be shot with live ammunition in pursuance of the normal procedure for the arrest of suspects. Amnesty International was just one of the human rights organisations to express disquiet at the new guide-lines insofar as their investigations seemed to suggest 'that the Israeli government is condoning and in effect encouraging extra-judicial executions'. In its statement issued in May 1990 Amnesty went on to voice its concern that the new directions 'appear to permit unjustifiable killings by allowing firearms to be used against people involved in activities which do not necessarily endanger life, or who are suspected of having been involved in such activities, or who are simply wearing masks.'[27] After three years of the Uprising Palestinian sources estimated the number of deaths due to gunshot at 890.[28]

Deportations

Amongst many Palestinians, the grief and mourning experienced at the death of a loved one was countered to some degree by feelings of pride for one who has joined the ranks of the 'martyrs'. Indeed, it seemed to many observers that amongst the young members of the strike forces who confronted the Israeli army with stones and Molotov cocktails, the fear of death had all but disappeared. Difficult though it may be in such cases to separate rhetoric from reality, some voiced the wish for martyrdom rather than the the 'living death' of expulsion from their homeland.

A total of 56 Palestinians were deported during the first year of the Intifada as part of the Israeli attempt to remove from the arena those they considered to be the ringleaders of the Uprising. Community leaders and grass- roots activists were targeted alongside trade unionists, lawyers, and journalists.[29] On occasions, however, it seemed as if the Israeli authorities had resorted to deportations in order to assuage the wrath of settlers and right-wing groups demanding punitive action against Palestinians. For example, following the tragic events at the village of Beita on April 6 1988 when an Israeli settler killed two Palestinians and one of the teenagers he was supposed to be guarding, demands were heard 'to raze the village of Beita and expel all rioters from the territories'. Responding to this lynch-mob atmosphere, the authorities immediately expelled six residents of the village who were allegedly involved in the incident. Such expulsion orders were based on an administrative decision against which there was no right of appeal. As such the practice was condemned by the international community, but this did not prevent Israel from expelling four Gazans in December 1990 following the fatal stabbing of three Israelis a few days earlier. Some months later, in March 1991, deportation orders were issued against a further four activists from the Gaza Strip after one Israeli was killed and five wounded in stabbing attacks during the previous week.

Demolition and collective punishments

The deportation of any individual imposes a severe emotional and economic penalty on the family that has to bear the loss of separation, with little or no hope of reunification in the short or medium term. A similar form of collective punishment resorted to by the Israeli authorities has been the demolition of homes, when the whole family is punished for the alleged crimes of one of its members. It is hard to convey the trauma of being given just a few minutes to collect your most precious belongings before your family home is either dynamited or bulldozed to the ground. You and your family are reduced to the status of refugees living in tents, years of hard labour and financial investment reduced to rubble.

According to Palestinian sources 668 homes were demolished or sealed for alleged security purposes during the first three years of the Uprising.[30] In an earlier report the Israeli Information Centre on Human Rights in the Occupied Territories (*B'Tselem*) pointed out that only 30 percent of the demolished homes in the West Bank, and 20 percent in the Gaza Strip, belonged to people suspected of being connected with a killing. Others had their homes destroyed on suspicion of incitement, resisting arrest, or throwing a petrol bomb. In some cases the homes belonged to relatives of the suspects and not to the suspects themselves, and in most cases the demolition was completed before the legal proceedings against the suspects had been concluded.[31] Within 48 hours of the incident at Beita in April 1988 15 homes were destroyed and another eight damaged by the blasts. In at least one case the home of a Gazan family was demolished because they failed to inform the authorities of the whereabouts of their son.[32]

In February 1990 a new and harsher policy was introduced of sealing the homes of Palestinian youths caught throwing stones. Such a threat of losing the family home was intended to act as a powerful disincentive for any parents who were tempted to encourage and applaud their offspring's harassment of settlers and Israeli forces. In a similar measure designed to pressure parents into preventing their children from taking part in protest activities, the practice was introduced of fining the parents of children caught throwing stones. Another form of collective punishment regularly imposed by the Israeli occupying authorities was that of the enforced confinement of people to their homes. It has been estimated that during the first year of the Intifada somewhere in the region of 1,600 curfews were imposed on areas of the West Bank and Gaza Strip. At least one quarter of these were of a prolonged nature, lasting between three and 40 days.[33] This meant that almost every Palestinian within the occupied territories suffered the disruption of daily life and the associated economic losses and costs to health of being imprisoned in his or her home during curfew.

It was during the period of the Gulf War that this method of collective punishment was imposed with unprecedented severity. A blanket curfew was imposed on the whole of the occupied territories at the outbreak of the war. For the next forty days Palestinians were only allowed out of their homes for a few hours every three or four days - once a week in the case of the Gaza Strip. From late February the situation began to ease somewhat, but the whole of the West Bank and Gaza Strip remained closed military areas, with travel between areas strictly controlled by a permit system and the discretion of the area military commanders. The impact of these measures on an already impoverished population was nothing short of catastrophic. Some 1.5 million people were imprisoned in their homes. Economic life was totally disrupted. Farmers could not tend their crops or livestock. People could not obtain medical assistance or supplies. Children could not go to school. The degree of trauma is difficult to comprehend. Moreover, the authorities maintained the restrictions on travel after the cessation of the war, further contributing to the deep bitterness felt by the vast majority of Palestinians towards the occupying power.[34]

Imprisonment and detention

Imprisonment within the home is only one form of incarceration. After three years of the Uprising the Israeli Chief Military Prosecutor estimated that somewhere in the region of 70,000 Palestinians had been arrested. At that time, in December 1990, there were a total of 9,972 in Israeli military detention centres and a further 4,000 in civilian prisons. Of those in military prisons, 762 of them were in administrative detention.[35]

Any Palestinian apprehended by the Israeli authorities and found guilty of a security related offence can expect a disproportionate sentence compared to that meted out to settlers who have committed more serious offences. One man from the Gaza Strip was sentenced to 14 years imprisonment for throwing stones and petrol bombs which did not injure anyone.[36] Another man, from Issawiyeh just outside Jerusalem, was sentenced to eleven years for throwing a petrol bomb at an Israeli army jeep and leading a 'local organisation'.[37] By comparison, a 38-year old settler was sentenced to three years in prison for killing a shepherd and wounding another one. He was also ordered to pay the equivalent of $15,000 to the murdered man's family. He had shot the men after they had refused to heed his demands that they leave the area outside Shilo settlement where they were grazing their sheep.[38] Perhaps the most notorious case of selective sentencing concerned Rabbi Moshe Levinger, a leader of militant settlers, who was sentenced to five months imprisonment for killing a Palestinian shopkeeper in Hebron. That same week a Palestinian was sentenced by a military court to life imprisonment and an additional 28 years for planting bombs in Tel Aviv. No one was injured by the explosions. In August 1990, Levinger was released from jail after serving little more than three months on the grounds of his good behaviour and overcrowding in the prisons.[39]

The largest prison facility for Palestinians, Ktzi'ot Prison (labelled Ansar III by Palestinians) was located inside Israel in the

Negev desert. At any one time somewhere in the region of 6,000 detainees were imprisoned there under the harshest of regimes. In a report of the New York based Lawyers Committee for Human Rights it was alleged that detainees were housed in primitive conditions, which did not provide adequate protection against the cold of the winter months and the heat of the summer. It was charged that discipline was imposed in an arbitrary fashion, with confinement in isolation cells as the most common form of individual punishment. Collective punishment such as the denial of cigarettes, soap and newspapers was imposed 'in arbitrary fashion for minor infractions' according to the report, which also recorded prisoners' allegations that medical services were unnecessarily withheld from prisoners who were ill and in need of treatment.[40]

Green cards

It is a familiar phenomenon that it is in prison that offenders receive the best grounding in methods of organisation and resistance. According to two Israeli observers:

> The political consciousness of the young people who are released after a stay of several months is immeasurably higher than it was prior to detention. Their self-esteem rises, and they return to their homes as local heroes. In many cases they try to retroactively justify their detention, and perhaps also get revenge, as they renew protest activity with a vengeance. Many, who were detained for minor offences, like throwing stones, burning tyres and other 'Intifada crimes' emerge from imprisonment as leading activists. Thousands of these young people have been transformed into the locomotive that leads the train of the continuing Uprising.[41]

For understandable reasons these former prisoners and detainees were marked for special attention by the Israeli security forces by means that included colour-coded identity cards. I had personal experience of how this scheme operated after I had been visiting a friend in Fara'a refugee camp, north of Nablus. When it came time to take the taxi back to Nablus, three of us walked through the camp to the road where the large Mercedes 'service' cars used to stop to pick up passengers. As we waited two soldiers emerged from the camp and demanded to see our documents. One of my companions produced a green ID card. He was promptly escorted away, whilst checks were made to see whether or not he was on any 'wanted list'. I had to follow them down the road to witness that he was not beaten, and to reassure the soldiers that he was merely escorting me to the taxi halt. Radio checks having been made, he was released. My two friends promptly disappeared back into the camp. This took place in September 1989. Some months earlier the Israeli authorities had started issuing ex-prisoners and activists with special green identity cards. Identity cards at that time were colour-coded, (like the licence plates of cars). Blue indicated East Jerusalem or Israeli residency, orange indicated West Bank and red indicated Gaza Strip. The new green cards were for 'security risks' - their bearers were barred from entering Israel.

In November 1990 the Israeli military authorities began a radical extension of the 'green card scheme', allegedly as a security measure in response to the Palestinian-Israeli violence inside Israel. By May 1991, there were estimated to be 27,000 West Bankers barred from entering Israel or East Jerusalem. In the Gaza Strip a slightly different practice was implemented. To travel into Israel all Gazans were required to use one of the magnetic cards that were introduced in August 1989. Those who were deemed security risks were simply not issued with them.[42]

'Death squads'

Most of the Intifada-related deaths amongst the Palestinian community were caused by soldiers firing at stone-throwers and those they judged to be potential assailants. But evidence emerged that a more sinister method had been adopted on occasions to eliminate those considered to be particularly dangerous security threats: so-called 'death squads'. As early as January 1988 there were reports that an undercover military unit code-named *Shimson* (Samson) had been operating in the Gaza Strip using a car with 'foreign press' stickers. Another unit, code-named *Cherry*, was later alleged to be deployed in the West Bank with verbal orders 'to shoot to kill fugitives with blood on their hands'. Israeli sources claimed that 'killings were not the unit's prime task, although it had shot dead several Palestinians in ambushes and undercover operations'[43] The Israeli authorities denied these reports, revoking the press credentials of those journalists who dared to suggest the existence of such squads.[44]

There were a number of well-documented accounts of Palestinians being kidnapped and shot by armed 'civilians' dressed as Arabs and driving vehicles with West Bank and Gaza license-plates. Thus, two leaders of the Shabiba (youth) movement in the village of Yatta near Hebron were killed in suspicious circumstances on October 9 1988.[45] A month earlier a resident of Silat al-Harithiya in Jenin district was killed in similar circumstances, whilst another man was killed in Jenin on November 13 1988.[46] It is of course difficult to come up with incontrovertible evidence to support such suspicions, but the use of such undercover squads to eliminate key figures in the Uprising was a logical extension of the Israeli policy of targeting leading activists and organisers. The most widely publicised use of this technique was the assassination of Khalid al-Wazir (Abu Jihad) in Tunis on April 16 1988. As Yasser Arafat's deputy with responsibility for activities in Israel and the occupied territories he was widely presumed to be responsible for the overall guidance of the Uprising, and consequently fell victim to a raid by an undercover Israeli commando unit.

The role of the settlers

In addition to adopting the guise of Palestinians, Israeli security forces were widely accused of impersonating journalists in order to photograph and arrest Palestinian suspects. The use of 'press' signs on vehicles was also a favourite ploy of settlers on vigilante patrol, enabling them to gain access to villages and neighbourhoods in order to carry out reprisal raids. The Hebron area suffered more than most from the provocative actions of settlers, with reports of Palestinians being shot at by settlers cruising round the town in vehicles carrying 'press' signs.[47] In other instances settlers literally ran amok in Palestinian communities such as happened following the injuries sustained by a settler family of four after a stoning incident near Issariyah on the eastern outskirts of Jerusalem on May 21 1989. After news reached the settlement-suburb of Ma'aleh Adumim hundreds of settlers piled into vehicles and headed for Issariyah seeking revenge. They rampaged through the village, smashing cars and destroying property, clashing with those soldiers who tried to restrain them. Other soldiers actively participated in the raid, with reports of army jeeps picking out targets with their headlights, soldiers throwing rocks, shooting tear-gas into a mosque, and lending settlers a crow-bar with which to open up the doors of a garage before setting the premises on fire.[48] A few days later, on May 29 1989, a group of settlers went on an alleged pilgrimage to a holy site at the village of Kifl Harith near Nablus. They clashed with villagers, leaving a 13-year old girl shot dead and a number of others seriously injured. Denying the charge that such a 'pilgrimage' was a highly provocative action during the Intifada, one of the settlers later claimed that 'at the entrance to the village it was clear we were surrounded. There was danger to our lives. The law enabled us to hit back.'[49] The villagers, on the other hand, claimed that the settlers came through the village wreaking havoc and firing indiscriminately. The evidence appeared to support the villagers' version:

> The village bore traces of a systematic, military-style operation of destruction. On either side of the main road, stacks of fresh straw had been set alight. A ewe had been shot through the head. On roofs, scarcely a water tank had not been punctured by shots. Three vehicles were damaged and a house was firebombed.[50]

Four of the settlers, students from the Tomb of Joseph Yeshiva in Nablus, were subsequently charged with manslaughter. At the time of the indictment one of them was already serving a prison sentence for an armed attack on two Gazans committed near Tel Aviv barely a month after the assault on the villagers of Kifl Harith.

According to a settler from the Hebron area, interviewed in 1989, a standard procedure had been worked out for when any of their vehicles was attacked by stone-throwers:

> A stone is thrown. Right there, the car stops and the passengers storm out and fire at the site from which the stones were thrown. Then shots are fired at water tanks and windows. People open fire. They shoot and then get back into their car and continue on their way. They don't shoot in the air. They try to hit the person who threw the stones. There's no other choice. You have to fire if you want to hit as many as possible.[51]

In the early weeks of the Intifada settlers began to form action committees for 'Security on the Roads'. Their argument was that if the security forces could not protect them, then they were obliged to take the law into their own hands. Here are some accounts of the kind of 'law and order' actions in which groups from the Hebron area engaged:

> In January 1988 we carried out our first operation after two Molotov cocktails were thrown at Jews in Hebron. Four people worked an entire night in Hebron and they didn't leave one car (undamaged). They wrecked about 400 cars. ... Since then we have carried out a lot of similar actions but in a more concentrated manner. ... We had one mishap: we accidently damaged the car of a collaborator. After that we called it quits for a while, but then we started up again.
>
> More than once we staged clashes. We rolled a few rocks onto the road and reported that we had come up against a road-block. Then we damaged the Arabs' homes near the road. It's first class chaos here. Anyone can do as he pleases. It's another planet. You're the law. You have to defend yourself, because there's no one to defend you. And if you don't defend yourself, you'll end up in the hospital or the cemetery. I've already shot a few Arabs in the legs. I haven't yet killed anyone. ... We go out at night, with our license plates covered, and enter a nearby Arab village and start up a ruckus.
>
> People walk around with knives in their pockets and every now and then they slash the tyres of parked cars. When it's possible, and the army isn't looking, they also pelt them with stones and torch them. The Arabs know they shouldn't park their cars near areas where Jews live. Our latest ploy is to quickly break into the car and release the brakes. The car starts rolling and … Peace to Israel, we didn't see anything and we didn't hear anything.[52]

Such accounts made a mockery of claims that settlers only reacted to attacks by Palestinians, particularly in the light of the evidence that settlers had produced a manual on how to shoot Palestinians and avoid legal retribution. At the very least the short-term aim would appear to have been to intimidate Palestinians into submission and to instil fear into Palestinian communities. A related purpose was undoubtedly to exert pressure on the Israeli authorities to pursue more punitive repressive measures and to forestall any peace initiative that might involve any kind of concessionary 'carrot' to the Palestinians. According to a political scientist from the Hebrew University their longer term aim was,

> … to force the Palestinians to take up arms, to provoke a real war. This would enable the IDF to shed its inhibitions in dealing with a civilian Uprising and use its full military force. In the end the settlers want to see the Palestinians smashed into submission, a state that would be so unbearable to them that they would voluntarily transfer themselves across the river to Jordan leaving the West Bank entirely to the Jews.[53]

Despite reports of clashes and fist-fights between settlers and soldiers trying to restrain them, many Palestinians remained convinced that the settlers enjoyed the active cooperation of the military in pursuing their strategy. They were of the firm belief that the IDF were using the settlers to do the kind of intimidatory 'dirty work' that the soldiers felt unable to commit for fear of disciplinary action and public outrage. Whether or not this was the case, there was clear evidence that in some situations soldiers turned a blind eye to the carryings-on of the settlers and even encouraged them in their activities. It was common knowledge amongst Palestinians and Israelis who had served in the territories that certain units were more sympathetic to the settlers than others, just as certain categories of soldiers (especially reservists) were rather more 'law-abiding' than others in their treatment of Palestinians. Certainly in the higher reaches of the IDF command structure the activities of the settler vigilantes caused considerable concern and occasioned criticism and condemnation.

Major-General Mitzna, the officer then in command of the West Bank, expressed the view in May 1989 that Jewish settlers were the primary problem as far as IDF operations in the region were concerned. This concern heightened when evidence came to light that settlers were staging stone- throwing and petrol bomb attacks on Israeli cars in an effort to incite settlers and draw attention to 'security problems' in the occupied territories.[54] Amongst the military the paramount concern was that the violent actions of the settlers would provoke reprisals from Palestinians, with a consequent heightening of the tension all-round and an accelerating spiral of violence and counter-violence, the burden of which would fall on the shoulders of the IDF. For Israeli politicians the spectre raised by settler violence was of a three-sided conflict between the Palestinians, the IDF and the settlers and the consequent drift into a chaotic civil war situation that might ensue as law and order and the state's monopoly of the use of violence was challenged from all sides. Indeed, in the summer of 1989 politicians from across the Israeli political spectrum joined voices in condemning those settlers 'who would arouse fanatical strife'.[55]

The costs of repression

The physical toll of the Intifada upon the Israelis would appear to have been minimal when measured against the deaths and casualties borne by the Palestinians. By the end of June 1990 48 Israelis had been killed since the beginning of the Uprising, as compared with over 800 Palestinians killed during the same period.[56] By mid-1990 somewhere in excess of 150 soldiers had suffered serious disabling injury, whilst Palestinians estimated their seriously injured and disabled at over 2,500. When it comes to estimating the number of Palestinians who suffered some form of injury, the truth of the matter is that no one knows with any degree of certainty - some Palestinians put the figure as high as 80,000 who required some form of medical attention during the first two years of the Uprising.[57] What is clear is that during the third year of the Intifada the number of injuries and deaths dropped significantly. The main reason for this was that the new Minister of Defence, Moshe Arens, instructed the military to avoid needless provocation of the Palestinians in their camps, villages and quarters - instead they should concentrate their attentions on the main highways and roads. As a consequence there was a marked reduction in the number of confrontations between the military and the Palestinians, but despite this some Palestinian sources put the number of injuries suffered during the third year in the region of 26,000.[58]

Whilst the costs of the Intifada, as measured in terms of injury and death were relatively low for the Israelis, the self-confidence and morale of their army suffered as the IDF became increasingly frustrated and demoralised by its role in the occupied territories. In March 1988, during a visit to the Gaza Strip, Defence Minister Rabin pronounced that 'the residents of the territories are beginning to feel exhausted.' In November of that year he expressed the wishful hope that 'within six months the Intifada will the out'.[59] His chief of staff, Dan Shomron, was never as sanguine - arguing that 'there is no such thing as eradicating the Intifada because, in essence, it expresses the struggle of nationalism'.[60] In December 1989 even Rabin was forced to admit that the IDF had failed to suppress the Uprising and acknowledge that it could go on for another two years.[61] There seemed to be a growing awareness amongst the military community of Israel that it was in the very nature of a popular civilian-based uprising that, whilst certain forms of resistance activity might be crushed by physical means, new forms of resistance would emerge, hydra-like, to replace the old patterns. As the respected Israeli military commentator, Ze'ev Schiff, wrote in the summer of 1988 concerning the role of the IDF in the Gaza Strip:

> We shall win the confrontations in the Gaza Strip, but we must not delude ourselves. There is lava boiling underground there, the basic cause of the Uprising. This lava will burst out again in one spot or another. All we can do, via the Israeli armed forces and the other security arms, is locate the fire - not extinguish it.[62]

In expressing this view he was clearly reflecting the mood within the general staff of the IDF and within the Shin Bet internal security service, who were reported to be feeling demoralised and angry that politicians continued to expect them to maintain order by military means, when only a political settlement of some sort could provide any long-term solution.[63] Indeed, Shomron told the Knesset Defence Committee in June 1989 that there were 'only three ways to eliminate the Intifada: transfer of the Arab population of the areas, starvation or physical elimination, in other words, genocide'.[64] Such a perspective was diametrically opposed to the critical voices coming from the right wing of the Israeli political spectrum. Echoing the demands of the settlers, people like Ariel Sharon urged a radical hardening of the Iron Fist policy, calling for mass arrests and deportation of all known activists, the sealing off of the entire West Bank from Israel, and a massive increase in the military presence as a means of punishing the population into submission. For such people, physical force and might continued to hold the key to the solution of the 'Palestinian problem'. Those with a somewhat deeper understanding of the nature of the Intifada, however, realised that each act of repression might only serve to feed the will to resist, and strengthen the solidarity of the Palestinians. As Dan Meridor of the Likud bloc observed, 'there is no greater error than to harass an entire population. It is a mistake to do so for operational, legal and moral reasons.'[65]

In acknowledging the fact that a straightforward military victory could not be achieved, Rabin pursued a twin-track policy based around the assumption that success in the conflict would go to the side that had more staying power, and could wear out and grind down the other. The aim was to continue wielding the stick of repression in order to maintain the burden of hardship borne by the Palestinians. Eventually their will to resist would be undermined to the extent that they would agree to accept, however reluctantly, any carrot that was held out to them which promised some relief from their suffering. What was on offer was the Israeli peace initiative put forward by Prime Minister Shamir in May 1989 that proposed elections within the occupied territories and the eventual devolution of some limited degree of autonomy. The scenario, then, was that the Palestinians would eventually realise that the Intifada was only increasing their hardships, whilst failing to break Israel. They would then opt for talks. As such it was a classical 'throffer' - a combination of threat and offer, stick and carrot.[66] A major problem with this strategy was that in acknowledging the long- term nature of the struggle, it demanded patience and perseverance from the Israeli public and their politicians, and from the security forces who were required to continue wielding the stick. It was a measure of the costs incurred by Israel, in its struggle to suppress the Intifada, that as early as February 1989 some observers began to question whether the level of morale within the IDF was sufficient for it to continue performing its allotted role, without risking permanent damage to its status and effectiveness as a military force. This point was put particularly strongly by Professor Martin van Creveld of the Hebrew University:

> By virtue of its questionable legitimacy and, even more, the tremendous disparity in power involved, the attempt to put down the Intifada has put the IDF troops into a false position. What used to be one of the world's finest fighting forces is rapidly degenerating into a

> fourth-class police organisation. To realise the way such a force will fight when confronted with a real army, one need look no further than the Argentinians in the Falkland Islands.[67]

During my fieldwork I heard reservists saying they would prefer to serve in southern Lebanon or sit facing the Syrians in the north-east, rather than spend their time 'maintaining law and order' in the occupied territories - a role for which they had not been trained and which many found militarily futile and morally distasteful. In a series of interviews with reservists serving in Gaza in February 1989 Abraham Rabinovich elicited some interesting comments on this theme from the soldiers.[68]

Danny, a 32 year old from Tel Aviv:

> Last year they looked us in the eye, and we could see the hate. Now, they look past us. And we look past them. ... There is a resignation on their part that the Intifada is going to continue for a long time. ... They know they're going to win, and a lot of us know they're going to win as well. ... Before, we used to see that every burning tyre was cleared away. Not anymore. Almost no one wants to chase after 14-year-olds any more. What do you do if you catch them? Hit them? Or if they're over 16, put them in jail for a few months? People realised it wasn't doing any good. ... After spending 75 days in Gaza in the past year, the main feeling is apathy and disgust... I'd prefer four weeks in Lebanon to two in the territories.

Ra'anan, a kibbutznik:

> Our object now is to get through our reserve stint without getting hurt, or hurting. There is an understanding that catching the stone-throwers and punishing them won't lead to an-

> ything. So we try not to get involved. Before, we would never let anything go by; if someone threw a stone we gave chase. Now, we usually just ignore it.

On the basis of such remarks, it is clear that part of the reason for the army's relative failure in the occupied territories was due to the lack of motivation of the officers and soldiers. This was most publicly displayed when Prime Minister Shamir paid a flying visit to a parachute battalion operating in the Nablus area in January 1989. The reservists who addressed him made clear their frustration and the weight of their moral burden as one of them complained:

> In order to enforce order in the casbah, we must be brutally violent against people who are innocent of any crime. I violate army regulations every day, and this weakens me and strengthens them. This dead-end situation is a disaster. Everything we do bolsters the Intifada.[69]

A significant number of reservists and young people confronted this moral dilemma by refusing to serve in the occupied territories. In excess of a hundred people were jailed as conscientious objectors within the first 18 months of the Uprising, including one sergeant in a combat engineers' unit, Kami Hason, who served four periods of imprisonment totalling 140 days in jail.[70] The actual number of 'refusers' was known to be far in excess of those who went to jail. In order to minimise controversy the army authorities found a variety of ways of getting around the issue. As one reserve officer in an elite infantry unit explained:

> Ninety percent of the guys in my unit are simply not psychologically built for clubbing little kids who throw stones at them. I don't know if they'll refuse, but neither does the army. The fact is, we haven't been called up for reserve duty, and in the statistics we figure among

> those who don't refuse. I'm an officer - the army has invested considerable money and energy in me - but I'm also the child of Holocaust survivors, and I'm not ready to enter the homes of civilians at night and scream at them to wake up and hear their children cry. ... If it comes to it I'll refuse and I'll protest in a manner that will make people very uncomfortable - including the chief-of-staff, with whom I flew in the same plane to Entebbe. Understand, he'll have a hard time explaining how it came about that a reserve officer who fought against PLO terrorism and risked his life now finds himself forced to refuse to serve.[71]

The distress experienced by such people was a symptom of the malaise brought about by the army's unhappy role in confronting the Intifada. Senior officers felt they had been made the scapegoat of the government's 'non-policy' in the territories. Consequently, they found it difficult to issue clear directives, and as a result those in the field complained that they were constantly told by their superiors what not to do, instead of being directed what to do. Meanwhile, the army was being pilloried at home and abroad for acts of brutality which contradicted the values upon which the Israeli Defence Force was established. At the same time, officers and soldiers were being criticised and disparaged by settlers and their allies for their inability to suppress the Uprising. As the editor of the army officer's journal *Ma 'arachot* observed:

> The Intifada is a slap in the face for the IDF - it's caught between the demand to curb the violence and the limits imposed on it through Israel being a democratic society. The result is a little of this and a little of that - the worst of possible compromises. Young officers are as aware as anyone else that there is a negative

> public image. Now they see the most senior commanders dragged into the mire as public scapegoats.[72]

Called into question for the way it performed its role in the occupied territories, the army was challenged also for taking on what many came to view as an impossible role in itself. The result was that the IDF, which had hitherto been the most sacrosanct of Israeli institutions, began to lose its self-confidence. According to one military researcher,

> During the Lebanon war there was disenchantment, but it was limited to a particular political sector, it was based on moral reservations and it was directed almost exclusively at the politicians who had launched the war. There has never been such delegitimisation, such an attack on the professional integrity of the army as we have seen recently. This encompasses far wider sections of the public and has focused on popular symbols or figures such as the Chief of Staff.[73]

Evidence to support this view emerged when, in June 1989, General Amram Mitzna, who had been in command of the West Bank since the beginning of the Intifada, asked to be relieved of his post. Considered by those who knew him to be of a liberal disposition, it was known that he had not enjoyed fighting the 'children of the stones' and sought to point out to people that the Uprising was not like invading Lebanon or Syria 'but a question of dealing with civilians, and whatever happens we are going to have to live with them in the future'.[74]

It was this question of the future that exercised the worst fears of many Israelis about the ultimate cost they would have to pay for attempting to suppress the Intifada by violent means. Advocates of nonviolence have always argued that violence is like a cancer: it spreads and distorts all with which it comes into contact. It corrodes the moral fibre of those who employ violence as much as it hardens the will for revenge of those who are its target. An indication of the nature of this process is provided in the following account by an Israeli officer of a tour of duty in the Ramallah area:

> The first night we had to make arrests in a village according to a list drawn up by the security services. The village was sleeping when we began rapping on metal doors with clubs and shouting '*Iftah el bab!* Open the door!' It was a terrible noise. They were poor villagers and they huddled together and tried to protect themselves.
>
> Then the search began. Some of the soldiers didn't give a damn and just threw everything around. A woman began to cry when we arrested her teenage son. I felt terrible. How could I participate in something like this?
>
> The next night we did the same thing. This time I said to myself, 'Well, what do you expect? You look for suspects and you make arrests. Just be sure you don't hurt people unnecessarily.' The third night it was already routine, and when the woman starts to cry you say 'Oh God, is that wailing beginning again?' The fourth night you're shouting at the woman, '*Uskut!* Shut up!'
>
> I felt us hardening from day to day. Not becoming brutalised - we were never brutal - but it could lead to that, or at least to acceptance of excesses that others perpetrate.[75]

Despite his protestations to the contrary, what this officer was describing was a process of brutalisation: the erosion of respect for any kind of humanitarian moral code brought about by the everyday practices required of those charged with controlling the Intifada. It was a process through which violence, intolerance, and contempt for the 'other' became the norm, a routine part of everyday military life. The soldiers exposed to this process were not separate from Israeli society, they were an integral part of it. What does it bode for the future of Israeli society when intimidation and the threat of violence become the accepted methods of dealing with people? What will happen to the values of tolerance, respect for the law, and all those other humanitarian principles that Israel used to claim it honoured? As the head of the military tribunal judging the case of the four soldiers from the Givati Brigade involved in the beating to death of a Gazan commented, 'We must preserve at all costs the rule of law from which derive the values that are at the foundations of our existence as a cultured people'[76]

As the Intifada continued, month after month, year after year, the fear grew that these foundations might be undermined to such a degree that the whole edifice might fracture. Although the Gulf War and the fear of Saddam Hussein and his Scud missiles, possibly bearing chemical warheads, caused the overwhelming majority of Israelis, 'doves' as well as 'hawks', to join together in solidarity against the external threat, the fear was that this would prove to be only a temporary respite from the unprecedented divisions that the Intifada created within the Israeli political system and society. Under the impact of the Uprising the society had become increasingly polarised between those who believed that popular resistance could be overcome by force, and those who saw the futility and danger of such a path and, however reluctantly and fearfully, urged some kind of political settlement. The accompanying erosion of the moral basis of the society was evidenced by the spectre of 'mob rule', which began to raise its head as settlers clashed with soldiers who dared to interfere with their vigilante raids. Even Prime Minister Shamir was moved to warn of the danger of civil war if extremists did not restrain themselves, after he had been jostled and abused as a 'traitor' at the funeral of a West Bank settler killed by Palestinians.[77]

Moreover, the violence did not stop at the Green Line but spread across into Israel itself. One of the most shocking incidents occurred in August 1988, when three Gazans were burned to death in an arson attack upon a hut adjacent to the construction site where they were employed in Or Yehuda, a development town outside Tel Aviv. In May 1989, crowds in Ashkelon and Ashdod, incensed by the discovery of the body of a soldier who went missing whilst hitch-hiking, drove Palestinian workers from their towns screaming 'Death to the Arabs!', and began stoning the vehicles of Palestinians. It culminated in the death of a Palestinian driver hit by a stone. That same month an Arab youth was fatally stabbed in Acre, and the mayor of Petah Tikva decided to ban Palestinians from moving freely about the city. He ordered the construction of a terminal on the outskirts to which all Palestinian workers would be bussed in the morning. The mayor explained that 'All Arab workers who come to Petah Tikva will either be at work or at the terminal. We don't want them on the streets; they are taking over the city'.[78] In May 1990 an Israeli civilian took such racist attitudes to their barbaric extreme when he lined up Palestinians who were waiting to be hired for work in Rishon Lezion and shot dead seven of them. The fear and hatred within Israel that was at the heart of such incidents grew to a new pitch in the months following the October 1990 killings on Temple Mount, when the spate of knife attacks by Palestinians seeking vengeance led to a hardening of attitudes, and an unprecedented lynch-mob atmosphere was discernible in the streets of Israel.

Israeli morale and self-confidence had not been helped by the censure that its treatment of the Palestinians had attracted from the international community. Such criticism, and the consequent damage to Israel's image, had come not just from international non-governmental agencies such as Amnesty International and the International Committee of the Red Cross. States noted for their sympathetic attitude towards Israel had also felt constrained to express their concern. Particularly damaging was the 1988 US State Department report on human rights abuses, which accused Israel of a 'substantial increase in human rights violations' in the West Bank and Gaza Strip, and expressed the view that many of the practices adopted by the Israeli government were illegal in terms of both Israeli and international law. Furthermore, in October 1990 the United States felt constrained to take the unprecedented step of supporting UN Security Council resolutions censuring Israel following the slayings on Temple Mount.

Even the staunchest of supporters expressed their unease with Israel's repressive policies. Thus, a poll conducted early in 1989 amongst American Jews revealed a clear majority (54 percent) opposed to the methods used by Israel to put down the Intifada.[79] At about the same time as the poll was taken a number of prominent US Jewish intellectuals, associated with the Committee for Judaism and Social Justice, published a full-page statement in *The New York Times* denouncing the policies of the Israeli government as 'immoral, contrary to what is best in our Jewish tradition and destructive to the best interests of Israel and American Jewry'.[80] Perhaps the most vivid expression of the fear that was gnawing away at the self-confidence of Israelis was the outburst from Prime Minister Yitzhak Shamir, after he had listened to the complaints of soldiers during his visit to Nablus in January 1989: 'We hate these terrorists, these PLO men, because they force us to kill children. But we have to do it to protect ourselves'.[81] A few months later in May, after a Palestinian had run amok in the main street of West Jerusalem and fatally stabbed two Israelis and injured another three, he encouraged Israeli Jews to exact vengeance if attacked, when he declared:

> I think that the public, the Jewish public, has to do everything possible to defend itself to prevent murderers from carrying out their

> plots and to prevent them coming out in one piece if they succeed in doing anything.[82]

The nightmare that must concern all is the way in which fear and hatred, and the urge to retaliate, could become the accepted norm on both sides of the conflict - with each side using the outrages of the other to justify its own pursuit of revenge. The costs borne by both sides in terms of loss of life and physical injury could be such as to render the toll imposed during the Intifada pale by comparison. Moreover, the damage in terms of the brutalisation and traumatisation of whole generations would cast an even darker shadow over future prospects of peace between Palestinians and Israelis - as people, let alone as states.

---

[1] See C. Boggs, *Gramsci's Marxism*, London: Pluto Press, 1976, especially ch. 2.
[2] G. Sharp, *Nonviolent struggle: An efficient technique of political action*, Jerusalem: Palestinian Centre for the Study of Nonviolence, nd.
[3] Punishing a nation (1988), p. 5.
[4] See A. Mosley Lesch, 'Israeli deportation of Palestinians from the West Bank and Gaza Strip, 1967-78', *Journal of Palestinian Studies*, Summer & Winter, 1979.
[5] *Twenty years of Israeli occupation of the West Bank and Gaza*, Ramallah: Al Haq, 1987, p. 26.
[6] Israeli spokesperson quoted in J. Metzger et al, *This land is our land*, London: Zed Press, 1983, p. 78.
[7] *Twenty years of Israeli occupation* (1987), p. 27.
[8] *The cost of freedom,* Jerusalem: Arab Studies Society, 1988, p. 33.
[9] Quoted in *Jerusalem Post*, September 11, 1988.
[10] J. Law, 'Letter from Kufr Malik', *Middle East International*, November 4, 1988, p. 24.
[11] K. Kaplan, 'An onerous duty that must be done', *Jerusalem Post*, September 8, 1988.

---

[12] For interesting insights on the nature of such forms of symbolic 'semi-resistance', see J. C. Scott, *Domination and the arts of resistance: Hidden transcripts*, New Haven, CT.: Yale University Press, 1990.
[13] Brian Martin has written extensively on this type of phenomenon which he has termed 'backfire'. See B. Martin, *Justice Ignited: The Dynamics of Backfire*, Lanham, MD: Rowman & Littlefield, 2007.
[14] Quoted in *Jerusalem Post*, January 26, 1988.
[15] Quoted in *Jerusalem Post*, February 24, 1988.
[16] *Jerusalem Post*, October 5, 1988.
[17] *Jerusalem Post*, May 26, 1989.
[18] Quoted in *Ha'aretz*, March 11, 1988.
[19] *The Observer*, February 14, 1988.
[20] *The Guardian*, May 12, 1989. At a subsequent trial the officer, Colonel Yehuda Meir, alleged that both the Defence Minister and the Chief of Staff had personally ordered such beatings, claiming that the army had two separate policies on beatings, one for the public record and the other for the soldiers in the field. See *Middle East International*, July 6, 1990, p. 8.
[21] *Jerusalem Post*, May 23, 1989. According to figures produced by UNRWA, of the 65 children aged under 16 who were killed between December 10 1987 and April 10 1989, 19 died from the effects of tear-gas. See *The Independent*, April 27, 1989.
[22] *Punishing a nation*, p. 31.
[23] *Jerusalem Post International Edition*, May 26 1990, p. 6.
[24] Palestinian Human Rights Information Centre, *From The Field*, v 1, no 4, December 1990.
[25] Personal communication, December 31, 1989.
[26] *The Guardian*, September 28, 1988.
[27] *Al Fajr*, May 28, 1990. IDF standing orders concerning the arrest of a suspect stipulated that soldiers must first give a verbal warning, fire shots in the air and shoot at the suspect's legs before resorting to direct fire.

---

[28] *From the Field*, v. 1, no 4, December 1990

[29] On May 1988 Israeli security reported they had a list of 1200 Palestinians slated for expulsion. (*The cost of freedom,* p. 15).

[30] *From The Field*, v. 1, *n.* 4, December 1990.

[31] See *Jerusalem Post (International Edition)*, October 7, 1989, p. 3.

[32] *Al Fajr*, March 20 1989, p. 3.

[33] Punishing a nation, p. 177.

[34] See report of *B'Tselem* reviewed in *Al Fajr*, February 18 1991, p. 4.

[35] Palestinian Human Rights Information Centre, *Update*, v. 3, *n.* 13, December 1990, p. 530.

[36] *New Outlook*, February 1989, p. 43.

[37] *Al Fajr*, February 6, 1989.

[38] *Al Fajr*, December 12 1988, p. 15.

[39] *The Independent*, August 15, 1990.

[40] *Jerusalem Post*, April 6, 1989.

[41] U. Nir & D. Sagir in *Ha'aretz*, April 14, 1989.

[42] I. Black, *The Guardian*, May 2, 1991.

[43] *Jerusalem Post,* October 23, 1988.

[44] *The Guardian,* October 26, 1988.

[45] See *Al Fajr,* October 30, 1988, p 10.

[46] *News from Within*, February 26, 1989, pp. 14-15.

[47] See *Jerusalem Post*, April 2, 1989.

[48] See *Jerusalem Post*, May 28, 1989.

[49] Quoted in *The Independent*, May 31, 1989.

[50] Charles Richards, *The Independent*, May 31, 1989.

[51] Quoted in *Ha'aretz*, May 26, 1989.

[52] *Ha'aretz*, May 26 1989. Also quoted in *Al Fajr,* June 5 1989.

[53] E. Spinzack, quoted in *Middle East International*, June 9, 1989, p. 8.

[54] *Jerusalem Post*, September 26, 1989.

[55] See Middle East International, June 9, 1989.

[56] This figure does not include the Palestinians killed by their fellow citizens in attacks on alleged collaborators, estimated to have been in the region of 228 by the end of June 1990. (*B'Tselem,* quoted in *Al Fajr,* July 9, 1990, p. 3.)

---

[57] Personal communication from surgeon at Maqassed Hospital, December 31, 1989.
[58] *From the Field*, v. 1, n. 4, December 1990.
[59] Quoted in *Ha'aretz*, April 7, 1989.
[60] Quoted in *New Outlook*, February 1989, p. 42.
[61] *Jerusalem Post*, December 6, 1989.
[62] Quoted in *The Independent*, July 4, 1988.
[63] *Ha'aretz*, July 8, 1988.
[64] Quoted in *Jerusalem Post (International Edition)*, June 24, 1989.
[65] Quoted in *Jerusalem Post*, August 17, 1988.
[66] See M. Taylor, Community, anarchy and liberty, p. 12.
[67] *Jerusalem Post*, February 18, 1989.
[68] *Jerusalem Post*, February 18, 1989.
[69] Quoted in *The Guardian*, January 18, 1989.
[70] See *Jerusalem Post*, May 21, 1989.
[71] Quoted by S. Tal, *Hadashot*, March 18, 1989.
[72] Quoted by David Richardson, *Jerusalem Post*, May 26, 1989.
[73] *Jerusalem Post*, May 26, 1989.
[74] Quoted in *The Guardian*, June 14, 1989.
[75] Quoted by A. Rabinovich, *Jerusalem Post (International Edition)*, March 4, 1989, p. 7.
[76] Quoted in *The Guardian*, May 26, 1989.
[77] *The Guardian*, June 22, 1989.
[78] Quoted by Yehuda Litani, *Jerusalem Post*, 26 May 1989. Following the lead of Petah Tikva, the mayor of the West Bank settlement of Ariel, with a population of 6000, proposed that Palestinians employees should wear tags saying 'foreign worker'. The parallel between this and the forcing of Jews in occupied Europe to wear a yellow star in the Second World War period outraged Israelis from across the political spectrum.
[79] *Jerusalem Post*, March 17, 1989.
[80] *Jerusalem Post*, April 5, 1989.
[81] Quoted in *The Guardian*, January 18, 1989.
[82] Quoted in *The Independent*, May 6, 1989.

Andrew Rigby

4

COPING WITH THE 'EPIDEMIC OF VIOLENCE'

The struggle to dislodge the occupying force of the Israelis during the Intifada incurred many costs for the Palestinians. Perhaps the most immediately obvious of these were the injuries and casualties suffered at the hands of soldiers and settlers. The beatings, the tear-gas and the shootings resulted in an unprecedented demand upon medical services and health care facilities in the occupied territories. Before going on to examine how the Palestinians sought to cope with the mushrooming toll of injuries, disabilities and other health-related problems, it might be worthwhile to sketch out the condition of the Palestinian health services in the West Bank and the Gaza Strip prior to the Uprising.

Background

As with almost every aspect of life (and death) in the occupied territories, the issue of health care has been a focus for polemic and argument. Israelis have selected certain indices and cited particular statistical sources to illustrate the degree of development made in health care under their occupation. Palestinians have selected other indices and quoted their own statistical sources to prove that military rule has damaged the health of the Palestinian people. What is clear is that in absolute terms the state of health within the occupied territories showed a marked improvement during the years of occupation between 1967 and

1987. By the outbreak of the Intifada, health conditions within the West Bank and Gaza Strip compared quite favourably with those in neighbouring Arab states.

However, it is equally clear that comparing Palestinian morbidity rates with those of Israel reveals a marked disparity. Thus, if we take infant mortality rates (death in the first year of life) as a key indicator of the general condition of health in a society, we find that in 1985 Israel had a rate of 14 deaths per 1000 live births. For the West Bank and Gaza Strip the figure was 70 per 1000, whilst the figures for Jordan and Syria were 55 and 60 respectively.[1] Despite this difference, the figures do seem to indicate a basic trend: health conditions in the West Bank and Gaza Strip improved during the period of military occupation prior to the Intifada. The rate of improvement bore comparison with other parts of the Arab world, although the statistics show that a Palestinian child born after 1967 was far more likely to die before its first birthday than an Israeli child. The inequalities in health have not been confined to the Israeli/Palestinian divide, however. As in other societies, there has been a clear pattern of class and gender related inequalities within the Palestinian population, with the children of working-class families, particularly girls, revealing relatively high infant mortality and other morbidity rates.[2]

What about the actual health services and facilities? Palestinians consistently alleged that the provision of health care had always been an integral part of Israel's overall strategy of occupation - obstructing the development of indigenous medical facilities in order to render the population dependent upon the Israeli health sector. It is indeed the case that the bulk of the health services within the occupied territories had been supplied through the governmental sector, supervised and controlled by the military government and financed from tax revenue and a voluntary governmental health insurance scheme. On the other hand health service provision for the refugees remained the responsibility of the United Nations Relief and Works Agency

(UNRWA). These two main sources were supplemented by a relatively small private sector and a larger number of hospitals and health centres funded from charitable sources, particularly through the Red Crescent Society. Due to lack of funding, poor coordination between the different sectors, and other reasons associated with the peculiar conditions of military occupation, a pattern of inequality between Israel and the occupied territories with regard to health service provision persisted, compounded by inequalities within the occupied territories themselves. Statistics tell a part of the story. In 1986 there were approximately eight physicians per 10,000 population in the West Bank and Gaza Strip, one third the figure for Israel where there were 28 doctors per 10,000 population.[3] The hospital bed/ population ratio revealed a comparable state of affairs, with 1.6 beds per 1000 population in the occupied territories - a fraction of the Israeli ratio at 6.1 beds per 1000 population.[4] According to Meron Benvenisti the average expenditure by the Israeli authorities on health services in the occupied territories up to 1986 was the equivalent of $30 per person per year, by comparison with the figure of $350 per Israeli over the same time period.[5]

Moreover, within the occupied territories, health services had been disproportionately located in the main population centres, and in the central region of the West Bank in particular. Thus, Hebron in the south of the West Bank with a population of some 300,000 was served by only one hospital. Approximately half the 500 population centres of the West Bank (villages, refugee camps and towns) lacked any form of health care centre.[6] The Gaza Strip, with a population of around 650,000, was served by three main hospitals. In the UNRWA clinics in the Gaza Strip doctors became accustomed to examining an average of one patient every three minutes - barely enough time to write a prescription! The Rimal Clinic in Gaza City served almost 60,000 refugees, with each doctor seeing an average of 100 patients a day.

Union of Palestinian Medical Relief Committees

It was as part of an attempt to tackle the unequal and underdeveloped nature of health care provision that the Union of Palestinian Medical Relief Committees (UPMRC) was launched in 1979. Like other Palestinian grass-roots organisations of the time this movement, staffed by volunteers largely drawn from the medical professions, was established not only to fill the institutional gaps left by the military government but also to mobilise local people to meet basic community needs. As such, the medical relief committees (MRCs) were an integral part of the process of informal institutional resistance to Israeli occupation referred to previously. The aim was to lay the ground- work for a national health service beyond the control of the Israeli authorities, specifically oriented to the needs of the deprived sectors of society, particularly the women and children in the villages, refugee camps and other areas where health services were either non-existent or woefully inadequate. Amongst the projects they undertook were local health surveys in order to assess the needs of a locality. Self-help preventative health care was promoted through the production and distribution of educational materials dealing with matters of public and personal health. Local women were chosen for special training as paramedics and local health workers, and 17 primary health care centres were established. The wider socio-political dimension of the work of the MRCs was consciously pursued, as the following depiction of the role of the primary health care services illustrates:

> Primary health care services are not only curative services, nor are they only health education and environmental sanitation and immunisation campaigns, among other activities. Primary health care services are also nuclei for community centres, foci where communities can be mobilised to have their needs met, be it in

> health, or in literacy, in school health or in the provision of health services to the community's nursery schools and kindergartens. Primary health care centres must be at the core of social relations at the community level. For health is not only the absence of disease, but rather the provision of economic, infrastructural and social opportunities that would ensure that a human being can live an active and happy life.[7]

The duality of Palestinian health problems

It was through the work of the medical relief committees that a significant aspect of the Palestinian health profile came to light. Compared to their Israeli neighbours, the Palestinians suffered from a relatively high rate of disease associated with poor environmental conditions and services, such as malnutrition and vitamin deficiency, a number of infectious diseases, anaemia, and a high infant mortality rate. This in itself was not surprising. However, it was also discovered that the population suffered from an accelerating incidence of so- called 'modern-day complaints' such as hypertension, diabetes, cancer, ulcers, heart disease and psychiatric problems. Thus, whilst research in the late 1970s revealed that three quarters of childhood deaths were due to infectious diseases, the most frequent cause of death among adults was heart disease.[8] In a survey of one area in the West Bank during the mid-1980s it was discovered that 15 percent of the families had at least one member suffering from hypertension, 10 percent had a member with diabetes, 7 percent had a member suffering from asthma, and 7 percent had a member suffering from psychiatric illness.[9]

This relatively high incidence of stress-related illnesses could have been attributed in part to the economic and social changes undergone in the occupied territories since 1967: the changes in lifestyle and consumption patterns resulting from the exposure to their economically dominant neighbour, the substitution of processed Israeli products for home-grown food, the changes in agricultural practice with the increased use of chemical fertilisers and pesticides and so forth. However, a more obvious factor had to be the psychological stress created by living under military occupation. This 'duality' of health conditions within the occupied territories, with new patterns of disease superimposed upon a pre-existing situation where basic health-related problems such as poor sanitation and inadequate water supplies to villages and camps still remained unsolved, was further complicated in the months following the outbreak of the Intifada. The new situation brought with it a new tier of health-related problems, thereby intensifying the demand for creative solutions to an unprecedented 'life and death' situation.

The Uprising: its consequences for health

As was seen in the previous chapter, the Israeli occupying forces reacted to the demonstrations, street confrontations and strikes that marked the outbreak of the Intifada by resorting to physical intimidation. The aim, to quote Prime Minister Shamir, was to 'put the fear of death into the Arabs of the areas so as to deter them from attacking us anymore.'[10] The result was a mounting toll of injury and death. By the end of 1989, after two years of the Intifada, Palestinian physicians estimated that they had dealt with somewhere in the region of 600,000 Intifada-related injuries. They estimated that after three years some 3,000 had suffered major injury involving amputations, colostomies, shattered joints - a figure which included over 100 paraplegics and quadriplegia and nearly 300 who had lost an eye. They estimate that 600 a year had been permanently handicapped in one way or another.[11] These casualties were the most obvious indicators of the physical suffering endured by the Palestinians during the Uprising. However, like the tip of the iceberg, they represented only the most visible and dramatic consequences for health and well-being of the on-going civilian resistance.

Whole strata of the population suffered damage to their health in less immediate but no less real ways than the direct victims of Israeli violence. Imagine a family of ten living in a few rooms, confined there under siege conditions for days on end, allowed outside for an hour every other day, during which time they have to try and obtain the supplies necessary to get through the next 48 hours. Such was the experience of many village and refugee camp dwellers under curfew. The 7,000 inhabitants of Jalazoun camp, near Ramallah, were under curfew for over a month in the spring of 1988. The soldiers stationed at the camp entrance attempted to stop people entering or leaving, the passage of food supplies into the camp was obstructed, the one hour in 48 when the curfew was lifted did not allow sufficient time for residents to get to Ramallah to stock up with essential items, the stores within the camp could not replenish their shelves. The inhabitants suffered from severe food shortages. Of particular concern was the plight of the youngest - no fresh milk for over a month. The electricity and telephone lines were also cut. People had to resort to burning whatever they could lay their hands on as a substitute fuel supply for the preparation of food. Piles of garbage accumulated in the streets as the sanitation workers were denied entry and the residents did not have sufficient time to dispose of it themselves, giving rise to fear of the spread of contagious disease. Those residents in need of medical treatment were not allowed out to visit doctors, clinics or hospitals. Health care programmes within the camp were totally disrupted. UNRWA medical teams had difficulty in obtaining permission to enter the camp. And underpinning all this, there was the enduring psychological stress and tension of living under siege.

The curfew at Jalazoun took place during the early months of the Uprising, when people were still relatively unprepared. Subsequently the regular experience of living under curfew meant that people learned how to cope to some degree - holding stocks of food and basic medical supplies within the home and other similar precautionary measures. However, little could have prepared the residents of the occupied territories for the blanket curfew that was imposed during the first three months of 1991 at the time of the Gulf War. Confined to their homes, the majority had insufficient living space to prepare a spare room sealed off in case of the feared gas attacks from Iraqi missiles. Moreover, out of the whole population only 50,000 adults were provided with gas masks, and none were distributed to children. Under the curfew conditions people were unable to gain access to medical services. This included emergency cases and chronic sufferers such as cancer patients who needed regular specialist treatment in Israeli hospitals. The problems were compounded by the fact that an estimated 30 to 40 percent of medical staff were prevented from travelling to work. The resultant staffing shortage in hospitals and medical centres meant that all preventative treatment and care, including non-urgent operations, had to be postponed for the duration of the curfew.[12]

The Gulf War experience can be viewed as a microcosm, albeit intensified, of the health situation throughout the occupied territories during the Uprising. Thus, access to medical services was curtailed throughout the Uprising because of the reluctance of people to travel far from their own locality to the centres where the physicians and clinics were based out of fear of check-points and associated harassment by the military. Moreover, due to the difficult economic conditions during the Uprising people did not have the disposable income to pay for travel and medical fees. This in turn highlighted a significant feature of the Intifada - the unequal burden borne by the weakest sections of society. The direct victims of Israeli violence, the wounded and the dead, were disproportionately drawn from the ranks of the poor, the sons (and daughters) of workers and peasants. Likewise, it was the women and the youngest children who suffered most from the collective punishment of curfews. It was the pregnant and those already suffering from respiratory diseases and related ailments who suffered most from the effects of tear-gas.

That said, no sector of Palestinian society remained untouched by the Intifada. Here is one doctor's depiction of the general health situation confronting the medical services in Gaza during the summer of 1988.

> It is well-known that people are suffering more because of the Uprising and the security restrictions. ... The psychological state of the people has meant that a great number of diseases have become incurable. Many new illnesses have appeared. For example, diseases of the digestive system, stomach ulcers - these are due to psychological factors. Chest diseases resulting from tear-gas, which we consider to be poison-gas. It has caused deaths and respiratory diseases among the people, diseases of the digestive system. Many have developed a sensitivity in the chest and many have begun spitting blood from the lungs. Finally, heart diseases of course increase, cancer, skin diseases as a result of burning, illnesses which might have been prevented but for the declaring of closed military zones. There is a lack of water, adequate sanitation in the streets and the houses. All this creates contagious diseases and in the end we're under a lot of pressure because of this increase in disease. There are many problems. During a military ban, people can't get to the clinics for treatment, be they private or government ones.
>
> The problems will become very evident in the future. First of all, many of the injuries - loss of eyes or limbs - are permanent and this will cause social problems in the future. Many of the cases of miscarriage which result from tear-gas being thrown in large quantities ... these

> problems will go on as long as the Uprising continues. The other health problems are psychological problems that people are exposed to. There are a lot of people walking round in a state of hysteria. …
> There are economic problems of course. The labourer isn't going to work. The clerk isn't going to work. And with the many taxes, this affects the medical services. He who has to pay taxes doesn't have any money for medical insurance and won't be able to treat his son or himself or his wife or anyone else.[13]

Coping with emergency: the initial response to the 'epidemic of violence'

Like everyone else, the personnel of the health services were caught unawares by the outbreak of the Intifada. Largely untrained in the skills of trauma medicine, the medical staff were faced with a sudden influx of injured people suffering from broken limbs, bullet wounds of various kinds, and the effects of gas. As the director of the Palestinians' premier hospital, Maqassed in East Jerusalem, observed in 1988, 'Israel is one of the most advanced countries in the world in everything related to the treatment of war injured and their rehabilitation... We, in comparison, are at zero.'[14]

Apart from the need to acquire the necessary skills whilst 'on the job', physicians faced a related dilemma. They had too little time to devote to the care of the chronically ill, such was the demand created by the 'epidemic of violence'. One doctor employed by UNRWA in the Gaza Strip recalled the predicaments he faced during the early months of the Uprising.

> Dealing with incidents is the first priority, injuries and casualties that are occurring in our area. There are new things to deal with which we

had only previously read about as medical cases while we were studying. We weren't really prepared for these things - like gas. Unfortunately, when the use of gas started against demonstrators and citizens in the Uprising, we didn't know about the medication to use specifically for its treatment. So our task in treating the patient was extremely difficult, especially with regard to pregnant women in whom we have noticed that the number of miscarriages and still births has increased during the Uprising. We've suffered from a great shortage of laboratory facilities....
There have been many injuries where there was no difference between old people and children. A lot of the injuries I've seen have looked as if they were deliberately inflicted. Bones have been deliberately broken, broken arms, heads deliberately cracked open... Bullet wounds, as they call them, rubber bullets or actually rubber casings containing iron or some other metal. I don't know which exactly. As doctors in UNRWA we do what we can and we transfer the cases which require hospital treatment or surgery to a special hospital. There have been many. The numbers are painfully disturbing... We used to see only one or two a day, on an ordinary day. Someone who had stepped on a nail, a car accident... someone who'd fallen off his bicycle, someone who'd cut himself, a small child ... trivial things like that. The incidence of injury has increased.... it comes to more than I5 or 20 a day, if we take an average over 30 days. On some days you get 60 or 70 cases: gas, beating, breaking of bones. ...

> To be a doctor and to have to forego treating someone, treating chronic illnesses and the illnesses that people suffer from in any case, in order to concentrate most of your attention on these new cases, is of course another burden on our medical capabilities.[15]

The burden on those working at the local primary level was made more problematic by the reluctance of patients to be transferred to hospitals where they faced the risk of harassment from Israeli soldiers who proved themselves not above searching the wards for wounded 'trouble-makers' and removing them from medical care under arrest. As the orthopaedic surgeon Dr Swee Ang witnessed during her time working in Gaza City's Ahli hospital:

> Dealing with wounds and fractures is just one aspect - perhaps the technical and straightforward aspect. Dealing with wounded patients who are threatened with arrest is the real difficulty ... There are two parties who are victimised in this process. The obvious victim is the patient, but the not-so-obvious victim is the medical team. I felt as though the army was forcing me to violate medical ethics. It was not only denying my patient the right to be treated; it was also denying me the right to treat my patient.[16]

The normalisation of emergency work

The inadequacy of the existing infrastructure in the occupied territories when it came to coping with the epidemic of violence was apparent to all. However, the work and experience of the medical relief committees prior to the Intifada proved an invaluable base for the mobilisation of personnel and resources to cope with the new situation. The decentralised nature of their organisational structure gave them the flexibility necessary to adapt to new circumstances. Their philosophy and practice of grassroots health care directed towards the underprivileged sectors of Palestinian society provided a crucial background of experience when it came to delivering basic medical services to the victims of violence. In examining their response to the new circumstances, attention will be focused upon the work of the Union of Palestinian Medical Relief Committees (UPMRC), the largest and best known of medical relief networks established under occupation.

By the end of the first month of the Uprising, the Union had begun to establish the basic pattern of its response to the Intifada. The most pressing need was for the immediate relief of the injured and traumatised. A call went out for volunteer doctors, nurses and other medically trained professionals. Eventually some 800 medical staff were recruited, half of them physicians. They worked in their free time, and were organised on a rota basis into mobile relief teams. Groups of up to a dozen would travel to the scenes of violence to minister to the victims. In the first week that these teams were in operation, 13-19 January 1988, seventeen refugee camps and three villages in the West Bank and Gaza Strip were visited, and 2,599 patients examined, of whom somewhere between 10-15 percent were suffering from wounds and injuries inflicted by the military. This level of activity was to continue throughout the following weeks and months.[17] As a doctor in Gaza explained,

> The principal aim of the establishment of the Medical Aid Committee was to raise people's consciousness about preventative medicine. .... As soon as the Uprising began the Medical Aid Committee became an emergency service. The tactics of the Committee used to be to have one team throughout Gaza. In the situation of the Uprising we formed three teams. A team for the southern regions, a team for the middle regions, and a team for Gaza Town and the

> north including Jabaliya and Beit Hanoun. Each team operates independently according to the conditions pertaining in the area where they are working.[18]

It was eventually decided to supplement the eight mobile teams (three in the Gaza Strip, five in the West Bank), by establishing a number of permanent emergency first aid centres in those densely populated neighbourhoods where clashes with the military were an almost daily occurrence.

One of the many obstacles with which the medical teams had to contend was the problem of gaining access to patients within closed military zones, such as when curfews were in operation. On one occasion a mobile dental clinic was marooned in the village of Kufr Ni'meh for two weeks during a curfew. For the predominantly middle class residents of Beit Sahour (where, to the casual visitor, it seemed as if every other family possessed at least one member who was either a doctor of medicine or of philosophy) curfews presented rather less of a problem. They formed their own mobile clinic, going from house to house treating the sick and the wounded.[19]

However, not all Palestinian communities had such indigenous resources upon which to call during curfews. In May 1988 the village of Kufr Malek in the Ramallah district was under curfew for over 40 days. Word was passed out via neighbouring villagers that there was a desperate need for medical services. Some two dozen volunteers decided to take up the challenge and carrying all their equipment by hand succeeded in entering the closed area by means of back roads and little known paths. As they made their way towards the centre of the village they attracted quite a number of villagers. Eventually they were confronted by a squad of Israeli soldiers, who demanded to know their purpose. Whilst negotiations ensued, some of the volunteers began there and then to examine those of the villagers displaying obvious signs of injury. Faced with something of a *fait accompli* the soldiers (one of whom was himself a trained nurse) allowed the 'intruders' to set up their clinic in a nearby house. The team of general practitioners, paediatricians, dentists, pharmacists, technicians and nurses succeeded in treating nearly 200 patients during the day, in addition to providing the community with basic first aid training.[20]

Despite such successes, it became increasingly apparent that as the use of various forms of collective punishment placed more and more centres of population under siege conditions with ever greater frequency, a change of approach was required. Instead of a whole team of volunteers trying to enter a closed area, a single doctor was sent to stay for four or five days before being replaced. As one doctor explained:

> We have faced many problems in the course of our work as a result of the imposition of curfews and security sieges ... This used to create big problems for us. So, we changed our tactics to deal with this business of closed military zones. We placed a doctor or nurse in each area under military ban. They would let us know what they needed and we would send it to them. ... This method worked very well. We were able to provide the people with medical services.[21]

Another innovation of the UPMRC was the establishment of a 'roaming physiotherapist' programme. Prior to the Intifada there had been a permanent physiotherapy centre based in Nablus in addition to a couple of physiotherapists who used to visit rural areas. With the dramatic increase in the numbers of those suffering limb injuries from beatings and gunshot wounds, this embryonic community-based programme was adapted to one of home visits to those struggling to regain mobility. An important part of their work was to convince people that physiotherapy was not the luxury they had traditionally considered it to be, but was an essential form of therapy. They also concerned themselves with teaching family members basic patient-management techniques, focusing on elementary massage and physiotherapy that would help in the rehabilitation of the wounded.

The training of lay-people in methods of health care and first aid constituted the second major component of the work of the UPMRC. It was a natural extension of the basic health education work that had always been a priority of the Union. Before the outbreak of the Intifada it had begun publishing leaflets, pamphlets and posters as part of its health awareness programme. In addition it had established a training school for village health workers in association with the Community Health Unit of Birzeit University, where predominantly women trainees received a basic grounding in various aspects of personal, public and community health over a period of nine months. This work continued during the Intifada, but in addition a crash programme for educating the public in the rudiments of first aid treatment was also launched. As in other constructive forms of community-based resistance activity during the Intifada women were particularly prominent in this programme.

From the earliest days of the Uprising volunteers were recruited to prepare and pack first aid kits for mass distribution. They were handed out at meetings and lectures where medical personnel would explain the rudiments of wound and fracture management. By the end of the first year of the Intifada 860 presentations had been made, attended by around 22,000 people, at which 12,000 first aid kits were distributed. Although the packing and distribution of the kits was initially based in Jerusalem, within a few months this was decentralised to regional centres. Following the establishment of the popular neighbourhood committee infrastructure throughout the occupied territories in the spring of 1988, members of the medical relief committees worked closely with local women's committees and health committees, training people in basic methods of first aid. The physicians and medical professionals, in their turn, learned from the local people of their own 'make-do' remedies, such as the use of onions, lemons, and even *eau de cologne* to counteract the effects of tear-gas.

By mid-February 1988 a third dimension of the UPMRC's work was launched. The upsurge in the numbers of injured had revealed a desperate shortage of blood supplies for transfusion purposes. It was therefore decided to initiate a Blood Typing and Donation Campaign, a drive to screen the population for blood type so that any emergency need for blood transfusions could be met from local donors with the minimum of delay. By November 1988 somewhere in the region of 25,000 people had been screened and their blood type recorded. The value of this project was proven over and over again. In one recorded case, following an army helicopter attack on the villages of 'Arura and 'Abwein in the Ramallah district, 22 people with the required blood type presented themselves at Ramallah hospital within half an hour of the emergency call to the Union. The worth of this programme was revealed in rather more dramatic fashion in October 1991. Within a short time following the shootings on Temple Mount, people were reporting to Maqassed and Augusta Victoria Hospitals in East Jerusalem to offer blood, each one of them knowing their blood type. Maqassed took blood from 250 volunteers that day.[22]

A fourth element of the work of the UPMRC was to improve the level of coordination and cooperation between the different tiers of the health service. Prior to the Intifada the provision of health care had not been immune to the deleterious effects of political factionalism, leading to the wasteful duplication of services in some areas where rival nationalist groups associated with different charitable and voluntary associations competed with each other in the provision of medical and health care facilities. Closely associated with the mainstream of Fatah, the UPMRC itself had not remained unaffected by the emergence of an institutional rival in the form of the Popular Committees for Health Services. The new found degree of unity between the nationalist factions during the Intifada, under the leadership of the UNC, along with the unprecedented urgency of the situation, proved a powerful stimulus to greater cooperation between the different sectors of the Palestinian health service.

At the local primary level patients were charged only a nominal fee for the treatment they received, but under the conditions of economic hardship during the Intifada the costs of hospitalisation became prohibitive for many Palestinians. Thus, one of the first tasks taken up by the UPMRC was to negotiate with the charitable hospitals for a number of free beds to be made available to those patients who could not afford the cost of treatment. A fund-raising campaign was also launched to help the families of the injured meet medical costs. The situation with regard to the Israeli-administered government hospitals was more difficult. Only a minority of Palestinians were covered by the government health insurance scheme. Several months into the Uprising the Israeli authorities sought to increase hospital charges. They insisted that patients be charged for three days treatment in advance (the equivalent of £300) before they were admitted to government hospitals. To their credit, the directors of the government hospitals refused to implement the instructions, arguing that it was the responsibility of the ruling authority to provide medical treatment for the victims of war. Faced with such determined opposition, the head of the 'civil administration' finally gave way and served official notice that Palestinians injured by the Israeli army could be treated in government hospitals without charge.

Health care as an instrument of collective punishment

The attempt to raise the charges for hospital treatment was only one element in the attempts of the Israeli authorities to interfere with the provision of medical aid for the casualties of the Intifada. This led to allegations that health care was being used as an instrument of collective punishment. Thus, whilst hospital fees were being raised, the actual health budget for the occupied territories was being reduced. In particular, the funds earmarked for the treatment of Palestinians in Israeli hospitals was slashed. Prior to the Intifada, the Israeli government had always justified its relative underfunding of the secondary and tertiary sectors of the Palestinian health service on the basis that specialist facilities were available in Israel for Palestinians in need of such treatment. As such there was no need to duplicate services. This explanation had always been read by Palestinians as a thinly-disguised rationale for maintaining the situation whereby Palestinians were rendered dependent upon their Israeli occupiers for adequate health care.

Rejecting the humanitarian appeals of Israeli and Palestinian doctors alike. Defence Minister Rabin justified the health service cuts as an economic necessity. The tax revolt in the occupied territories had so reduced the income of the civil administration that corresponding cuts had to be made in expenditure on health services in the territories. Such was his argument. His promise was that 'the minute that our budgetary situation improves, we will return to our past practices'.[23] The message was plain - if the Palestinians wanted to enjoy government health facilities, including continued access to the specialist treatment available in Israeli hospitals, then they should resume their tax payments and wind down their resistance activities. Physicians were appalled. The head of internal medicine at Tel Aviv's Belinson hospital was just one of those to express their concern at this mockery of medical ethics:

> We are shocked to see the extent to which the authorities are using medicine as a stick to beat people with, and I don't mean just against those wounded in the Intifada, but also against the sick among the civilian population.[24]

Similar sentiments of concern were expressed at press conferences in Israel and elsewhere by Israeli and Palestinian physicians. Tales of Palestinian children being denied treatment in Israeli hospitals, some of them dying as a consequence, were a public relations nightmare for the Israeli authorities, coming as they did in the wake of international concern at the policy of beatings and unnecessary force being used against protesters. In January 1989 the policy was reversed.

It is obviously very costly for an occupying power concerned about its international image as a humanitarian regime to be revealed as directly interfering with the provision of medical aid to those in need. During the course of the Intifada there were allegations that soldiers had prevented ambulances from picking up those injured in confrontations with the army. It was alleged that on occasions soldiers have commandeered ambulances in order to enter 'no-go' areas. There were also numerous reports of military personnel interfering with the attempts to minister to the wounded and of soldiers entering hospitals to apprehend injured suspects. Allegations were also made that medical personnel were singled out for harassment and intimidation.

All these charges had been levelled against the Israeli security forces at some time or another during the Intifada, and they proved extremely damaging. It is one thing to dismiss allegations made by Palestinians as propagandist in purpose and substance, it is quite another thing when allegations concerning the violation of medical rights emanated from relatively unimpeachable sources such as Israeli physicians and representatives of the international medical community. Thus, the report of the North American based Physicians for Human Rights, published in the summer of 1988, attracted media attention throughout the world, whilst the work of the Tel Aviv based Association of Israeli and Palestinian Physicians, which was formed early in 1988 in response to the way medical ethics were being abused during the Intifada, proved to be an on-going irritant to the Israeli state authorities.

Faced with the damaging consequences of its own policies, Israel began to seek rather more indirect ways of using medicine as a means of punishing the Palestinians. A key method was that of administrative delay and bureaucratic obfuscation. This ranged from withholding travel permits requested by Palestinian physicians to attend overseas conferences, through to delays in granting permission for the installation of a telephone at the hospital in Hebron, and delays of several months before the Swedish-funded rehabilitation centre at Ramallah was able to obtain the necessary documentation to allow it to open. One of the better documented cases of bureaucratic interference in the provision of medical aid concerned the Palestinian ambulance service. It became apparent during the early days of the Intifada that this underdeveloped service needed to be modernised and extended in order to cope with the casualties of the conflict. The problems faced by the Palestinians in obtaining the necessary permission to operate the new ambulances bordered on the Kafkaesque. Difficulties in obtaining the necessary import permits resulted in the decision to purchase ambulances made in Israel. There was then the problem of obtaining the necessary operating licenses. The Israelis made this contingent upon there being specially licensed ambulance drivers to operate the vehicles. The prospective drivers would have to take and pass a training course, just as Israeli ambulance drivers did. But before taking the course, unlike Israeli drivers, they needed the permission of the Civil Administration, who in turn needed reassuring that the drivers had paid all their taxes and had a satisfactory security clearance. Those who passed this obstacle, and successfully completed the course, were then forced to wait several months before actually receiving the driving licences necessary for the ambulances to be awarded their operating permits.

For the Israelis, such bureaucratic delays enabled them to assert their control over the provision of health care, whilst avoiding the stigma of appearing to play the dirty game of punishing the victims of ill-health and injury. Moreover, a security-related reason could invariably be produced to justify their 'caution'. Thus, a spokesperson for the West Bank Civil Administration was able to explain with regard to the case of the ambulances:

> We believe there are links between some medical organisations and groups that are not medical. ... Because the situation is very delicate today we have to check to see that the PLO or other extremist groups are not part of the request. ... So, they have to be checked out to know exactly why they are trying to get permits for those ambulances.[25]

For the Palestinian medical institutions, the circumvention of the Israeli reluctance to grant operating permits for ambulances did not present too great a problem. Normal commercial vehicles were purchased by some of the medical committees, and then converted into 'quasi-ambulances' of varying degrees of medical sophistication. Another tactic involved listing the ambulances as 'health buses', thereby side-stepping the need for specially licensed drivers.

Conclusion

With the ingenuity born of necessity, the Palestinians had to cope with the demands on the medical services during the Intifada as best they could, and with a considerable degree of success. The pre-intifada trend towards increasing dependence upon Israeli medical facilities was reversed. As in other spheres of life, the crisis facing the medical and health care institutions had forced the personnel to overcome past rivalries based to a significant degree on political factionalism. The result was that in the process of responding to situational imperatives, the infrastructure of a Palestinian national health service began to emerge which provided some with a degree of optimism for the future – an emotion that was common during the height of the unarmed resistance up to 1990. This hope for the future was tinged, however, by mounting concern regarding the future of the disabled and handicapped. As early as spring 1988 Dr Al-Namari of Maqassed hospital was warning:

> The problem of treatment and recovery is small compared to the huge problems related to the rehabilitation of the disabled and his absorption into the community. ... The hospital is only a way station … . At one time they would lock up a handicapped person in a back room so that no one would see him. We have already passed this stage. Those injured in the Intifada are received with honour by their friends, but the average family still lacks the knowledge and the psychological readiness to deal with someone who is disabled.[26]

As the Intifada continued the shortages of such basic items as wheelchairs, artificial limbs and other aids grew increasingly acute. But these concerns were overshadowed by worries over the long-term future of the disabled, the vast majority of whom were under 18, in a society lacking the institutional, material and psychological resources necessary for their rehabilitation.[27]

For the young victims of the Intifada, their status as heroes was continually reaffirmed during their hospitalisation. Friends, family, dignitaries and hospital personnel were in attendance. They were at the centre of concern and attention. Honour required that they display the necessary signs of steadfastness and high morale. The secondary trauma came when they were discharged. The majority of them came from poor families in villages and refugee camps. They returned to the family home, confined, lacking mobility, dependent on others - separated from the life of collective struggle going on outside. In such circumstances dreams about the national destiny of the Palestinian people could give way to nightmares about their own personal future. The consequent depression, in the absence of adequate therapeutic support services, could be profound and led to suicide in a number of cases.

As the Intifada progressed it became increasingly clear to those involved in the medical care of the victims of Israeli violence that a massive injection of funds, expertise and facilities was needed if the physiological and psychological wounds inflicted upon a whole generation of young Palestinians were to be healed. Hopes of such an input of finance took a severe jolt in the months following Iraq's invasion of Kuwait, as the loss of funds from the Gulf States placed all Palestinian institutions, including those in the medical sector, in dire financial straits. Construction work on new hospitals at Tulkarm and Hebron had to be halted, whilst plans for a new UNRWA hospital in Gaza had to be shelved. There was particular concern at Maqassed Hospital, where 70 percent of its $15 million annual budget came from the Gulf States, the majority of it from Kuwait. [28]

The concern of medical personnel about the long-term psychological damage inflicted upon the young during the Intifada was widely shared. A number of researchers claimed that one consequence of the Intifada was that Palestinians had forfeited their childhood during the years of struggle and confrontation. As one observer commented,

> They do not play like normal children elsewhere in the world. Their games reflect their daily life: children with stones facing heavily armed Israeli soldiers. The older children carry makeshift toy guns while the little ones throw make-believe stones at them. Some pretend to be hit and fall to the ground while their friends carry them to hospital. [29]

It was scenes like these that constituted one of the driving forces behind the efforts of parents, teachers and educationalists to maintain some form of educational system in the face of the tremendous obstacles created by an occupying power determined to make the people of the West Bank and Gaza Strip pay dearly for their resistance.

---

[1] Israel Ministry of Health, *Report to World Health Organisation*, 1986, p. 8.

[2] See *An Overview of health conditions and services in the Israeli Occupied Territories*, Jerusalem: Union of Palestinian Medical Relief Committees, August 1987.

[3] *Overview of health conditions*, p. 12.

[4] *Overview of health conditions*, p. 15.

[5] M. Benvenisti, *The 1986 report*, Jerusalem: West Bank Data Base Project, 1986, p. 17.

[6] *Overview of health conditions*, p. 13.

[7] *Overview of health condition*, p. 47.

[8] J. H. Puyet, Infant mortality studies carried out among selected refugee camp communities in the Near East, Vienna: UNRWA, 1979.

[9] *Profile of life and health in Biddu: Interim report*, Ramallah: Union of Palestinian Medical Relief Committees and Community Health Unit, Birzeit University, 1987.

[10] *Jerusalem Post*, January 26, 1988.

[11] Figures quoted by Dr. R. Al-Namari at *Workshop on health*, Jerusalem, December 31 1989 (Part of the *Time for Peace, 1990* activities.) See also *Al Fajr*, December 10, 1990, pp. 8-9.

[12] Report of *B'Tselem*, reviewed in *Al Fajr*, February 18, 1991, p. 4.

[13] Interview with doctor at Shafa Hospital, Gaza, June 1988 (*Voices from Gaza*).

[14] Dr R. Al-Namari, quoted in *New Outlook*, June 1988.

[15] Voices from Gaza.

[16] *The Guardian*, January 28-29, 1989.

[17] UPMRC, *Emergency Newsletter no. 6*, April 1 - May 15, 1988.

[18] Voices from Gaza.

[19] *News from nowhere*, v. 7, n. 4, April 3 1991, pp. 12 - 13.

[20] Emergency newsletter no. 6.

[21] Voices from Gaza.

[22] *Al Fajr*, December 10, 1990, pp. 8-9.

[23] Quoted by T. Segey, *Ha'aretz*, January 6, 1989.

---

[24] E. Theodor quoted by E. Pallis, *Middle East International*, February 3, 1989.
[25] Quoted in J Levin, *The Palestinians' ambulance problem: a health care Catch-22 in the West Bank and Gaza*, mimeo, 1989, p. 9.
[26] Quoted in *Koterest Rashit*, May 18, 1988.
[27] During the Uprising three new rehabilitation centres were established: Friends of the Patient Society at Ramallah, the Arab Rehabilitation Centre at Beit Jala, and the Beit Sahour YMCA Rehabilitation Centre. See *Al Fajr*, December 10, 1990, pp. 8-9.
[28] *The Guardian*, August 30, 1990. See also *Financial Times*, September 28, 1990.
[29] N. al-Helo, 'The trauma of growing up in Palestine', *Al Fajr*, August 13, 1990, p. 7.

5

THE STRUGGLE OVER EDUCATION

Introduction

It has been a common observation that Palestinians in the diaspora and living under occupation have placed a particularly high value upon formal educational attainment. In uncertain circumstances education has been seen as an important form of investment for the future, providing people with a passport to greater economic security and enhanced life-chances. The Israeli authorities were well aware of this attitude towards education on the part of Palestinians and therefore it came as no surprise that educational institutions became a specific target in the power struggle that lay at the heart of the Intifada.

The use of education as a means of collective punishment was a particular feature of Israeli policy towards the West Bank. They did not attempt to 'outlaw' educational activity with anything like the same rigour in the Gaza Strip. In part this was because the direct economic dependency upon Israel of the majority of the Gazan population rendered them far more vulnerable to economic sanctions. Thus, whilst the Islamic University in Gaza was closed after December 1987 the schools in Gaza remained open - except for those areas under curfew and individual schools closed for specific periods as punishment for particular acts of defiance on the part of their students.[1] Consequently, in this chapter the focus will be upon the West Bank and the battle of wills that took place there over education.

Background

Schools, colleges and universities represent a considerable problem to any occupying power. Educational institutions are one of the places where people gather and meet together as a group to discuss issues of common concern. They are key agencies for the transmission not only of substantive knowledge but also of cultural values and dominant world views. In the occupied territories the world view of the Palestinians has been crucially shaped by the perception of the injustice and illegitimacy of occupation, and the values that have been transmitted have been nationalist ones. Consequently schools and colleges have been the sites of demonstrations and protests against Israeli rule since the occupation began. The response of the Israeli authorities was fairly predictable - students and teachers were harassed, arrested, deported. Schools and colleges would be closed down for varying periods of time as a form of collective punishment aimed at subduing unrest. Universities in particular came in for special attention as Israel sought to prevent and frustrate the emergence of any autonomous indigenous political, social and cultural leadership amongst the subject population.

To some observers there was a ritualistic quality to the regular confrontations that took place between students and the military during the years prior to the outbreak of the Intifada. The students would demonstrate by blocking a road and setting fire to tyres; stones would be thrown at the advancing soldiers, who would reply with tear-gas, rubber and occasionally live bullets. A chase would then take place. Those unfortunate enough to be caught would be beaten and arrested. The school or university would then be closed by military order, and the academic year would have been interrupted once again. Universities, and to a lesser degree secondary schools, became accustomed to spells of closure and enforced inactivity, followed by periods of intensive instruction and study in order to make up the lost time so that students might complete their courses before the commencement of the next academic year.

For the schools in the West Bank the major matriculation exam was the Jordanian *tawjihi*, which was a requirement for entrance to university and to a number of white-collar and professional career paths. It consisted of a number of compulsory examinations, sat in two blocs - the first in January and the second in June. Failure to sit and pass any of the exams resulted in failure to matriculate, and the student had to wait another year before trying again. This meant that students prevented from sitting the exams (because of arrest, curfews, school closure or some other reason) in effect lost a year's schooling.

The universities in the occupied territories were modelled to some degree on the North American system of course credits, with students taking a range of different courses in order to obtain the required number of credit hours to graduate. In both schools and universities the methods of teaching was very traditional, and before the Intifada there had been little attempt to develop any indigenous model of education with regard to teaching methods and curriculum content. Paradoxically, the impetus for such a revaluation emerged during the Intifada as the Israeli authorities, fully aware of the value placed on education by Palestinians, sought to impose a mighty cost on the resistance through a massive disruption of the educational system.

The struggle over schooling

As in other areas of life, the response of the Israeli administration to the challenge posed by students and institutes of education during the Intifada did not represent any markedly new departure, but rather an intensification of established patterns of individual and collective punishment. From the Israeli point of view, if the schools and colleges could not control their students in the interests of 'law and order', then they would have to bear the resultant cost.[2] The hope was that if sufficient sanctions were imposed upon the Palestinians, they would eventually 'come to their senses' and follow the more rational course of quiet acceptance of the status quo. They would then be in a position to resume their pursuit of knowledge and the associated educational qualifications that represented necessary passports to economic and social mobility.

On February 3 1988 a military order was issued closing down until further notice all schools in the West Bank because they had become 'centres for organising and stimulating violence'. A few days later on February 13 this closure order was extended to all government schools in East Jerusalem. This meant that over 1200 schools were shut down, affecting more than 300,000 students. The schools were allowed to reopen on May 23 but were closed down again two months later and remained closed from mid-July until December 1988. On January 20 1989 all the schools in the West Bank were closed down once again, only one month after the secondary schools had reopened. They remained closed until the last week of July 1989, when the Israelis allowed them to start reopening once again.

The initial response of teachers and school administrators to the closure order of early February 1988 was uncertain. They received no advance official notification of the closures, many of them hearing the announcement over the radio or arriving at school to find the gates locked. They therefore had no opportunity to meet collectively in school to prepare contingency plans. Moreover they had no idea how long the Intifada would last and how long the schools would remain closed. As the weeks passed depression spread amongst teachers. More and more of the government schools were being taken over by the military as barracks, temporary detention centres, and storage bases. Teachers and administrators felt helpless and frustrated. They were reluctant to call for student demonstrations against the closures for fear of injury to the students. Indeed it was reported that one of the wry jokes of the Intifada during this early period was 'Don't ask him to demonstrate. He's a teacher; he might dirty his hands'.[3]

The position of teachers in the government schools was particularly difficult. Deprived of their salaries, they suffered economically. In addition, locked out of their schools without warning, they had no access to teaching materials and no means of meeting with their pupils. Teachers could still gain access to the private schools, and so they could continue to meet with their colleagues to restore their flagging spirits and discuss contingency plans. The administrator of one such school told me of their efforts to frustrate the closure order by preparing self-study packs for pupils, meeting with them on an individual basis at regular intervals to discuss their work and set them their next assignment. However, such attempts to 'teach from a distance' were somewhat half-hearted. For one thing the teachers themselves were not trained for such a task and lacked experience and expertise. For another, they lacked the equipment and the means necessary to duplicate the teaching materials and distribute them throughout the private school network. There was also a strong feeling that at a time when the Palestinian people, in their resistance to Israeli occupation, were experiencing an unprecedented degree of unity that transcended divisions of class, religion and family it was inappropriate to discriminate in favour of the children of middle class families who could afford the fees of the private schools. By continuing to make educational provision for these already relatively privileged pupils, they would in effect be discriminating against the relatively disadvantaged pupils of the government schools. However unintentionally, they would be contributing to a widening of the social gulf between the classes, something that was contrary to the whole ethos of the Intifada.

Towards the end of March 1988, well into the second month of closure, the unified leadership of the Uprising began to urge students and teachers to return to schools and universities and 'to practice their legitimate right to education'. March 24 was declared a 'Day of Education' by the UNC, which prompted a number of private schools to open on that day.[4] It was a short-lived act of defiance. As the administrator of one school told me, within minutes of the pupils arriving the military appeared on the scene and threatened to use tear-gas if the school was not emptied within five minutes, intimating that any repeat would risk incurring permanent closure.

A more sustained form of constructive resistance to the suppression of formal educational activity was launched towards the end of March 1988. This was the attempt by popular neighbourhood committees to organise alternative classes for school children which were held in private homes. This development was heralded as a significant move in the strategy of resistance through progressive disengagement from the occupation authorities. It was also depicted as a first tentative step towards the development of a truly indigenous Palestinian educational process that was organically based in the community. For all those who were involved it was an exciting innovation. Teachers were faced with the challenge of motivating students without recourse to the traditional sanctions of the classroom, the formal school system of grades, and the 'carrot' of accreditation for the diligent student.

However, the actual implementation of this programme of popular education varied in quality and coverage from neighbourhood to neighbourhood, and a number of serious problems were encountered that were not satisfactorily resolved. In middle class communities, where there was a ready supply of teachers and members of other professional groups, there was little difficulty in finding people to service the alternative classes. However, in many of the villages, camps, and neighbourhoods there were few people with appropriate experience to take on the role of teacher, with the result that the classes suffered. Added to this problem of uneven development, there was no central coordination of what to teach and how to go about it. There were no back-up services to assist those lacking relevant previous experience. Moreover, a common problem was encountered in trying to motivate the students. The traditional process of schooling in the occupied territories involved a lot of 'chalk and talk' from the teachers and rote learning from the students. The prime aim seemed to be to enable the students to gain the necessary accreditation to move on to the next year of study. The popular education classes could not provide the students with that accreditation, and it would appear that, as a result, the pupils failed to appreciate the need to study.

Despite these problems, this community based system of education was seen by many as a significant 'challenge to the occupier's ability to control the process and contents of Palestinian education and ... another grave threat to Israel's failing efforts at maintaining authority over the population'.[5] Perhaps the Israeli military authorities also saw it in such a light for, much to everyone's surprise, they announced on May 23 1988 that schools would be allowed to reopen. The elementary schools were the first to be allowed to welcome their pupils again, followed a few days later by the secondary schools. For the teaching staff a major concern accompanying the reopening of the schools focused on the motivation of the students. Would the young people generalise their defiance of the Israelis to defiance of authority in general, and the teacher's authority in particular? In fact they were pleasantly surprised by the initial enthusiasm shown by the pupils on their return. However, this began to wear off, and after a few weeks there was a certain amount of tenseness in the classroom. Schools continued to abide by the directives of the UNC to restrict their hours in line with the daily commercial strike. As a consequence, with teachers feeling the need to 'make up for lost time', schools started 'doing away with fun classes such as art, physical education and home economics, to concentrate on the more serious subjects.'[6]

This attempt to cover the ground in examinable subjects during the restricted school day was very demanding of both staff and students, particularly when events outside the classroom intruded. As one young student at a school in Ramallah wrote, 'Lots of time while we are in class we smell tyres burning and hear shots in Ramallah. Our minds are outside so we can't do anything in class'. Another student admitted, 'Sometimes I feel bad in school. Everyone outside is in the Intifada and we're stuck in school.'[7] Indeed, teachers found themselves unable to prevent secondary students from leaving the classroom before classes finished, as they made their preparations for the day's confrontation with the Israeli soldiers. These daily clashes with the military as the students emerged from school were a source of concern to teachers and parents alike who feared for the safety of the young. Eventually, early in July 1988, the schools were closed down once again.

If the aim of the Israeli authorities in allowing the schools to reopen for a few weeks had been to disrupt the development of an alternative Palestinian system of community-based education, then the plan succeeded. When the pupils had returned to the classrooms in May it was resolved that the informal sector of alternative education should be maintained. One student was quoted as saying 'We will not give up our classes. Schools teach in the morning, and our neighbourhood studies take place in the afternoon.'[8] Educationalists had also recognised the need for a thorough survey of the educational needs of the different villages and neighbourhoods throughout the occupied territories, so that a serious attempt could be made to match resources with expressed needs through developing contact lists, resource centres and the like. It was also realised that particular attention should be paid to assisting parents who, it was acknowledged, would have to play a key role in the educational classes. There were simply not enough professional and experienced teachers available to lead the home-based educational groups.

Despite such worthy and laudable intentions, the reality was that during the period that formal schooling was resumed, the popular education classes were allowed to lapse. When the schools were closed once again the following July, people were faced with the problem of rebuilding their underground educational infrastructure. This task was made more difficult and costly when, in mid-August 1988, the Israelis declared all popular committees illegal. In effect this meant that anyone involved with organising any kind of educational or cultural activity risked prosecution and imprisonment. That the Israeli authorities were serious in their attempts to suppress any form of educational activity was revealed by the arrest on September 2 1988 of a number of teachers and twelve students discovered when soldiers raided a classroom in Abu Diss College of Science and Technology. A couple of days later two teachers and two students were temporarily detained in Nablus following an army raid on the offices of the Society of Friends of al-Najah University. The head of the Society, Said Kanaan, had been organising classes in a range of subjects including physics, chemistry and English. He explained, 'We wanted to serve our people. We were involved in education and we were not doing anything against the security of Israel.'[9] In effect the Israeli authorities were attempting to outlaw all forms of educational activity, and to a considerable degree they succeeded, especially with regard to school-age children. During the 1987-1988 school year pupils lost 175 out of 210 school days. During the school year that began in 1988, students were allowed to attend school for only 40 days prior to the reopening of the schools at the end of July 1989. During 1989 the schools were in operation for a total of four months.[10]

The continued closure of the schools was a very heavy cost borne by the Palestinians of the West Bank. Their concern focused on both the short and long term consequences of this Israeli policy of 'cultural massacre', to quote the phrase used by one of my informants. Alongside the concern for the plight of the students prevented from completing their *tawjihi* examinations, there was considerable worry about the situation of the younger children. The fear was that the longer the children remained out of school, the greater the likelihood that they would lose their basic foundation in literacy and numeracy. Educationalists also emphasised the damage to those who had yet to acquire these basic skills, arguing that the longer the delay in teaching a child how to read the more difficult it became. There was also considerable trepidation about the administrative difficulties of coping with the return of the pupils to school. In the relatively normal times prior to the Intifada there had been approximately 28 - 30,000 children entering the school system. How could the schools cope with an entrance double the normal quota? Government schools in particular already suffered from over-crowding, with class sizes in the region of 45 - 65. How could they manage when the normal entry was supplemented by an equal number who had been prevented from starting twelve months previously because of the closures?

Beyond the concern with the consequences of lost qualifications and knowledge, and the organisational problems of coping with the return to 'normal' schooling, there were other issues causing anxiety amongst educationalists. A genuine fear had grown that during the Intifada the young had begun to lose their study skills in general, and that in future there would be a serious problem of motivation and discipline amongst the student body. During the period of school closure the students had a considerable amount of spare time when they could have been studying. Most found it almost impossible. As one student explained, 'I spend my time switching from one radio station to another, trying to find out what is happening around. When Palestinians of my age are being killed, I can't just sit and study.'[11] This was completely understandable – how could you expect a young person to sit down and concentrate on reading a history book when history was being made outside their very door? The helicopters are circling overhead, the smell of tear-gas is in the air, there are military patrols in the street and your friends are whistling for you to come out and join them in the fray. How could anyone concentrate with so much excitement and tension being generated? How mundane and tedious any classroom would appear after such periods of high drama? So, how prepared would the youth of the strike forces be to accept the discipline and order of the classroom in the future? How prepared would they be to make the necessary effort to make up for the lost time?

These were the questions that exercised the teachers, educationalists and parents. They were part of a wider anxiety about the deeper damage that the Israelis were causing, beyond the denial of access to formal education. Outside of school, on the streets and elsewhere, the young Palestinians were receiving an education. They were learning new things about themselves and about the 'enemy'. They were operating in a milieu where macho-courage and aggression was valued. As an onlooker who witnessed the daily confrontations with the military the thought would strike me that these clashes were reminiscent of encounters between rival youth gangs, taunting and harassing and attacking each other when fighting over their territorial rights. What kind of preparation was this for living and working cooperatively in a future Palestinian society? As one Palestinian mother expressed her hopes and fears about her infant son: 'I would like him to grow up to be a revolutionary, but I'm worried that he is growing up learning to resort to stone-throwing as a means of settling arguments and conflicts'.[12]

In November 1989 there was evidence that these fears were justified. During the *tawjihi* examinations, held six months later than usual, there was incontrovertible evidence of widespread cheating and intimidation during the course of the examinations, even though the students were tested on just half the normal syllabus in the light of the disrupted school year. Even more worrying was the repetition of such behaviour in the examinations that took place the following summer of 1990. Despite prior appeals for honesty by the UNC and other bodies, in a number of locations young activists entered the classrooms and ordered teachers and invigilators aside while they coordinated the cheating process. The result was that in at least one university in the West Bank the *tawjihi* results were dismissed as unreliable and applicants were required to take a separate university entrance examination.[13]

The administrators and teachers in the private school sector faced far more immediate fears - the threatened bankruptcy of their schools. Tuition fees were the major source of income and with the schools closed for month after month these were not being paid, and a severe financial crisis was the result. A substantial number of well-to-do families that had been sending their children to fee-paying schools in the occupied territories withdrew them, either out of fear for their physical safety or concern about the lost schooling. The children were sent elsewhere for their education - the Arab world, the United States, Europe, or perhaps just as far as East Jerusalem where the private schools remained open for longer periods than elsewhere in the territories. Not only did this contribute to the financial crisis of the private schools, it raised deeper fears of a more long-term nature. In effect what was happening was that those with the necessary resources were still managing to obtain schooling for their children, a schooling that would provide them with the necessary accreditation to proceed to higher education and beyond. At a time when social solidarity was claimed as a key factor in the continuation of the struggle against the occupation, the seeds of social division were being reproduced through different 'educational classes' being superimposed on existing social divisions: one class made up of a mass group of relatively disadvantaged, and a smaller group who managed to reap the benefits of uninterrupted formal schooling.

For many of the school-age young of the occupied territories, the costs of interrupted schooling would not have seemed too significant – after all the future is a long long time away when you are young. However, many educationalists were deeply concerned about the future of these 'children of the stones'. There seemed to be no satisfactory alternative except to struggle to keep the schools open as much as possible. The popular home and neighbourhood based educational classes had not really functioned adequately, for reasons already discussed. But even if this alternative system did succeed in some measure (providing the opportunity for peers to meet and study together, maintaining study skills and encouraging a basic coverage of texts and other materials), it could not hope to provide the accreditation that the formal school sector had traditionally supplied, and which the students needed to proceed to the higher education so valued by Palestinians. Of course, even with the schools open, many senior students might have asked themselves why they should trouble to study for examinations, as the universities in the occupied territories had been closed down more frequently and for longer periods than any other sector of the educational system.

The assault on academe

Until the summer of 1990, when a few higher educational institutes, including Bethlehem and al-Quds Universities, were allowed to reopen, all the universities and colleges of further education in the occupied territories had been under continuous closure order since January 1988. The faculty and students should not have been too surprised at this drastic punishment, as the institutions of higher education have been a special target of the occupying authorities over the years. The military intruded onto the campuses regularly, breaking up demonstrations, arresting students, confiscating books and materials. Military checkpoints and road-blocks around the campuses had also been an all too familiar feature, disrupting the daily life of students and staff. Even before the commencement of the Intifada the members of the universities suffered disproportionately from the whole gamut of repressive measures available to the Israeli authorities: short-term arbitrary arrest, restriction orders and 'town arrest', administrative detention without trial, and even deportation. In July 1980 the Israelis introduced Military Order 854 through which they sought to exercise broad powers of control over curricula, the admission of students, the hiring and firing of staff and other areas. Foreign and non-resident staff were asked to affirm a 'loyalty oath' that they would 'refrain from any act which is harmful to security and public order... and the rendering of any service, of a collaborative or helpful nature, to the PLO or any other hostile organisation.' Due to local and international protest, the operation of this order was allowed to lapse in November 1982 and the pledge was struck from work permit applications a year later. The experience of closure was also a familiar one before January 1988. Birzeit University near Ramallah had been closed on 15 separate occasions between December 1973 and December 1987 for periods totalling over 18 months, including one of four months during the 1986-87 academic year. In the 1981-82 academic year it was closed for a total of seven months.[14] Al-Najah University in Nablus was closed by military order on three separate occasions amounting to two months in total during the first six months of 1987. The universities and colleges at Bethlehem, Hebron, and Gaza had also suffered similar disruptions.

For their part, the Israelis justified their actions by claiming, not without some justification, that the universities were centres of protest and hot-beds of nationalism. 'If they wish to pursue their goal of instruction and research, then they should control their students', was the argument. Amongst the voices raised in protest against such reasoning and the punitive measures of the authorities were those of students and academics within Israel itself. In October 1981 five professors from the Hebrew University in Jerusalem published a report calling on the authorities to 'refrain from closing universities as a means of punishment or to prevent disturbances'. In November of that year 100 students and staff from the Hebrew and Tel Aviv universities who were associated with the Birzeit Solidarity Committee took part in a demonstration and sit-in at the Birzeit campus in protest against the two month closure order that had been imposed. To a far greater degree than the schools Palestinian universities had cultivated support not only from Israeli faculty and students but from the wider international academic community, who were urged to exercise pressure upon Israel in protest against the assault on academic freedom and higher education in general within the occupied territories.

Indeed, a key reference group for Palestinian academics was the international community of scholars and academics in whose institutions many of them obtained their higher degrees and upon which their own universities have been modelled. Palestinian universities were organised into faculties and departments along traditional subject lines: engineering, mathematics, social science, and so on. Teaching and assessment methods were likewise along the established lines of lectures, text-books, examinations and credits. Power was also distributed in a manner familiar to academics the world over - with students feeling relatively disenfranchised, junior faculty complaining that their voices remained unheard, and senior academics bemoaning the power of the administrators and the patronage of the university power elite. Palestinian universities also had their fair share of 'internal' conflicts, with sit-ins and demonstrations by students protesting over such issues as the level of tuition fees, assessment procedures and the like. In other words, prior to the Intifada there was nothing particularly unique about Palestinian universities, except for the circumstances under which they attempted to fulfil their functions. Added to this, Palestinian academics seemed to have enjoyed an unusual degree of prestige within the Palestinian community, a reflection of the value placed by Palestinians upon higher educational qualifications.[15] In response, Palestinian academics accepted as part of their function the role of opinion leader within the community, and also sought to champion the Palestinian cause on the conference circuits of the world, and within the ranks of international organisations and professional associations.

Sadly, it would appear that following the commencement of the Intifada and the consequent closure of the universities, the academics began to lose the respect that was once theirs. By September 1988 I was being told that 'Academics are one of the few groups that are not playing a significant role in the Intifada.'

'They draw their salaries, sit at home, and do nothing' was the feeling expressed by more than one observer; a verdict endorsed by some of the academics that I met at that time. 'I am not part of the struggle, I am doing nothing for the Intifada', bemoaned one of their number. 'All that we have done since the Intifada in terms of developing alternative teaching has been little more than symbolic, more an expression of inertia than of active and imaginative struggle', confessed a senior professor. 'The military have forbidden any teaching - what can I do?' queried another. What the teaching staff of the universities had done up to that stage had been to continue teaching final year students who had only a few credit hours to complete for their degree. Classes were held in private houses and elsewhere on a regular basis, coursework was assigned, course notes and other hand-outs distributed, problems discussed. Thus, Birzeit University ran classes between July and September 1988 for 240 students, 80 of whom graduated on completion of their courses.[16] Attempts to establish any wider system of alternative education were frustrated by the outlawing of the popular committees and the subsequent suppression of educational classes. As a consequence many university staff experienced a deep sense of impotence. They, like the other sectors of Palestinian society in the occupied territories, felt the need to play a part in the Intifada. But individually they feared the penalties that the Israeli authorities had shown themselves willing and capable of applying. Collectively, they had not developed the infrastructure to coordinate any joint action throughout the university sector. Once the universities were closed they had been unable to develop a means to facilitate the widespread discussion and concrete planning necessary for coordinated activity throughout the occupied territories.

Although there were demonstrations in protest against the closure of educational institutions during the first year of the Intifada, some activists were critical of the limited and uncoordinated nature of such actions.[17] Disappointment was expressed that no attempt had been made to organise a joint demonstration on all the campuses, perhaps supported by eminent academics from Israel and the international community, which could have attracted the attention of the world media and seriously embarrassed the military authorities. Likewise, whilst there was a fair amount of discussion around coffee tables and within individual homes about the possibility of engaging in a radical review of the existing structure, content, and process of higher education in the light of the needs of the Palestinian community during the Intifada, little progress was made at the collective level during that first year.

This relative failure could be attributed to a number of factors. First of all, most Palestinian academics had been trained in traditional university environments and had accepted the established norms, practices and patterns of education as their own. They had proven themselves reluctant to develop new paradigms and approaches to teaching with all the associated risks of failure and the damage to one's career prospects that can result from being labelled a 'trouble-maker'. Of equal importance had been the nature of the relationship between the universities within the occupied territories, characterised more by rivalry and competition rather than cooperation and open communication. As the Intifada advanced into its third year the situation changed somewhat. When I returned to the West Bank during the autumn of 1989 I was heartened to discover that the alternative 'universities without walls' had become rather more firmly established over the previous year. Serious attempts had been made to expand and develop the framework of underground teaching and assessment. Perhaps this was in response to the criticism to which they had been exposed. There was also a fear of losing valued faculty members who were beginning to seek posts abroad as academic life in Palestine continued to remain moribund. And also there was a growing realisation that 'things could not remain as they were'.

Given the inadvisability of holding lectures and classes in a single centralised location, which would attract the attention of the military, a radically decentralised mode of teaching had been established. Classes were held for a maximum of six or seven students in different locations. This meant, for instance, that if 36 students were registered for a course, the lecturer would hold the same class up to six times in six different locations. Typically, it would appear that each course was arranged to last between six and eight weeks, during which time the students were assessed and course credits awarded. In the absence of normal library and study facilities, due to the closure of the campuses, maximum use was made of photocopied readings and texts, duplicated lectures notes and other study aids.[18] In order to preserve some degree of academic quality under such difficult circumstances, the general practice was to restrict students to two courses per session, although those near to graduation were allowed to take three. It had been estimated that if the universities could continue to hold three sessions or semesters each academic year, then it would take students seven years to complete their 'underground degree'. Although this might seem an abnormally lengthy period, even before the Intifada it was not unusual for undergraduates to take six years to obtain a degree, due to university closures and other interruptions of the educational process.

A major problem was encountered with this decentralised, covert, off- campus mode of teaching. It proved impossible to provide the facilities for the practical, laboratory-based work that is a fundamental part of any course in the pure and applied sciences. The same obstacle applied to all forms of research that required such facilities as scientific equipment, computers and the like. The closure of the libraries also meant that even faculty members and researchers in the arts and humanities found it difficult to keep abreast of the latest work in their field. Moreover, despite precautions to avoid attracting attention - a basic rule being that students and staff should not arrive at classes together carrying bags full of incriminating books - there remained the risk of discovery. Thus, in April 1989 it was reported that 'a network of illegal classes held by two West Bank universities at private high schools in East Jerusalem' had been uncovered. It was claimed that Birzeit and Bethlehem Universities had been holding classes for some 300 students on the school premises.[19]

Conclusion

This chapter has examined the struggle that took place over education in the West Bank within the context of the wider power struggle of the Intifada. There can be no doubt that through their closure of schools, universities, and other educational institutions, and their attempt to prohibit educational activity in general, the Israeli administration succeeded in imposing a severe collective punishment upon a people who placed a high value on educational attainment. In trying to counter these measures, the Palestinians met with only partial success. During the long period of school closure, despite some initial enthusiasm, the exercise in establishing neighbourhood classes would appear to have achieved only a limited coverage of the school-age population, not least because such 'schools' could not provide the formal accreditation held in such high esteem by Palestinians. The fact that the universities maintained at least the skeleton of their formal system of assessment might help to explain why the condition of higher education achieved a relatively healthier state than the alternative school system, although even here only about one tenth of the normal number were graduating with their degrees. For many Palestinians, these short-term costs were of less concern than the longer-term consequences of what they saw as a sustained attempt to destroy the infrastructure of Palestinian education. However, throughout the first six months of 1990 there were repeated rumours that the universities and colleges were about to be reopened. Hebron Polytechnic and the Arab Medical College at al-Bireh were the first to be allowed to open their doors. Israeli officials stated that if classes were resumed normally at these institutions they would be prepared to consider the gradual reopening of the other educational institutions, and at the end of August it was decided that Bethlehem University should be allowed to open once more, after nearly three years of official closure. The re-opening of Birzeit and al-Najar Universities was made dependent upon the 'good behaviour' of the students of Bethlehem. Most Palestinians viewed these steps with caution, seeing them as little more than public relations exercises aimed at appeasing world opinion and under- mining the Palestinian will to resist. They were fully aware that the institutions of higher education, like the schools, could be closed down again at any time.

It seemed as if the Israelis had learned an important lesson - rather than impose blanket closure orders on schools and colleges and incur the cost of widespread and damaging domestic and international censure, the selective closure of 'troublesome' institutions could achieve the same end of collective punishment without attracting the same level of opprobrium. Thus, by mid-1990 there still seemed little likelihood of the Palestinian educational process being restored to anything like 'normal', and generations of young people would consequently continue to be denied their right to learn and develop their potentialities to the full. But how could it be otherwise under conditions of occupation? In this bleak scenario, some Palestinians pointed optimistically to the emergence of the new 'colleges of education' in the detention camps such as Ansar III in the Negev. Thousands emerged from detention more politicised, more skilled in the techniques of resistance, and more committed to the continuation of the Intifada. They might also point to the impetus that the Intifada had given to what many feel was a much-needed and long-overdue revaluation of the structure, process and content of education in Palestine. Despite such claims, it remained clear that a major priority for all those concerned about the future of the Palestinian people was the development of an adequate alternative educational structure that would be sufficiently flexible to adapt to the ever-changing conditions in a land under occupation.[20]

And what of Israel? What costs were incurred through the actions of its soldiers and citizens in denying the Palestinians the freedom to learn? At the most obvious level they faced a barrage of international censure.[21] Israel found it particularly difficult to convince world opinion of the legitimacy of its denial of the Palestinians' right to education. At a deeper level, perhaps a greater cost was incurred by the heightening of divisions within Israeli public opinion itself. It was not easy for those Israelis who were justifiably proud of their liberal values and the great Jewish intellectual, cultural and academic tradition to accept silently, let alone endorse, a policy designed to deprive a people of the most fundamental of human rights. One of their number compared the situation to George Orwell's *Nineteen Eighty Four*, observing: 'In Israel in 1989, a military occupation is organised by the "Civilian Administration" and the main responsibility of the "Office of the Director of Education, Judea and Samaria" is to close down schools and universities.'[22]

Perhaps, at the end of the day, it will be the self-interest of all those who have the long-term future of Israel at heart that will bring about a resolution of the conflict between Israelis and Palestinians. If this turns out to be the case, it might be due in no small measure to the perceived damage inflicted upon the 'moral fibre' of Israel by policies and practices such as those that attempted to criminalise educational activity in the occupied territories during the Intifada but such a day does not seem to get any closer.

During the Gulf War and the draconian curfew measures imposed upon the whole population, all formal educational activity came to a halt. Once the war was over Palestinians faced the kind of restrictions that were to become commonplace over subsequent years. These involved the unprecedented restrictions on travel imposed by the Israeli authorities, which prevented any Palestinian from entering Israel without a special document, which seriously disrupted the covert educational activity within the higher education sector. These restrictions also prevented people from the Gaza Strip travelling to the West Bank and vice versa, thereby heightening the division between the two stretches of territory. It also meant that Palestinians in the West Bank were prohibited from making any journey that involved traversing East Jerusalem, thereby planting the seeds for the further isolation of East Jerusalem from the rest of the occupied territories. As a consequence students living in the southern area of the West Bank could not attend classes at universities such as Birzeit or Nablus without risk of arrest, unless they had the necessary travel documents – a phenomenon that was to become commonplace by the late 1990s.[23]

---

[1] For details of school closures in Gaza, where it is estimated that 35 - 50 percent of school days were lost during 1988 due to curfews and other interruptions, see *Punishing a nation*, p. 314.

[2] On December 24 1988 Defence Minister Rabin stated his intention to 'close schools which have ceased to fulfil their function as educational institutions and which have been consistent in allowing their children out into the street'.

[3] Lindsay Cooper, *The Guardian,* August 5, 1988.

[4] 'The lessons of occupation', *News From Within*, May 31, 1988.

[5] 'The lessons of occupation', p. 7.

[6] West Bank school-teacher quoted in *Al Fajr*, May 29, 1988.

[7] *Friends Schools Newsletter*, v. 2, n. 3, Summer 1988, p. 3.

[8] *Al Fajr*, May 29, 1988.

[9] Quoted in *Jerusalem Post,* September 5, 1988.

[10] For figures on the closure of schools, see S Cohen, 'Education as crime', *Jerusalem Post,* May 18 1989 and *Al Fajr*, January 15 1990, p. 1. According to B 'Tselem West Bank schools were open for an average of 99 days out of a planned 210 days during the 1989/90 school year. See *Information Sheet: Update* September-October 1990, p. 10.

[11] Quoted by R. Nuseibeh in *Al Fajr*, March 27, 1988.
[12] Personal communication.
[13] D. Kuttab, *Middle East International*, August 3 1990, p. 10, and personal communication (al-Najar University, April 1991).
[14] See *The Twentieth Year*, Birzeit University, 1988, p. 7.
[15] One anecdote to illustrate the prestige enjoyed by those with higher educational qualifications: I once asked a Palestinian student why he was studying for a doctorate – 'I want to go into politics' was the reply.
[16] Birzeit University Newsletter, no 18, March 1989.
[17] During the first week of March 1988, students and faculty at Bethlehem University attempted to enter the campus in defiance of the closure order but were stopped by soldiers at the entrance. A similar attempt was made at Birzeit University on March 7 with the same result. On November 7 1988 there was a clash with the military in Nablus when more than a hundred students marched in protest against the continued closure of the university.
[18] This of course was before the days of the internet and electronic 'distance-learning'.
[19] *Jerusalem Post*, April 19, 1989. In developing a network of underground classes, the universities of Bethlehem and Birzeit benefited front their relative proximity to East Jerusalem where circumstances were more conducive to holding clandestine classes than elsewhere in the occupied territories.
[20] In 1991 a Palestinian 'open university" of the airwaves was launched, using programmes transmitted by Jordanian television. It was claimed that it would focus on 'non-traditional" subjects not normally found within university curricula and specially catered to meet the educational needs of Palestinians living under occupation. See *Al Fajr*, January 7, 1991, p. 3.
[21] The decision of the European Community in February 1990 to suspend all scientific cooperation with Israel was in protest

---

against the continued closure of Palestinian universities, amongst other human rights abuses.

[22] S. Cohen, *Jerusalem Post*, May 18, 1989.

[23] In the aftermath of the Gulf War the educational institutions also suffered from the drastic loss of funding from Kuwait and other Gulf States. See *Al Fajr*, September 10, 1990, p. 2.

6

ECONOMIC ASPECTS OF THE INTIFADA

Introduction

One of the main aims of civilian-based resistance to occupation must be to impose such a cost on the occupier as to make the option of withdrawal more attractive than maintaining the occupation. Likewise, the aim of any occupying force must be to impose, or threaten to impose, such a punitive cost upon those civilians who dare to resist their rule that any attempt to launch such a struggle is still-born or aborted. One of the key areas in which this battle can take place is in the economic sphere. The purpose of this chapter is to examine the nature of this economic struggle during the Palestinian Uprising.

The economic background

After Israel occupied the West Bank and Gaza Strip in 1967 it sought to integrate the territories into the economy of Israel. As Salim Tamari has pointed out, it pursued this aim through three main processes.[1] 1) It began to restructure the transport and communications network in order to physically integrate the occupied territories with the state of Israel. This process also included restructuring the water and electricity grids so that Palestinians became dependent upon Israeli-controlled public utilities. 2) The Israeli labour market was opened up to Palestinian labour, at the same time as obstacles were created to prevent the development of indigenous sources of employment in the occupied territories. 3) The integration of markets was the third mechanism, with the result that the occupied territories became captive markets for Israeli industrial and agricultural products. By the 1980s nearly 90 percent of all goods imported into the territories came from Israel. At the same time Palestinian products were denied free access to Israeli markets. The result of these three processes was to render the population of the occupied territories economically dependent upon Israel, a situation that constituted a fundamental basis for Israel's political control of the territories. Once that control was challenged with the outbreak of the Intifada in December 1987, a serious attempt was also made to erode the economic foundation of the occupation.

The early days of nonviolent 'blitzkreig'

During the first few weeks of the Uprising its character resembled what Gene Sharp has termed a 'nonviolent blitzkreig' - a massive display of defiance and near-total non-cooperation with the Israeli occupiers. It was a period of almost complete economic shut-down, the paralysis of everyday economic life caused by general strikes and 'stay-at-homes' by employees that accompanied the daily demonstrations and street confrontations. The result was that both sides in the struggle suffered severe economic dislocation.

Prior to the Intifada some 110,000 Palestinians from the occupied territories travelled to work in Israel each day, some 60,000 from the Gaza Strip and the remainder from the West Bank. During the first few weeks of the Uprising it was estimated that up to 70 percent of this number failed to attend for work, either because they were responding to general strike calls, could not attend because their homes were under curfew, the buses on which they travelled had been fire-bombed or they had been intimidated in some way or another. The consequences were felt immediately within Israel, particularly by the agricultural sector. The Uprising coincided with the citrus harvest and Palestinians normally constituted one third of the workforce for picking and packing the fruit. There were reports that the Israeli agricultural marketing body Agrexo lost $500,000 during December 1987 and January 1988 as a result of not being able to fulfil orders for the British market.[2] In response Israel threatened to stop workers who had participated in the strikes from travelling into Israel, and a number of workers were sacked from their jobs. Attempts were made to recruit high school students for the citrus harvest, guest workers were recruited from the Israeli controlled 'security zone' of southern Lebanon, and work permits were issued for labourers from southern Europe and Cyprus.

Agribusiness was not the only sector to suffer. A large proportion of Palestinians worked as day labourers on construction sites in Israel, and their absence from work caused severe disruption to building projects. There were reports of construction sites in Jerusalem offering Jewish workers double the normal wages of Palestinian labour in a vain attempt to attract replacement labour.

Alongside the withdrawal of labour in response to calls for general strikes, there was also a call during the first week of January 1988 for Palestinians to boycott Israeli products in general, and in particular for people to boycott those Israeli products for which Palestinian alternatives were available.[3] According to an army-commissioned report published towards the end of January the consequent loss in sales and production had cost the Israeli economy some £28 million. The loss of markets in the occupied territories was particularly serious for many of the small enterprises in Israel - the sale of textiles, food products and soap powders was particularly badly hit.[4]

However, the Palestinian economy was also suffering. As one observer commented after the first six weeks of the Uprising:

> … the economic effects of the continued unrest in the West Bank and Gaza have been far more devastating for the Palestinian population

> of these territories than for the Israelis. Many Palestinians have found themselves without any form of income for weeks.[5]

It was estimated that Palestinian industry, although not occupying a major role in the economy of the occupied territories, had suffered a drop of between 25 - 30 percent in sales during the first months of the Intifada. However the drop in demand consequent upon consumers having reduced disposable income was offset to some degree by the increased purchase of local Palestinian products in preference to Israeli ones. Indeed, some companies, such as the Jneidi Dairy Products factory in Hebron, recorded improved sales due to the boycott of Israeli products.[6]

The pressure on the Palestinian economy appeared likely to intensify in March 1988 when the ninth leaflet from the Unified Command of the Uprising called on all those Palestinians working for the Israelis in the occupied territories to resign 'and stop betraying their people'. It has been estimated that somewhere in the region of 17,000 Palestinians were at that time in receipt of wages and salaries from the Israelis for their work in the police force and the various wings of the 'civil administration'. Whilst the mass resignation of all these workers would have represented a most powerful symbolic victory for the leadership of the Uprising, it would also have been a severe economic blow to all those families and households who would have been deprived of the major source of their income. As it was, a number of tax officials and other workers with the civil administration resigned, along with the majority of the police officers. However, it seems clear that the leadership of the Uprising realised that their call for mass resignations was premature, just as it was unrealistic to expect each and every Palestinian who normally worked in Israel to stay at home. Particularly for the people of the Gaza Strip, the majority of them living in refugee camps without any other source of income, the day labour in Israel was an economic necessity. It was apparent that if the Uprising was to be sustained, the period of the 'economic blitzkreig' needed to be curtailed. Modes of struggle had to be developed that could be maintained over time, methods of resistance generated that, whilst imposing costs on the occupier, would limit the hardship and suffering incurred by the civil population who were being called upon to make the sacrifices necessary for ultimate victory.

Thus it was that from March 1988 onwards the nature of the resistance began to take on new forms. The struggle appeared to be less intense at the surface level. The aim was, however, for the attitude and practice of resistance to become so deeply embedded in people's everyday way of life that it would become 'second nature', and as such sustainable for 'as long as necessary'. This was particularly apparent with regard to the demands made of business and the retail distribution sector of the Palestinian economy.

Business and commerce in the Intifada

One of the most important aspects of daily life to which any visitor to the occupied territories during the Intifada had to become accustomed was the opening hours of the shops and stores. Except on general strike days and special occasions when shopping hours were lengthened, the stores were open for only three hours each morning. I recall the weird experience of visiting East Jerusalem for the first time since the outbreak of the Uprising: from nine o'clock until mid-day the streets were busy and the shops appeared to be doing good business. At 12.00 the stores closed, the streets started to empty, and within a few hours they were almost deserted. This daily closure of the shops after three hours trading, interspersed with total closure on general strike days, became a major symbol of the struggle taking place between the Palestinians and the Israeli state.

During the first few weeks of the Uprising virtually every day was a general strike day. The response of the security forces was to try and force the shops to open, breaking the locks of those that were closed. A variant of this was to weld shut the doors of shops closed in response to strike calls. The costs of this blitzkreig of commercial strikes was heavy. As one observer remarked at the end of January 1988, 'The total commercial strikes in key business centres like Nablus, Ramallah and East Jerusalem have ... left many Palestinian merchants on the brink of bankruptcy.'[7] Realising that such a level of resistance could not be maintained, the unified command of the Uprising stipulated that traders might remain open for three hours each morning. What followed was a struggle for control over the closing hours of shops and businesses, a struggle of great symbolic significance. For the leaders of the Uprising the closure of the shops each day demonstrated to the Israelis that the situation was not normal, and that the unified command was in control of the situation rather than the Israelis. In order to assert their claim and demonstrate their capacity to control all aspects of life in the territories, the Israeli authorities adopted a number of counter-measures. One tactic was to announce that shops were only to trade in the afternoons. They then sought to close those shops trading in the mornings. The result was that in a town like Nablus during the month of March 1988 the shops were closed for over a week, as the battle of wills between the Israeli occupation force and the young strike forces of the Uprising was fought out.

A key feature of the Israeli response to such acts of defiance of their authority as the closure of stores in the afternoons was to focus attention upon one particular shopping area or town, attempting to break the resistance of that particular target group, and thereby intimidate all other storekeepers into compliance with their will seeking to make an example of a few as a salutary lesson for the many. Thus, towards the end of April 1988 fourteen merchants in East Jerusalem were arrested and charged with disobeying military orders to open their stores.[8] The following month the Israelis adopted another counter-measure, announcing that stores would be compulsorily closed for three days for each day that they answered the call for a general strike.

In such ways the Israelis sought to impose an economic and financial burden on those merchants and traders who actively displayed their solidarity with the Uprising. The Israelis hoped that they could thereby break the resistance of these 'front-line forces' who persisted in presenting such a visible and public display of the vitality of the Uprising. The 'defeat' of the traders would represent a powerful symbolic blow to the Palestinians within the occupied territories.

There can be no doubt that shopkeepers, traders and small businesses suffered financially as a consequence of the Uprising, and there were many bankruptcies. During the first year this was due more to the fall off in consumer demand than to Israeli sanctions. By the second year of the Uprising, the punitive tax burden imposed by Israel began to take a greater toll. Some Palestinian economists estimated that during the first year of the Intifada there was a decline in consumer expenditure within the occupied territories of some 40 percent. A number of businesses suffered terminal damage - especially those dealing in luxury items, electrical goods, furniture and the like - non-essentials that people were obliged to do without in a siege situation. The order of the day was to 'tighten one's belt" and confine purchases to basic needs. However, the majority managed to survive. The reduction in opening hours resulted in an intensification of business during the time the shops were open. Whilst income from sales declined, so did costs and overheads. Moreover, despite the 'official' restrictions on trading hours, merchants found ways of extending them. Some converted their homes into storehouses and sales areas. Garages continued to repair vehicles behind closed doors. Furthermore, the poorest traders - the street vendors - were exempted from the daily strike calls. Bakers and pharmacists were also allowed to remain open by the leadership, albeit on a rota basis, in order to maintain a supply of essential food and medical requirements for the population - the UNC feeling obliged to remind such retailers on occasion that they were to confine their sales during such times to basic essentials.

One of the key strategies of any occupying force must be to focus their attention upon the most vulnerable sections of the society, hoping that by fracturing the 'weakest link' they might thereby break the chain of resistance. This is what Israel tried to do with regard to the commercial sector in the occupied territories. However, any trader who felt tempted to place their economic interests above compliance with the collective will risked the prospect of having their premises fire-bombed by the local strike forces. The dilemma faced by many in the business sector was brought home to me in a conversation with a wealthy merchant from Nablus who recalled an exchange he had with a youth who was instructing him to abide by the new 'winter time' closing hours, which entailed closing the shop an hour earlier than in the summer months. When the businessman complained that this would seriously affect his business, the reply came: 'We are prepared to give up our lives for the struggle, is it too much to ask you to give up some of your profits?'

The tax war

It was the merchants who bore the brunt of the struggle over taxes that was an enduring feature of the Uprising.[9] Early in 1988 the leadership of the Uprising had called upon Palestinians to refuse to meet the Israeli tax demands, as part of the overall strategy of disengagement from the occupying power and its 'civil administration'. At the same time an alternative taxation system was being developed, with popular committees collecting money and supplies from those that could afford to give for distribution amongst the needy.[10]

It was estimated that Israel collected some $160 million in tax revenue from the West Bank in 1987 which helps explain the determination with which they sought to break the tax strike - both for financial reasons and in order to assert their power over the occupied population.[11] Various tactics and measures were adopted in pursuance of this goal. Stores were raided, identity cards and business documents of merchants confiscated, reclaimable only after the merchant had reported to the tax office and paid the amount of tax the authorities claimed was owed. Tax officials accompanied by the military commandeered merchandise from shops in lieu of unpaid taxes. Other businesses were closed and their owners jailed because of the refusal to pay taxes. In East Jerusalem 17 hotels had their bank accounts frozen for failure to pay the municipal tax. The hotel and tourist trade was particularly badly hit by the Intifada. There was a 15 percent drop in the number of visitors to Israel during 1988, although numbers picked up again during 1989, earning Israel a reported $1.8 billion.[12] In East Jerusalem a number of hotels closed down due to lack of business. In June 1988, at the time when their bank accounts were frozen, the occupancy rate in East Jerusalem hotels was around 18 percent, compared with 32 percent in June 1987.[13]

The Israelis took advantage of curfews to collect taxes, raiding the houses of merchants and workshop owners to seize property. In Tulkarm, where a 29 day curfew was imposed during June and July 1988, the curfew was lifted on June 14 for six hours to allow the residents to purchase basic items. Road blocks were set up throughout the town, and local residents were stopped for tax and vehicle licence checks. Apparently some 400 residents had to pay sums ranging from $300 to $3,000.[14] Road blocks were set up on the outskirts of towns and villages, each passing vehicle being stopped to allow tax officials to check whether the occupants had paid their taxes. The cars and the drivers' licences of those deemed to owe money would then be confiscated until the sums demanded of them were paid. On July 5 1988 over 300 cars were seized in this manner in Ramallah. A few weeks before, in May 1988, the Israelis seized 40 taxis operating between Jerusalem and Ramallah in lieu of taxes they claimed had not been paid. Driving school instructors had their identity documents seized when accompanying students for their driving test. In Ramallah 14 vehicles belonging to driving schools were seized by the authorities, and it took an interim order from the Israeli High Court to prevent the tax officials auctioning off the vehicles to raise money to pay the taxes.

Another method adopted by the Israeli authorities was to insist upon Palestinians producing a document of clearance proving that they have paid their taxes before being issued with any kind of official document such as travel or export permit, birth certificate, driver's licence, or renewed identity card. In May 1988 400,000 Gazans were ordered to renew their identity cards. In order to obtain the new cards they were required to prove that they had paid their taxes. The following July a new measure was adopted in the Gaza Strip, later to be imposed on West Bank residents - the changing of the licence plates of cars. To obtain the new plates, which were of a different colour than the old ones and therefore instantly recognisable at any road block, the owners had to obtain clearance from the Israeli tax and customs officials and pay the 'special tax' levied on vehicles.

How did Palestinians respond to such punitive measures? Many had no choice but to meet the tax demands of the Israelis. Gazan taxi drivers, for instance, had to comply with the new regulations if they wished to continue in business. Others were prepared to suffer the confiscation of their property rather than cooperate with the tax demands of the occupier.[15] One of my hosts in Gaza was defiantly driving round Gaza City with the old licence plate attached to his car, some months after the new measure had been announced. However, for those who had their identity cards confiscated for any reason, there often appeared to be little alternative but to obtain the certificate of tax clearance necessary to regain their ID, without which anything resembling a normal life under occupation would have been impossible.

In one notable case however over 300 villagers of Beit Sahour, near Bethlehem, turned in their identity cards to the municipality in a collective act of defiance and solidarity with those of their number whose houses and shops had been raided by tax officials. The Israeli response was to impose a two-week curfew on the village and to place 16 residents in administrative detention.[16] A year later the inhabitants of Beit Sahour were to suffer a further penalty for their continued commitment to the principle of 'no taxation without representation', when the Israelis embarked upon a draconian attempt to collect taxes from this defiant community. For six weeks, starting in September 1989, Israeli troops kept the village under siege whilst soldiers escorted tax collectors round the village, accompanied by removal vans, confiscating property in lieu of unpaid taxes. Road blocks were set up around the village, a strict curfew was imposed and all telephone communication with the outside world was cut. Machinery and workshop equipment was seized, leaving craftsmen deprived of their means of livelihood. Shops and stores were left empty of goods. People's homes were stripped bare of household items. According to Israeli army figures property worth £1 million was expropriated, although residents later claimed that the actual figure was up to three times that amount. The UNC called for an unprecedented five day general strike in response to the Israeli actions. Storekeepers in the town launched a commercial strike that lasted three months in protest against the confiscation of property. Members of the Israeli Knesset, foreign diplomats, church leaders and others protested against the sanctions imposed on the village.

Collective economic punishment

However severe the sanctions imposed upon Beit Sahour might appear, in essence they represented a continuation of the Israeli policy of inflicting collective economic punishment upon those Palestinian communities that dared to oppose the occupation. Thus, in March 1988, following the murder of a Palestinian collaborator in the town of Qabatiya, a ban was placed on the export of building stone and agricultural produce from the town to Jordan - the major sources of income. In similar fashion, the water-melon growers of the Jordan valley and Jericho area were prevented from marketing their crop within Israel, and whilst they were not prevented officially from exporting their crop to Jordan, the requirement that the hauliers obtain tax receipts, licences for the trucks, certificates of good conduct for the drivers and other forms of documentation made it virtually impossible to ship the produce. Similar attempts to restrict the transfer of produce from the centres of production to surrounding markets during the peak season had been a recurring feature of the economic struggle between the occupying power and the Palestinians. Gazans were forbidden from marketing their fruit in the West Bank. Fruit and vegetable growers in the West Bank were prevented from transporting their crops to wholesale markets. Bans were imposed on selling produce in Israel. Loads of fruit destined for Jordan were held up at the bridges until they rotted in the trucks.[17]

The major agricultural crop in the West Bank has traditionally been olives, estimated to provide up to 30 percent of the West Bank's income during the period immediately prior to the Intifada.[18] 1988 was a bumper year for the olive crop and the Israelis made it clear to producers that they intended to use the economic importance of the crop as a weapon to restore their control. They refused to grant export licences to olive press owners without the down-payment of 10,000 Jordanian dinars (JD) for 'anticipated taxes', about £20,000 at the exchange rate pertaining in October 1988.[19] Access roads to 'troublesome villages' were blocked during the harvest season. This form of collective economic sanction was practised on the village of Tell, near Nablus. Famous for its figs, the village was sealed off on August 13 1988, just as the time for the fig harvest approached. Whilst the inhabitants were allowed to leave and re-enter their village, they were prevented from going to their fields, their agricultural implements were confiscated, even their donkeys were requisitioned. This village, which had declared itself a 'liberated zone' during the early months of the Intifada, was sealed off for 35 days. The message to all the other villages in the West Bank was clear: if you want to avoid the fate of Tell, then do not cause trouble to the occupiers. As one Israeli military commander remarked,

> We will not accept a situation in which villages or areas riot... and then be able to act as though nothing had happened. This was the policy during the plum harvest and during the grape harvest. It will also be in effect during the olive harvest.[20]

Certain villages that sought to disengage themselves from the 'civil administration' of the West Bank refused to pay their water bills to the Israeli-appointed local councils. In retaliation the supply from the Israeli Mekerot Water Company was cut off. The villagers found that whilst they could obtain sufficient water for domestic use from local wells, the supply was insufficient to irrigate their crops. They were forced to pay their bills in order to restore the supply. Villages that refused to pay their electricity bills for the same reason had a similar experience, with the electricity supply being severed until they had paid. The occupation forces and in some cases settlers also destroyed crops and orchards as a form of collective punishment of 'troublesome' areas. On one occasion in 1989 there were reports of vineyards around Hebron having been sprayed with toxic weed-killer by settlers from Kiryat Arba. The Palestinians, for their part, also took to destroying Israeli crops and forests. The UNC declared June 22 1988 a 'Day of Arson', and during the months of May and June of that year it was reported that over 25,000 acres of forest had been burnt in Israel.

Perhaps the most drastic form of collective punishment employed by the Israeli security forces was the curfew. Whilst the human and psychological costs borne by families confined to their homes for day after day should not be disregarded, the economic consequences of curfews were particularly severe. People were prevented from attending their place of employment, with the consequent loss of income. They were prevented from tending their crops, which in certain areas could have a disastrous effect on the local economy. Thus, the town of Qalqilya was put under a 29-day curfew during August 1988. The town is in the middle of a major citrus growing region. Citrus trees need irrigating every 10-15 days if the crop is not to be damaged, whilst any vegetable crop left unwatered for such a period would be totally destroyed. Here is an extract from an Israeli soldier's diary of that curfew:

> As we reach the end of a night patrol (to ensure nobody tries to rescue their dying crops), we spy a family bringing in a bucket of tomatoes. Suddenly our jeep springs into action. ... We corner them. ... They tell us they have no food, are simply starving to death and had no choice. At which point the old woman, 90-years old, falls to her knees, kisses my hand, and begs me not to send her away. 'We really needed tomatoes' she tells me.

Over time, and with experience, the residents of the refugee camps, villages and towns that had been subjected to curfew learnt how to survive. Most families stored up to two months' supply of basic food and other necessities in the home. Those who could afford the expense constructed water cisterns to serve their house. Under cover of darkness adjacent villages would send in supplies, to be distributed by the youths according to instructions from the popular committees. In those areas not too far from the 'green line', supplies were delivered from Palestinian villages and towns within Israel.

Whilst the majority of Palestinians learned to live with the economic consequences of their collective resistance, the overall impact of the economic sanctions should not be underestimated. One researcher estimated that the volume of losses incurred by eight villages in the West Bank over a period of ten months between January and October 1988 totalled $6.5 million. This figure becomes even more staggering when one realises that there are 420 villages, 30 refugee camps and 15 cities in the West Bank and Gaza Strip.[21] Take the case of Gazan fishermen. Approximately 80 percent of the estimated 2,000 who depended upon fishing as their prime means of livelihood lived in Shatti refugee camp. During 1988 the camp was under curfew for more than 250 days, during which time they were denied access to their boats and hence their livelihood.[22]

It was in the Gaza Strip in the summer of 1989 that Israeli collective economic sanctions took on a new dimension. Early in June 1989, following the imposition of a three-day total curfew on the Strip during May, the Israelis began issuing new plastic entry permits for those wishing to travel into Israel. On August 18 they began to refuse entry to any adult male Gazan who did not possess one of the new magnetised cards. Those Gazans who depended upon work in Israel for their livelihood found themselves caught in a battle of wills between the Israelis and the leadership of the Uprising, as the UNC called for a boycott of work in Israel and activists of the strike forces confiscated thousands of the newly issued cards in order to enforce the ban. The intention behind the introduction of the new cards was clear: to show the Gazans that it was Israel that held the whip-hand over their lives and not the underground leadership, and if they wished to enjoy the fruits of labouring in Israel then they would have to earn such a right by good behaviour and the payment of all outstanding taxes. Thus, the new cards were only issued to those Gazans who did not have any record of resistance activity against the occupying power. It was a typical Israeli strategy - 'rewarding' good behaviour and punishing 'trouble-makers'. Just as any Palestinian who was 'cooperative' might find the level of their tax assessment halved whilst that of others might be doubled, so it was with the new cards. The aim was not only to impose suffering on the population but also to foment divisions within the Palestinian community, and to heighten tension between the local population and the underground leadership. In this they were successful. Considerable bad feeling developed amongst Gazans, directed at West Bankers who were allegedly taking the jobs left vacant by the strikers.

The struggle over the new cards continued throughout August and September 1989, with the Gazan population experiencing new levels of deprivation as the Israelis tried to enforce their policy and the UNC exhorted the people to maintain the boycott. Somewhere in the region of 35 - 45 percent of the population in the Gaza Strip depended upon income earned in Israel for their livelihood. With the loss of their wages they were forced to draw upon their meagre savings and rely upon occasional cash hand-outs from the local popular committees in cases of exceptional hardship. Even non-refugees began to turn to UNRWA in the hope of obtaining work, cash, or food relief. Such hopes were ill-founded. According to Hashim Abu Siro, an UNRWA official, their annual budget of $48 million was totally inadequate. He estimated that it would take $300 million to satisfy the requirements of all those who relied upon work in Israel.[23] By October 1989 more and more Gazans were having to face up to the reality of their situation and the economic necessity of returning to work in Israel. Faced with the problem of sustaining the Uprising, without at the same time imposing unbearable hardship upon the population, the leadership in Gaza was forced to recognise that the battle with Israel over the new entry permits was not one that they could win, given the chronic weakness of the Gazan economy and the consequent dependency of such a large proportion of its population on the Israeli economy.

The household economy

Compared to the economic deprivation and loss of income suffered by the Palestinians as a consequence of Israeli sanctions, the attempts to alleviate the suffering by the regeneration of small-scale household-based economic activity might seem rather risible. However, the development of what became known as the 'household economy' became a key feature of the survival and resistance strategy developed by the Palestinians in the occupied territories during the Intifada. As the concern of the leadership of the Uprising turned to methods of sustaining the struggle, they began to exhort the people to 'intensify the home grown economy through farming their land, rearing poultry, decreasing expenses and boycotting Zionist goods'.[24] The economic necessity of relying on one's own indigenous resources became a matter of political pride. In terms reminiscent of the Gandhian concept of *swadeshi* Palestinians began to talk of the political imperative of 'going back to basics', rediscovering the simple lifestyle of previous generations. [25] The boycotting of Israeli products, the closure of the shops, the loss of income due to strikes, the increased amount of time spent at home, combined with fears of Israeli attempts to 'starve them into submission', were all relevant factors pushing people to respond to the promptings of their leadership, as they tried to become more self-reliant through simplifying their lifestyle and meeting more of their basic needs through their own efforts. As one resident of the Gaza Strip explained, by the summer of 1988 he had adapted to his new circumstances:

> It's true it's difficult, but for a particular goal, for my cause, I'm prepared to overcome the circumstances in which I live, using things I have and which are available to me. ... For example, on the roof I keep a few pigeons, a few chickens. So, I can save. Instead of buying from outside, I feed the birds our scraps and I eat them. And this is a saving. It's not a problem...
>
> This Uprising has created an atmosphere which we didn't have before of kindness and brotherhood. For example, if I have something and my neighbour doesn't, I'll take something to my neighbour. If I didn't have anything but my neighbour did, he'd probably come and

> bring something to me, to help me. Conditions have changed. This Uprising has created a reality which didn't exist before. Everything has changed for us now. ... My average expenditure was 100 or 150 dinars, like most people. Now it's different. It's maybe 50 or 60 dinars. I can manage on that. It's a change. I used to work maybe 15 or 20 days a month. Now it's ten days a month or sometimes even less. I've had to adapt myself to my means.[26]

Of course there was little that was new in such practices for the peasants of the Palestinian villages, but for the middle class and professional strata it meant engaging in 'bread labour', working with their hands on the vegetable plots that they started in their gardens. With the women's committees in particular playing a prominent role in promoting new forms of home-based economic activity, more people began to keep a few chickens and areas of waste land were turned into communal allotments. Such enterprises had a symbolic value as great, if not greater, than the material one of providing a supply of home grown foodstuffs. As one observer explained, the prime aim of the 'digging for victory' project upon which a number of middle class neighbours had embarked in Ramallah was 'to sow the seeds of greater community feeling and propagate and nurture a sense of independence from Israel'.[27]

The more cynical might argue that the real purpose and value of the middle class experiments in ploughing the land and planting seeds was to give them reassurance that they too were playing their part in the Uprising. Be that as it may, the seriousness with which the Israeli occupation forces viewed such morale boosting activities was evidenced by their treatment of an agronomist in the village of Beit Sahour who decided to make his professional skills available to the community. With a few friends, he began to sell seeds and basic agricultural equipment and give advice to people on how to grow their own produce. He was threatened with 24-hour surveillance and arrest if he did not cease his activities, and was one of those sentenced to administrative detention following the mass surrender of identification documents in protest against the forcible seizure of property in the village by the tax officials. Undeterred by the ten-day curfew that was imposed on the village, the residents reported that it had in fact contributed to the strengthening of the local committee which had organised the distribution of food during the curfew, and thereby gave the villagers the opportunity to try out their preparations for self-sufficiency.[28]

External funding

Despite pursuing a simpler lifestyle, reducing their levels of consumption to disengage themselves as much as possible from the Israeli economy in their efforts to achieve greater self-reliance, Palestinians living in the occupied territories still required money to survive. Prior to the Intifada a major source of funds was the supply of regular remittances from family members living and working abroad in the Gulf and elsewhere, which amounted to an annual sum in the region of $120 million.[29] Such remittances would be transferred either through the Cairo-Amman Bank which had branches in the occupied territories or through couriers who would bring the money over the bridges from Jordan. With the commencement of the Intifada the supply of such funds took on an added significance as a result of the reduction in opportunities to earn income from employment and the general decline in business activity. At the same time, people were encouraged by the promises of financial aid made by the Arab states at the Algiers summit in April 1988, the reassurances about compensation coming from the PLO leadership outside, and the specific commitments made by Iraq and Jordan that they would pay pensions to the families of martyrs who lost their lives during the Uprising.

Consequently it became a major aim of the Israelis to stem this flow of funds. So long as Palestinians could receive finance from abroad, many of the economic sanctions imposed by the occupying power were rendered relatively ineffective. The Israeli counter-attack began by severely curtailing the activities of licenced money changers, and limiting the amount of money that could be brought over the bridges from Jordan without declaration to 400 dinars per person. This left the Cairo-Amman Bank, whose books and activities were closely monitored, as the only legal channel through which Palestinians could receive sums over 400 dinars. In March 1988 the Israelis issued an order that all transfers of amounts larger than 400 dinars required special permission from the authorities, and limiting to once a month the transfer of sums of up to 400 dinars. These restrictions were further intensified in August: individuals were only allowed to receive payments up to 400 dinars once every two months. In December 1988 the screw was tightened even further when it was announced that individual Palestinians coming from Jordan or Egypt would only be allowed to bring in amounts up to 200 dinars or its equivalent in other currencies. People seeking to bring in greater amounts would have to prove that it did not come from 'hostile sources', whilst people carrying amounts larger than 500 dinars risked its confiscation unless they could display special permission from the Israeli civil administration in the territories.

Faced with the blockage of open channels for transferring funds the Palestinians had to develop covert means in order to maintain the necessary flow of financial assistance from outside. The most straightforward was the simple device of tossing packages of money over the border fence with Egypt at Rafäh in the Gaza Strip. Another major conduit was through Israeli commercial banks, with deposits being made from untraceable bank accounts outside Israel, which could then be drawn upon by the account holder in amounts small enough not to attract unwelcome attention. Apparently another channel was opened through the purchase of Israeli government bonds by Palestinians living in the United States, who then sent them to individuals and institutions within the occupied territories to be redeemed.[30] Palestinian citizens of Israel, anti-Zionist Israelis, ultra-orthodox non-Zionist Jews, business people and tourists were amongst those who acted as couriers and 'go-betweens' - some out of a sense of solidarity with the resistance struggle, others for a percentage profit. A particularly important role in the transfer of funds was played by Palestinian money-changers with foreign bank accounts. It was a reasonably straightforward matter to have someone deposit a certain amount in one of these overseas accounts. The money changers would then pass on an equivalent amount, less their percentage profit to representatives within the occupied territories.

As part of their attempt to cut off the supply of financial support from outside the Israelis began to require voluntary organisations and UNRWA to account for their sources of funding. A number of voluntary associations and welfare organisations were closed down, partly in an effort to frustrate any form of Palestinian collective organisation and mutual aid, partly as an additional means of imposing economic hardship by closing down charitable institutions, and partly out of the belief that these associations were acting as a channel for funds into the territories. These efforts were intensified following King Hussein's formal relinquishment of Jordan's claim to the West Bank on July 31 1988. According to unofficial estimates Jordan had been spending up to $200 million a year in the West Bank and East Jerusalem - funding hospitals, agricultural development projects, Islamic institutions such as the Waqf religious trust, and providing aid to municipalities. The funds covered wages and pensions for about 21,000 Palestinian teachers, civil servants and other functionaries amounting to some $46 million a year.[31] The PLO promised to assume full responsibility for all those whose jobs and incomes were threatened by the Jordanian action. Quite how the necessary funds were to be made available through the narrow channels that existed was never made clear, not surprisingly.

In May 1989 the Israelis introduced new legislation aimed at further stemming the flow of financial support by making it an offence for any Palestinian or Israeli institution to receive funds or property known by the recipient to be connected to a 'terrorist organisation'. The new 'hostile funds' law also permitted the confiscation of property so received, and was made retroactive, thereby rendering funds already in the possession of associations liable to confiscation.[32]

As time passed it became increasingly clear that the Israeli measures to curtail the flow of external funds into the occupied territories was having an impact. My own experience was that despite the openness with which Palestinians were prepared to discuss most aspects of the Intifada, whenever the conversation turned to the question of how outside funding found its way through the Israeli net I encountered a 'red line' beyond which it was made clear I should not try to enquire. What was apparent was that the supply of funds from outside was drastically reduced during the summer of 1988 and the situation got steadily worse. By the late summer of 1989 many Palestinian institutions which relied upon external assistance for their survival were finding it hard to make ends meet. Moreover, one began to hear complaints about the system of distributing those funds that did get through. The spectre of factionalism began to reappear as rival nationalist groups accused each other of using outside funds for the purposes of political patronage. Allegations of corruption began to be made, with references to the number of people occupying strategic points along the distribution system who were appropriating money for their own purposes, with the result that by the time the funds had found their way through the network to those who were most deprived, in the refugee camps and elsewhere, there was barely enough left to meet basic needs.

Israel, for its part, did not escape without damage to its external sources of funding. In February 1988 the parliament of the European Community (as it was then called) refused to ratify an agreement to provide Israel with up to £50 million in cheap loans and privileged access to European markets as a protest against the repressive measures being taken in the occupied territories and the failure of the Israelis to honour an agreement to allow Palestinian agricultural products to be exported directly to Europe rather than through the Israeli state export board.[33] Two years later the European Community suspended all cooperation with Israel on high technology research as a further mark of protest against Israel's abuse of Palestinian human rights. At the same time the European authorities promised to double their direct financial aid to the occupied territories and increase its contribution to UNRWA. Palestinian support groups also tried to promote an international boycott of Israeli goods. However, such 'costs' were relatively insignificant when compared with the estimated $3,000 million Israel received in aid every year from the United States.

Other external factors

In any power struggle, the nature of the outcome can be crucially determined by the role of external actors and agencies. As has already been observed, the Palestinian economy of the West Bank and Gaza Strip was a peculiarly dependent one prior to the Intifada, and so it remained despite all the efforts to generate self-reliance and a degree of economic autonomy during the Uprising. Throughout the Intifada the economic well-being of the Palestinian population was subjected not just to the direct effects of Israeli sanctions and the uncertainties of external supplies of funding into the territories, but also affected by the economic conditions of their two more powerful neighbours: Jordan and Israel.

Palestinians in the occupied territories customarily kept their savings in Jordanian dinars, traditionally a far more stable currency than the Israeli shekel. Imagine the calamitous consequences for the Palestinians when, on top of all their other economic woes, the purchasing power of their savings was cut by over 50 percent in a period of less than a year. This is what happened to the dinar. Due to the political uncertainties accompanying Hussein's announcement of July 1988 there was a rush by Palestinians and Jordanians to unload their dinars in exchange for dollars. The result was that the dinar lost 17 percent of its exchange value during the month of October 1988. Worse was to come. Amid allegations that the Israeli banks were selling large quantities of dinars in order to flood the market, the exchange rate continued to plummet. By March 1989 the dinar had dropped to half its pre-intifada value against the US dollar. By the end of the year it was down 65 percent on its 1987 value, as the Jordanian economy reeled under the three-fold impact of a drastic reduction in foreign aid, a massive surplus of imports over exports, and a foreign debt of staggering proportions.[34] Whilst Palestinians suffered from the decimation of the dinar's purchasing power, their plight was compounded by the Israeli attempts to control their own inflation rate and budgetary crisis. In January 1989 the shekel was devalued by 13 percent. The following June it was devalued by a further five percent, and by another six percent in March 1990. It was estimated that the shekels earned by Palestinians working in Israel constituted 25 percent of the income of the occupied territories prior to the Intifada.[35] One can begin to picture the deep crisis in which Palestinians found themselves as both the major currencies upon which they relied for their everyday transactions continued to decline in purchasing power. Moreover, as part of its effort to reduce its budgetary deficit, Israel began to cut state subsidies on essential commodities. This contributed to an inflation rate of 20 percent for 1989, whilst the prices of the basic items upon which Palestinians spent the bulk of their income rose by up to 25 percent. As the economist Samir Abdallah described their predicament:

> ... citizens in the occupied territories are caught between a rock and a hard place. Their incomes are eroded by the deterioration of the

> Jordanian dinar on the one hand and by the rise in the prices of goods and inflation in Israel on the other.[36]

Squeezed between two troubled economies, Palestinians of all social groups suffered. But as always, some suffered more than others, and signs of internal economic conflict and social division became more manifest. Traditionally most property rental agreements in the occupied territories had been transacted in dinars. Faced with its devaluation landlords began to demand rent increases. Landlord-tenant conflict became sufficiently worrying for the UNC to intervene, calling on parties to 'maintain personal agreements and mutual understanding'.

During 1989 there was also a disturbing outbreak of labour disputes and strike actions by workers demanding increases to compensate for the deteriorating purchasing power of their wage packets. Once again the UNC had to intervene, instructing employers to raise the salaries of their workers. Some indication of the tensions that began to emerge within the Palestinian community during this period, brought about by the conflicting demands of national solidarity and class interest, was revealed in an interview with a Palestinian worker in August 1989:

> I can't remember things being so bad in the West Bank for a long time. Last year we were scraping the bottom of the barrel; this year we're not even managing to do that. Most people have no money in the West Bank, nor in the Gaza Strip. People are really suffering there. But at least we're suffering for a cause, for independence, which I'm sure will come sooner or later. There are always those who have money - lots of money. Maybe you can explain it to me - it seems that people who were rich before the Intifada are even richer now. I have a neighbour in Ramallah who behaves as if there were no Intifada in the world.

> His son and daughter are studying in some university in the United States; he himself told me that he wanted them as far from the Intifada as possible. He very often drives to Jerusalem and Tel Aviv at night in his plushy car and goes to night-clubs and restaurants. His refrigerator is always full of delicacies.[37]

In August 1990 the economy of the occupied territories suffered an additional blow consequent upon Iraq's invasion of Kuwait. Remittances, donations and export earnings from the Gulf constituted somewhere in the region of one fifth of the GNP of the West Bank and Gaza Strip. The most immediate impact of the invasion was a drastic drop in remittances from Palestinians working in Kuwait, which had previously totalled around $130 million a year. Institutions also suffered. Kuwait had been the biggest Arab donor to UNRWA, whilst Maqassed Hospital and other welfare organisations and West Bank universities were also heavily dependent upon Kuwaiti financial aid. This loss of external aid, coming on top of nearly three years of economic suffering and financial hardship, posed a serious dilemma to Palestinians in the occupied territories. However, for some it served to under- line the dangers of dependency upon outside financial aid and the vital importance of developing self-reliance in the economic sphere as the key to sustaining the resistance struggle and to laying the economic basis for an independent Palestinian state.

Conclusion

In the unequal battle between the Israeli state and the Palestinians in the occupied territories, the struggle by both sides to impose punitive economic costs on the opponent as a means of influencing the eventual outcome was of crucial significance. Whilst the daily street confrontations, the deaths, the beatings, the arrests and the deportations were the events that attracted world attention, a deeper clash of wills took place that cost both sides dearly.

Particularly during what might be depicted as the peak of the Uprising during 1988-89, the clear impression given by the Palestinians was of unbending resolve. The sufferings consequent upon their commitment to resistance had become an accepted part of their life. They were prepared to endure economic hardship with pride and not a little ingenuity. They were confident in the belief that through their resistance to the economic costs the Israelis sought to impose they were in fact laying the economic foundations of a future Palestinian state. However, as the Intifada moved into its third year with no significant sign of a political settlement, the leadership had cause for concern. Beneath the rhetoric of national unity there were signs that the stress lines that had always existed within the Palestinian community were beginning to reappear, in part because of the perceived unequal distribution of the economic burdens of the Uprising.

The fact is that by 1990 all social groups were suffering economic hardship. In some ways the professional and middle classes experienced greater relative deprivation than the poor, in the sense that they had more to lose and had to make more dramatic changes in their lifestyle. But at the end of the day it was the poorest sections of Palestinian society who suffered the most - the villagers and refugee camp dwellers. Alongside the loss of income, the devaluation of the dinar and the shekel, the inflation and the consequent drastic decline in living standards, the punitive tax-collection measures adopted by the Israelis became an increasingly heavy burden for many Palestinians living under occupation. Indeed, according to information acquired by a Palestinian economist, after an initially sharp drop in tax receipts during the early months of the Intifada, they had risen to around 95 percent of their pre-intifada level by July 1989.[38] This at a time when the unemployment level in the occupied territories was put at somewhere around 30 percent, whilst for those who were in employment the average monthly income was estimated to be in the region of $250-300, well below the minimum wage level in Israel. By 1990, before the impact of the loss of remittances from Kuwait had been felt, the annual per capita income in the West Bank was calculated to be in the region of $1,200, whilst for the Gaza Strip it was as low as $6 - 700.[39]

The radical decline in the levels of disposable income, coupled with the tax burden and the drop in the value of the dinar resulted in a wave of closures sweeping through small and medium sized businesses during the second year of the Intifada. Manufacturers came under considerable pressure to maintain wage rates and levels of employment, despite the downturn in the economic situation and the reduction in the number of days worked in a month. It was in response to the deteriorating economic situation that the number of general strike days was reduced in 1989 and factories were allowed to operate round-the-clock in an effort to maintain employment levels and avoid total economic collapse. In similar vein, enterprises received permission from the UNC to pay taxes and purchase Israeli-made inputs so that they could remain in business. One measure of the decline in economic activity was the increase in the number of Palestinians seeking work in Israel. According to the statistics of the military authorities the number of people from the West Bank working in Israel rose from a pre-intifada level of 45 - 48,000 to 60 - 65,000 by late 1989.[40]

Despite the general economic gloom that deepened with each passing month some businesses actually managed to increase profits. As many Israeli products started disappearing from the shelves of stores, Palestinian manufacturers took advantage of the opportunity to expand their sales. Free from outside competition as a consequence of the boycott of Israeli goods, companies producing basic commodities such as foodstuffs, soft drinks and cigarettes experienced increased sales of between 20 - 30 percent. Moreover, certain sections of the agricultural sector gained some relief as direct exports to Europe increased dramatically during 1989-90, with the citrus fruits from the Gaza Strip and winter supplies of aubergines from the West Bank constituting the major items. Some businesses proved themselves to be rather less than scrupulous in taking advantage of the boycott of Israeli products to increase their prices. On occasions the UNC felt obliged to warn sections of the community against taking advantage of the situation to make excessive profits. Thus, in Communiqué No. 40 issued in late May 1989 doctors were enjoined to lower their fees whilst bakers were urged to restrict their sales during strike hours to bread 'and not to turn the bakeries into shops selling food and drinks'. On a more anecdotal level, a friend of mine was outraged to discover that a Palestinian company supplying him with printing ink for his computer was demanding ten times the price being charged by a company in Tel Aviv, from whom the local company had purchased the supplies in the first place.

Despite the exceptions, the economic plight of Palestinians in the occupied territories continued to worsen as the Intifada continued into its third year. For the more aware amongst the leadership there was a growing realisation that any long-term strategy of disengagement from Israel, in the form of a thorough-going, mass-based campaign of civil disobedience, could remain little more than a dream so long as the occupied territories remained so economically dependent upon Israel and lacked the necessary indigenous economic base to sustain such a struggle. Indeed, in a paradoxical manner, the forms of resistance pursued by the Palestinians in terms of general strikes and limited commercial hours were rendering the population increasingly dependent upon the Israeli sector - as evidenced by the increased numbers seeking employment across the 'green line'.

However, the economic costs that Israel imposed upon the Palestinians was also a cause of concern to sections of the Israeli security establishment. The fear was that if the Palestinians were squeezed too hard, then they might feel they had nothing to lose - the consequence being an explosion of violence fed by feelings of despair. As early as February 1989 Defence Minister Rabin expressed the dilemma as he saw it:

> We have to strike a balance between actions that could bring on terrible economic distress and a situation in which they have nothing to lose and measures which bind them to the Israeli administration and prevent civil disobedience.[41]

Such strategic considerations were not the only problems Israel faced as a consequence of the economic struggle in which it was locked with the Palestinians. The economic costs of the Uprising for the Israelis were less obvious but they were real enough. In December 1989 the Minister of Economic Planning put the total cost of the Intifada at $1.5 billion. Perhaps a more authoritative figure was the estimate of Bank Hapoalim which gauged the accumulated cost to the Israeli economy after two years at $1 billion - a severe enough burden for an economy whose national output is about $27 billion. The costs were not just the direct military ones of ammunition, construction of detention centres, feeding and clothing detainees and the like.[42] There was also the loss of revenue from taxes, the loss of sales and production, and the loss to the economy occasioned by the mobilisation of reservists who, during the first year of the Intifada, were required to serve up to 60 days of duty and which resulted in a significant loss of key personnel in the Israeli economy.[43] The absenteeism of Palestinian workers, particularly during the first year of the Intifada, also contributed to Israeli economic difficulties, especially in the building industry. 1988 saw a 15 percent reduction in house construction in Israel, which in turn contributed to a 35 - 40 percent rise in house prices during 1989.[44] By mid-1990 the Israeli economy was sliding into stagflation as unemployment rose above 10 percent and inflationary pressures increased. All this at a time when Soviet Jews were entering the country at an increasing rate. 50,000 arrived during the first half of the year and the rate was expected to rise to 22,000 a month.

Government resources were stretched to the limit. The main pressure was on housing, and whilst plans were laid to import some 3,000 prefabricated homes as part of an attempt to increase the supply of housing units from 20,000 to 80,000 a year the deprived and homeless sections of Israeli society began camping out in parks in protest against the escalating rents and the privileged treatment being meted out to the new arrivals. The government budgeted $1.25 billion for the absorption of immigrants during 1990, most of which would have to be borrowed - adding further to the cost of servicing debts which already amounted to a third of the annual budget, with defence expenditure accounting for another 20 percent.[45]

Alongside the problem of housing the influx of immigrants, Israel faced the daunting task of finding employment for the newcomers. One obvious strategy was to replace Palestinian workers with Soviet Jews. This was the background to the temporary bans preventing Palestinians from entering Israel that were imposed after the al-Aqsa massacre and the subsequent spate of killings by Palestinian labourers towards the end of October 1990. It also helped explain the steps taken to prohibit the entry of thousands of Palestinian workers into Israel by the radical extension of the green ID card scheme. These sanctions were imposed upon a population that was already suffering under the traumatic financial and economic impact of the Iraqi invasion of Kuwait. The most immediate effect was the drying up of the flow of funds from Kuwait and the other Gulf states. This included remittances from Palestinians in the Gulf, as well as funding from Arab non-governmental institutions and banks that had provided support for Palestinian educational and medical institutes and projects. Furthermore, the PLO suffered a drastic drop in income with its budget cut by a reported 40 percent.[46] Not only did this mean a massive laying-off of staff within the PLO structure but also a severe curtailment of financial support for institutions and personnel within the occupied territories.

On top of this loss of external funding Palestinian agriculture and industry suffered severely from the loss of export markets in Jordan, Iraq and the Gulf. This in turn contributed to the rising tide of unemployment in the occupied territories, a level which was heightened by the return of Palestinians from Kuwait and the Gulf. Erstwhile financial supporters of their families in the occupied territories, they returned as refugees to constitute an additional burden on household incomes. The Gulf crisis also brought with it a complete halt to the tourist trade which had begun to revive a little during 1989-90. This also added thousands of unemployed to the labour market.

However, worse was to befall the Palestinians as 1990 came to an end. On January 14 1991 Israel imposed a total curfew upon the occupied territories which continued for 40 days. People were unable to go to work, children could not get to school, and the sick could not get to hospital. Crops could not be tended or harvested. People went hungry and fell further into debt. Meantime tax collection was pursued with renewed vigour amongst the captive population, whose plight went largely unnoticed as the world focused upon events in the Gulf. The curfew finally came to an end, but the restrictions on travel within the occupied territories and across the 'green line' into Israel remained in force. It became increasingly obvious that the Israeli authorities had used the opportunity presented by the Gulf War, and the consequent need to confine the Palestinians to their homes because of the alleged 'security risk' they posed, to accelerate the replacement of Palestinian labour within the Israeli economy by new Soviet immigrants.

Thus, after the cessation of hostilities, the border between the West Bank and Israel remained sealed and Israel began to apply the same conditions for entry to West Bankers as they had already implemented with regard to Gazans. Only those with a registered work permit were allowed to seek employment. Eligibility was restricted to married men with children over the age of 30 with no record of arrest or imprisonment for criminal or political offences. Furthermore, Palestinians could only be employed in the industrial, agricultural, and construction sectors. Those who had worked in the service sector were not permitted entry. Over and above these restrictions, measures were introduced to 'encourage' Israeli employers to find alternative sources of labour. Thus, employers were not allowed to hire Palestinians for night work. They had to hire a minimum of ten Palestinians and they had to provide transport to and from work for those Palestinians that they did hire. As a 'sweetener', the government began offering employers monthly subsidies equivalent to £250 for each new Israeli worker hired. The result of all these measures was that by May 1991 only 25 - 35 percent of the 150,000 or so Palestinians who were normally employed in Israel had resumed work.[47]

For Israel, the selective granting of work permits was a continuation of the established 'stick and carrot' policy. Thus, in villages where the mukhtar or village council had resigned in accordance with the UNC instructions concerning disengagement from the Israeli administration no permits were issued on the grounds that no official local authority existed to support requests for permits. In similar fashion only those who could furnish proof of having paid their taxes were granted authorisation to seek work in Israel, always assuming that they had no 'security record'. Thus it was that in the months following August 1990 all the major sources of income for Palestinians in the occupied territories were severely cut: remittances from Palestinians working in the Gulf, financial aid from the Arab world, financial assistance from the PLO, employment within the occupied territories and employment in Israel. In April 1991 I visited the occupied territories and the consequences of these calamitous developments were all too obvious. I found it difficult to comprehend how the impoverished occupants of the refugee camps were surviving. UNRWA was estimating that 80 percent of the families in the occupied territories were in need of urgent relief in basic necessities. Throughout the Intifada no one had starved.

Now there were widespread reports of malnutrition.[48] The situation seemed all the more desperate insofar as the indigenous relief and welfare services that had been based around the popular committees had been allowed to fall into disrepair, due in part to the misplaced faith of the population in the rhetoric of Saddam Hussein and his promises of liberation.

The view amongst Palestinians was that Israel was trying to starve them into submission, to force them to their knees, so that they would be amenable to any concessions Israel might care to grant them - some kind of limited autonomy, anything that promised some respite from their suffering. The risk run by Israel in pursuing such a policy was vividly expressed to me by a Palestinian acquaintance, someone renowned for his commitment to nonviolence, when he observed, 'At the moment all we can do is concentrate on survival. But if the suffering gets too much, the people will find flesh to eat - Israeli flesh. The Israelis must not squeeze us too hard.' The obvious implication being that desperation might lead to an explosion of violence directed against Israelis - soldiers, settlers, and civilians alike.

---

[1] S. Tamari, What the Uprising means', *Middle East Report,* May-June 1988, pp. 24-30.

[2] *The Independent,* January 30, 1988.

[3] This echoed a call made by Mubarak Awad of the Palestinian Centre for the Study of Nonviolence made prior to the outbreak of the Intifada.

[4] *The Guardian,* March 4, 1988.

[5] C. Richards, *The Independent,* January 30, 1988.

[6] *Al Fajr,* March 20, 1988.

[7] C. Richards, *The Independent,* January 30, 1988.

[8] A meeting of East Jerusalem merchants threatened an indefinite strike until the fourteen were released, see *Al Fajr,* May 1, 1988.

[9] According to some analysts Palestinians in the territories were taxed more heavily than Israelis. See S. J. Baxendale, *Christian Science Monitor*, August 15-21, 1988.
[10] A standard monthly payment equivalent to around £50 might be asked of an academic, whilst a more affluent landowner might donate nearer to £100 per month. Receipts were provided for such contributions in order to avoid charges of corruption and malpractice.
[11] See D. R. Francis in *Christian Science Monitor*, May 9-15, 1988.
[12] *Financial Times*, August 16, 1990.
[13] See *Al Fajr*, August 14, 1988.
[14] *Al Fajr*, June 19, 1988.
[15] One tactic was to make over the legal ownership of one's goods to a neighbour or relative, thereby avoiding their confiscation in lieu of unpaid taxes.
[16] *Jerusalem Post*, July 15, 1988.
[17] A farmer in the Halhoul region reported that his normal annual profit on the 1988 grape harvest of $10,000 had been reduced to $1,000. See *The Guardian*, March 16, 1988.
[18] Christian Science Monitor, October 3-9, 1988.
[19] *Financial Times*, 8 October, 1988.
[20] Quoted in *Christian Science Monitor*, October 3-9, 1988.
[21] Cited by Hisham Awartani, 'Impact of Israeli policies on the Palestinian economy and the role of Palestinian economic institutions', *International symposium on the role of foreign assistance in meeting the economic and social development requirements of Palestinian People*, Vienna, 1989, p. 5.
[22] *Al Fajr*, 27 November 1989, p. I.
[23] Quoted in *The Independent,* September 1, 1989.
[24] Quoted in *The Independent*, April 13, 1988.
[25] *Swadeshi* was an integral component of the Gandhian constructive programme, involving the reliance on local resources for one's basic needs.
[26] *Voices from Gaza.*

---

[27] Quoted in *The Independent,* April 13, 1988.
[28] D. Kuttab, *Middle East International,* July 22, 1988, p. 11.
[29] *The Independent*, August 23, 1990. Aid and remittances from the Gulf region constituted some 30 percent of the Gross National Product of the occupied territories, see *The Guardian*, August 30, 1990.
[30] *Middle East International,* June 24, 1988.
[31] Personal communication.
[32] See Fiona McKay, 'A draconian measure', *Middle East International,* June 23 1989, pp. 8 - 9.
[33] It was only in October 1988, some eight months later, that Israel issued the first permits to Palestinian producers in Gaza allowing them to export their fruit direct to the European Community in a successful attempt to clear the way for the ratification of the trade agreements with Europe. See *The Guardian,* October 11, 1988.
[34] It was estimated that somewhere in the region of $300 million was knocked off the value of Palestinian savings by the depreciation in the value of the dinar. Samir Hulaileh, *The Gulf crisis and the Palestinian economy,* East Jerusalem, PASSIA, 1991, p 5.
[35] Samir Barghouthi, in *Al Fajr,* January 23, 1989, p. 16.
[36] S. Abdallah, *Al Fajr*, August 7, 1989, p. 16.
[37] Quoted by Yehuda Litani, *Jerusalem Post (International Edition)* August 26, 1989, p. 17.
[38] H. Awartani, *International symposium* (1989), p. 3.
[39] Khalil Touma, *Al Fajr,* February 19, 1990, pp. 8-9.
[40] *Jerusalem Post,* November 27, 1989
[41] Quoted by Joel Greenberg, *Jerusalem Post (International Edition),* February 25, 1989, p. 5.
[42] Bank Hapoalim calculated the direct cost to the army of dealing with the Intifada at between $120 - 160 million for 1988, with a slightly lower cost incurred for 1989. The IDF's own estimates were considerably in excess of these figures: $260 million for 1988, $205 million for 1989, and the estimated cost

for 1990 was $225 trillion. See *Jerusalem Post (International Edition)*, January 6, 1990, p. 6.

[43] Israel's trade surplus with the occupied territories totalled only $56 million in 1988, a third of the 1987 figure of $174 million. (*Jerusalem Post International Edition),* February 18, 1989, p. 7.) Israeli food producers and processors were particularly badly hit with a reported loss of revenue of $100 million after two years of the Palestinian boycott. In retaliation Israel insisted that all goods produced in the occupied territories for sale in Israel must be labelled in Arabic to indicate their place of production. See *Jerusalem Post (International Edition)*, November 25, 1989, p. 21.

[44] *Financial Times*, January 16, 1990.

[45] *Financial Times*, May 2, 1990 and July 10, 1990.

[46] *The Guardian*, December 8, 1990.

[47] Details from Kav La'oved - Workers Hotline Newsletter, March 1991, Tel Aviv.

[48] Hulaileh, *The Gulf crisis and the Palestinian economy*, p. 5.

7

THE ROLE OF THE MEDIA

Introduction

Advocates of nonviolent resistance have highlighted a crucial insight concerning struggles against occupation - the most punitive costs that can be inflicted upon an invader or occupier are not necessarily those that can be counted in material terms (the number of lives lost, tanks captured, installations destroyed, and such like). Of potentially greater significance is the cost an oppressor can be made to bear in terms of social and political division at home and censure from abroad. Thus, a major concern of tacticians of unarmed civil resistance has been how to create situations that can cause moral outrage. The aim has been to 'stir sluggish consciences' by means of what has been termed 'shame power'. By creating situations in which the occupier is revealed as transgressing those values to which they lay claim (democracy, respect for human life and human rights, etc.), it is hoped that the seeds of moral doubt can be sown amongst the ranks of oppressors and onlookers. The fomenting of dissent and dissatisfaction amidst the occupying forces, the erosion of the occupying power's claims of legitimacy, the threat of social and political division on the home front, the loss of the support of allies and other third parties in the international arena - all these costly trends can be set in motion by means of nonviolent forms of resistance, such that even if the occupier is immune to moral qualms, expediency and self-interest can undermine their political will.[1]

The effectiveness of such undermining activities crucially depends on communication. The stories and images that reveal the barbarism of the opponent, the illegitimacy of their cause, and the unjustified suffering for which they are responsible, need to be transmitted to as wide an audience as possible. In the modem age this involves gaining access to the mass media and the electronic channels of communication. In the case of the Intifada, this meant that both sides engaged in a battle for public opinion in which they sought to present their respective versions of reality. It became a war over words and pictures every bit as vital as the 'real' struggle on the ground. The purpose of this chapter is to examine some of the features of this 'symbolic struggle': the fight to convey competing images of the Intifada to the wider world.

Background

In any conflict situation the parties involved will seek to purvey their own version of the truth. Indeed, there was considerable debate in Israeli government circles following the 1967 war as to whether or not a Palestinian press should be allowed to operate in the newly occupied territories. Eventually it was decided to allow newspapers to publish - as a safety valve for Palestinian political expression and as a valuable source of insight into the thoughts and feelings of the subject population. However, the freedom thereby granted was severely circumscribed. Since the formation of the state in 1948, Israel sought to control the flow of information into the public arena by means of regulations inherited from the British Mandate period, including the 1933 Press Ordinance and the 1945 Defence (Emergency) Regulations. These endowed the government and military authorities with broad powers to restrict or prohibit the import, export or printing of material which were deemed to threaten security or public order. Under the regulations the relevant authorities enjoyed the right to review materials before publication with a view to partial or full censorship. In addition, all newspapers, printing and press offices within Israel were required to hold a licence from the Ministry of Interior. The publishing of material without prior submission to the censor which occasioned official disapproval could result in such licences being revoked or suspended without explanation, although censorship decisions themselves could be appealed against through informal negotiations or formal channels to the chief censor in Tel Aviv.

In theory these regulations applied equally to all journalists based in Israel. This meant that what applied to the Israeli and foreign media (every Israeli-accredited journalist was required to sign a document agreeing to abide by the censorship rules) should also have applied to the Palestinian media based in East Jerusalem, annexed by Israel in 1967. The practice proved rather different. The distribution of newspapers in the occupied territories required a permit from the military authorities, whilst the military could also confiscate any publications they considered to be a threat to security or public order, even if the material had already been passed by the censor. Moreover, with regard to censorship, the chair of the Foreign Press Association (FPA) in Israel, Bob Slater, observed:

> Palestinians have to submit everything or they are closed down. Israelis technically should show everything, but even if they are accused of censorship violations they face less harsh reprisals. The foreign press has an unwritten understanding that we submit the material we feel may infringe on Israel's security system.[2]

Thus, between 1980 and 1986 the licences of six Palestinian publications were revoked, invariably on the grounds that they served as propaganda outlets for the PLO. In addition, during the same period, three of the four Arabic language dailies published in East Jerusalem (*al-Sha'ab, al-Quds* and *al-Fajr*) had their publishing licences suspended for periods ranging from several days to a month on the grounds that they had violated the censorship regulations. By such means the Israeli authorities were able to exercise tight control over the content of the Palestinian media, arguing, as did the State Attorney in April 1987:

> The areas of Judea and Samaria and the Gaza Strip are subject to military government and accordingly there does not exist there the fundamental right of freedom of expression in its various kinds and forms, and most certainly not that of an equal status to that existing in the State of Israel.[3]

With regard to the Israeli media, the controls over their functioning were customarily exercised by informal negotiations and tacit understandings, such that the formal legal powers rarely had to be invoked. Israel is a small-scale society, many journalists are reservists in the IDF, and they share the security concerns of a country that has been involved in successive conflicts with its neighbours. In addition, there were regular meetings between government and military officials, the editors-in-chief of the daily newspapers and the Israeli Broadcasting Authority for off-the-record briefings in return for their cooperation in 'eliciting support for the government's policies and actions.'[4]

The real problem for the Israeli authorities was how to control the activities of the foreign correspondents based in Israel. Claiming to be the only democracy in the Middle East, Israel used to be particularly sensitive to how she was portrayed to the outside world. A small, vibrant and democratic society that had succeeded in making the deserts bloom, whilst threatened on all sides by hostile Arab states who refused to make peace but sought the destruction of the state and its people - this was the image that the Israeli authorities sought to convey to the world in general, and to the members of the Jewish diaspora in particular. Obviously, one of the most important channels through which this picture was portrayed was the 2 - 300 strong corps of foreign correspondents based in Israel and accredited by the Government Press Office (GPO). One of the important functions of the GPO was to assist foreign correspondents by providing daily translations of all major news, features and editorials from the Israeli press, acting as a distribution point for all government press releases, providing access to photographic archives, arranging interviews, and alerting journalists to upcoming stories. According to a senior official, 'Journalists are grateful for this help. And we want them to be grateful. Our philosophy is to make his life as easy as possible.'[5] Foreign correspondents on a long-term posting to Israel knew that if they offended the Israeli authorities in some way they risked losing the support services of the GPO. Therefore, whilst over the years few foreign journalists had taken the trouble to submit their reports to the censor as formally required, they had become sufficiently attuned to render the official procedures virtually unnecessary.

Such had been the practice in what we might term 'normal times'. In 'abnormal times', such as during the 1982 invasion of Lebanon and in the years following the outbreak of the Intifada, Israel had cause to regret the limitations on its ability to keep a tight rein on the foreign media. Abnormal times in a world trouble-spot like Israel attracts hordes of correspondents who fly in to cover specific stories for a limited time period. Such people did not depend upon the long-term cooperation of the GPO for their livelihood. They were beholden to their editors in London, Paris, New York or wherever - not to the Israeli censor. They were employed by organisations that had become increasingly transnational in scale and commitment - media conglomerates with interests and consumers to satisfy far beyond the borders of a single state, particularly a small state like Israel. They were driven more by a fear of 'missing a story' than by any sensitivity to the security concerns of the Israeli state. Therefore they were far more likely to risk by-passing the censorship regulations and, as a consequence, Israel had to acknowledge that its ability to control the flow of information to the outside world was thereby drastically circumscribed. An associated reason for the decline in the state's capacity to control the flow of information was the changes in the nature of communications technology that had taken place by the late 1980s. Satellite links, the miniaturisation of cameras, long-range lens and directional microphones might seem 'old hat' to contemporary newshounds with their access to internet-based modes of communication and social networks – but back in the 1980s and 1990s there were changes that had a comparable impact. Communication satellites transcended national boundaries and made it extremely difficult for governments to exercise political control over the material transmitted. Likewise, direct dialling telephone technology meant that information - pictures and images as well as words – could be transmitted without the intervention of an operator. Using the same telephone links computers could transmit and receive lengthy reports in a matter of seconds via the relatively new phenomenon of the internet. In the midst of such technical innovation Israel was not alone amongst nation-states in having to face up to their relative impotence to censor information transmitted to the outside world. As a British Ministry of Defence spokesperson observed to a committee on censorship in the 1980s: 'Modem communications are making it easier for a journalist to pass his information, with or without approval, and making it more difficult for any authority to control the passage of information or even know that it is being passed.'[6]

The Israeli public relations disaster

Within a week of the outbreak of the Intifada television screens around the world were filled with pictures of the confrontations between the Palestinians and the IDF - unarmed civilians, including women and children, standing firm against the shootings, gas attacks and beatings. The Intifada became a global news story. During the first few months there were well over a thousand foreign media people milling around Jerusalem, filing front-page stories with pictures to match. It was an exciting time, not just for the hotel owners but for the Palestinian journalists who acted as guides, contacts, and information sources for the newcomers from abroad.

Just as the Israelis had no clear policy for dealing with the Uprising, they were similarly bemused about how to cope with the media. The familiar threat of terrorism was one thing - they knew how to deal with it, and 'Palestinian atrocities' commanded little sympathy in the world outside. But mass resistance and civil disobedience -- how could Israel portray itself as a fundamentally decent and moral society and state when its military were using all their might to suppress demonstrations by unarmed civilians? The nadir, from the Israeli point of view, came early in 1988. In mid-February reports sped around the world that the brutality of Israeli soldiers had reached new depths with the burial alive of four Palestinians. Commenting on the atrocity, General Mitzna, the army commander of the West Bank, confessed: 'Even in my worst dreams I would never imagine such a thing'. This story coincided with the publication of a report from the Boston-based Physicians for Human Rights group which blamed the Israelis for 'an uncontrolled epidemic of violence in the West Bank and Gaza'. Just a few weeks later, in early March, a CBS television crew filmed four soldiers subjecting two Palestinian youths to a calculated beating, in which heavy rocks were used to break their limbs. Within a day it was being shown on news programmes throughout the world. 'Bone-cracking soldiers break US Jews' hearts' was one headline above a story on the response of North American Jews to the Intifada.[7] The European Parliament passed a resolution condemning 'the instances of torture, arbitrary arrest, reprisals, expulsions and all acts of violence committed by the Israeli army against the Palestinian population'.[8] In an effort to counter the 'distorted image' of Israel being portrayed to the outside world, an information centre was hurriedly established at the GPO in Jerusalem. It was a failure. According to the British journalist Ian Black

> ... the daily bulletins it published tended to be late, laconic and partial. Army accounts of violent clashes often jarred with what journalists

> had seen for themselves. The Palestinians had a far better grasp of the importance of the information war. And on balance they won it.[9]

Attacks on the 'oxygen of publicity'

Much of the discussion amongst Israeli decision-making circles during the early weeks of the Uprising focussed on how to control the media's coverage of events. Indeed, there was a tendency in some quarters to blame the media for the events themselves, with allegations that the confrontations and demonstrations were merely performances presented to satisfy the media's thirst for news. 'What has the Intifada achieved? Only a media achievement,' claimed Shimon Peres in the spring of 1988.[10] Such attempts to deny the substance of the Uprising could not mask the significance of this 'media achievement'. The portrayal of Israeli brutality and repression in the press and on the television screens around the world had restored the Palestinian issue to the fore on the international agenda, and had seriously undermined Israel's standing in world opinion. It was clear that something had to be done to cut off the oxygen supply of publicity upon which the Palestinians seemed to be thriving. There were three related strands to the strategy adopted by the Israelis in 'managing the media': 1) Restricting the dissemination of information in the public domain, 2) Restricting journalistic access to information, and 3) Various forms of 'disinformation' and 'psychological operations'.

1. *'After the fact restrictions': the attempt to prevent the public dissemination of information*

In any civilian uprising against occupation the indigenous media plays a crucial role as a means of keeping the population informed, maintaining morale and unity, and countering feelings of isolation. Hence, one of the first reactions of the Israeli authorities was to restrict the distribution of Palestinian newspapers and magazines throughout the occupied territories. Thus, as early as December 14 1987, in the first week of the Uprising, all

East Jerusalem newspapers were confiscated. Subsequently all four daily East Jerusalem newspapers were served with orders banning their distribution in the occupied territories for varying periods of time. For example, between December 1987 and July 1989 *Al-Fajr* was banned five times for a total of nearly 100 days. Invariably such bans were imposed as penalties for publishing material that the censors deemed should have been submitted for clearance.

For years Palestinian newspapers and magazines tried to evade the wrath of the censor, not always successfully, by using material that had already appeared in the Israeli media. After the outbreak of the Intifada the incidence of publications being banned for carrying material that had already appeared in the Israeli press increased.[11] In addition to denying the population access to the printed word, the bans carried serious commercial implications for the publications affected. In addition there was the ever-present fear of permanent closure, as happened to the weekly *Al-Awdah* which was closed down on May 1 1988 on the grounds that it was funded by a 'hostile organisation' - the PLO. As a consequence editors had to act with great caution in order to cope with the increasingly stringent censorship. To reduce the chances of a permanent ban the owner and editor of the weekly *Al-Bayader Al-Siyassi*, Jack Khuzmo, began to submit everything to the censor during the Uprising.[12] Other editors estimated that during the Uprising the average amount of material prepared for publication which was censored was somewhere between 30 - 60 percent, a figure which occasionally rose to 80 percent.[13] What should be borne in mind is that this censorship took place following a process of careful self-censorship on the part of journalists and editors. Such self-monitoring has been a characteristic of the media throughout the world, but for the editors of the Palestinian press the cautiousness brought about by the fear of closure led some to feel as though they were little more than 'hired pens', working for the censor rather than their publication. As Sa'eb Eraqat, who was one of the editors of *Al-Quds* remarked, 'We are not the editor-in-chief, the head censor is.... It is not an exaggeration that the chief censor is the editor-in-chief of all Palestinian papers.'[14]

The cumulative result of all these pressures was a very inadequate coverage of events and issues of interest to the population in the occupied territories, and a general decline in the quality of the Palestinian press. Potential feature writers became reluctant to submit articles that they knew would be censored. The repeated frustration consequent on having work censored affected the morale and creative effort of journalists. They became resigned to writing pieces on innocuous topics. Moreover, the very tactics used to avoid the censor's pen such as understatement, the use of a virtual code-language of 'writing between the lines', the structuring of the writing so as to keep stronger statements in low profile, could result in a frustrated readership who found it difficult to understand just what it was the journalists were trying to communicate.

As was remarked above, a traditional tactic of the Palestinian press in coping with censorship had involved drawing upon items that had already been covered by the Israeli media. This practice had increased during the Intifada, with journalists feeding stories to the Hebrew press, then quoting the Israeli interpretation of their original material for inclusion in their own papers. Such were the contortions in the flow of information occasioned by occupation. However, even the Israeli media were not immune to the impact of the censor and the restrictive regulations governing the publication of information. In May 1988 the Israeli afternoon daily *Yediot Ahronot* appeared with a blank space in its columns - an article condemning the extent of censorship in the Israeli press had been censored. Another Israeli paper that suffered unduly from the attentions of the censor was the Arabic language daily *Al-Ittihad*, published by the Israeli Communist Party (Rakah). According to its editor 20 - 25 percent of its material had to be submitted, including everything related to the occupied territories, the armed forces and police.[15]15 In addition it had its publishing licence suspended at the end of March 1988 for the week prior to Land Day, when Israeli Arabs commemorate the death of six of their number shot by Israeli troops in 1976 whilst protesting against land expropriation. In early March 1989 the licence of the Nazareth-based *Al-Raya*, published by the Abna'a al-Balad movement, was withdrawn after allegations that it was financed by the Popular Front for the Liberation of Palestine.

Concern at the tightening controls on the media, and the realisation that the restrictions imposed upon the Palestinian press were beginning to filter across the 'green line' into Israel, led Israeli journalists in June 1988 to organise a symposium on the dangers posed by the erosion of press freedom in Israel. This followed the publication by over 100 Israeli journalists of a joint protest against the banning of the left-wing Israeli weekly *Derech Hanitzotz* the previous February. Published in Hebrew and Arabic, the magazine had only a limited circulation but it was widely respected as an authoritative source of information on the situation in the occupied territories, and had long been a thorn in the side of the military government with its damaging reports of Israeli brutality in the West Bank and Gaza Strip. The closure of *Derech Hanitzotz* was not on the grounds of censorship violations, but because of the alleged political affiliations and sympathies of the journal and its staff, who were later convicted of membership of a 'hostile organisation' - the Democratic Front for the Liberation of Palestine.[16]

None of the foreign correspondents covering the Intifada suffered such draconian measures. Although technically subject to censorship most of them felt free to file what they wanted. Occasionally, however, the authorities felt obliged to rebuke some of their number, if only to serve as a reminder to the others that there was a line beyond which they should not stray. Thus, two North American journalists had their press credentials suspended in the spring of 1988 after they had published leaked details of the Israeli assassination of Abu Jihad. The same fate befell three British journalists in October 1988 after they had filed stories on the Israeli 'death squads" operating in the occupied territories, whilst in June 1989 Reuter's chief correspondent in Jerusalem was threatened with having his visa revoked if he persisted in wiring material without submitting it to the censor. In all these cases the correspondents were based in Israel, and as such were sensitive to such threats to their continued professional activity. Less amenable were the hundreds of media personnel who were mere 'transients", on temporary assignment to cover the Intifada.[17] In order to cope with them the Israelis had to develop another ploy. Rather than trying to restrict what they published, a serious attempt was made to deny them access to the information and events themselves.

2. 'Before the fact' restrictions: the attempt to prevent access to information

One way to stem the flow of hostile information is to prevent the people with information passing it on to journalists who want to report and disseminate it. On occasions the Israelis tried to 'censor at source' by issuing specific orders forbidding personnel in such institutions as hospitals from talking to journalists. However they soon realised that such orders were virtually impossible to enforce. If you cannot stop people divulging information, then the obvious next step is to prevent the media from gaining access to the source of the information.

On March 29 1988 the Israeli authorities took the unprecedented action of closing off the whole of the West Bank and Gaza Strip for three days as a precaution against the disturbances that were expected to take place on March 30, the Day of the Land. The Israeli Arabs had declared a nonviolent general strike for that day as an expression of solidarity with their fellow Palestinians, and the leadership of the Intifada had called for a general strike and demonstrations against 'the forces of occupation and settlers'. By declaring both the West Bank and Gaza Strip closed military areas the authorities sought to prevent any contact between Palestinians and the Arab citizens of Israel, and also to deny the media access to the occupied territories unless accompanied by military escort. In so doing they were merely implementing on a larger scale a practice that was to become increasingly common in their attempts to manage the media.

Under the military regulations the military commander of a region could declare an area closed at any time. In January 1988 this power, along with the power to declare curfews, was devolved to the senior officer on the scene. This meant that if a soldier noticed the unwelcome presence of the media. he could order them to leave by producing a written order signed by a senior officer. As one correspondent commented, 'They all seem to have these papers ready anytime ... If a soldier spots you, he tells you to leave. If you challenge it, he just brings his officer who can sign a closure order on the spot.'[18] The frequency with which this method was used to keep the media away from the news rose markedly throughout 1988. Such 'pocket closures' proved almost impossible to challenge, insofar as the orders were issued at the location where the action was taking place and where observers could be forced away at gunpoint if necessary. The media might lodge their complaints after the fact, but by then the incident might well be 'old news'. The Israelis appear to have been particularly wary of film crews and photographers, aware that an image could convey far more than the written word in many cases. As a result camera-men and photographers developed the practice of filming and 'shooting' as soon as they arrived on the scene, in the expectant knowledge that they would have only a few minutes before they were ordered to leave. Another ploy that was practised with some success involved training local people in the use of small video cameras, so that even when the foreign film-crews had been denied access they could still get their footage 'second-hand'.

The Israeli practice of turning foreign correspondents back at road blocks, even when others - including tourists – were being allowed through was another source of frustration for the media. They were also excluded from areas and neighbourhoods that had been placed under curfew, although occasionally the military would permit a pool of journalists to enter if accompanied by a military escort, with the result that they only got to see what they had been allowed to see, with little opportunity to check the army's version of events. Thus, following the slaughter of seven Palestinians by an Israeli civilian just south of Tel Aviv at Rishon Lezion on May 20 1990, foreign correspondents issued a statement through the Foreign Press Association protesting that they had been prevented from covering the subsequent events in the occupied territories except under close military escort and then only within a very restricted area. They went on to complain that such restrictions had rendered them unable to fulfil their role as impartial observers, insofar as 'military escorts have prevented direct contact with the civilian population, as well as with soldiers engaged in the events.'[19]

Such restrictions impacted less heavily on the Palestinian media. No curfew or siege is hermetic, particularly for those with an intimate knowledge of the locality. Moreover, Palestinian journalists tended to have such a wide range of contacts within what was a 'small-scale society' that even if they themselves were denied access, they could always obtain reports from their network of contacts in the field. Even when the Israelis cut the telephone links from certain areas and confiscated the fax machines of journalists, the reports got through by one means or another – there were always people prepared to make the journey to the nearest telephone that was still live, crossing over the border into Israel if necessary or making the journey to East Jerusalem itself to report in person.[20] Thus, although the attempts to restrict the access of foreign journalists to newsworthy events were aimed at forcing journalists to rely upon military spokespersons for their information, one unsought for consequence was that correspondents began to rely more heavily on Palestinian sources, given the scepticism with which most of them came to regard the veracity of official Israeli sources.[21] As one correspondent observed, 'We find ourselves depending on Palestinian sources since the territories are usually closed to the press. ... The Palestinian sources turned out to be more reliable.'[22] In an attempt to disrupt the symbiotic relationship that developed between Palestinian and foreign journalists, the Israelis began to target the Palestinian press agencies. During the early months of the Intifada one of the main secondary sources of information for foreign correspondents was the Palestine Press Service. In March 1988 it was closed down for a period of two years. The same fate befell the Holy Land Press Service which was closed for a similar period in June 1989. Other press offices were closed for shorter spells of time. In addition, it seemed to many that those Palestinian journalists who specialised in accompanying foreign correspondents and film crews around the occupied territories became a particular target for harassment and intimidation by the Israeli authorities.

Palestinian journalists were subjected to the whole range of sanctions resorted to by the Israelis, ranging from administrative detention through to deportation. Foreign journalists did not escape intimidation either. By January 1989 the Foreign Press Association had been informed of over 150 incidents ranging from verbal abuse to physical assault and threats at gunpoint. They included occasions when film was confiscated and equipment and cameras smashed, instances of short term detention and other forms of harassment. Often this was at the hands of soldiers and military personnel, sometimes it was the work of Israeli civilians. Thus, after a bomb explosion in the Mahane Yehuda market in West Jerusalem on May 28 1990, bystanders attacked journalists who were photographing border police detaining Palestinians, accusing them of ruining Israel's image abroad. Cameras were smashed and two photographers required medical treatment for wounds to the head.

West Bank settlers were particularly active in the fight against the press. Thus, one group began distributing car-stickers promoting 'The People Against Hostile Media' and carrying an illustration of a snake flicking its forked tongue at a shield bearing the Star of David. Of greater concern to correspondents were the direct cases of intimidation and violence perpetrated by such 'people against hostile media'. Michael Rosenbaum, the director of CBS Television in the Middle East, recalled one such incident in an interview he gave in June 1989 in which he expanded on some of the problems involved in covering the Intifada:

> Israeli soldiers and the military authorities often carry out measures against TV crews, such as preventing them from entering areas where incidents are taking place. We also face harassment and even assaults from Israeli settlers. Just last week, settlers attacked and smashed the windows of a car which a crew of ours was using in the village of Izzariyeh. They prevented them from entering to film what was going on there.[23]

Joel Greenberg, one of the best informed Israeli journalists covering the occupied territories during the Intifada, expressed his fears concerning the erosion of press freedom within Israel, and the damage to democracy and human rights that this entailed. He focused in particular upon the growing hostility towards the media which he felt was orchestrated by the government and the IDF:

> Beyond the restrictions hindering news coverage, a palpable anti-media mood has been created in response to the graphic coverage by the press and foreign television of ugly confrontations in the territories and excesses by soldiers. The media is perceived as 'hostile' - focusing on the negative, serving Israel's Arab enemies ... The government and IDF, perceiving themselves to be at war, have clamped increasing restrictions on journalists for what they believe are overriding reasons of security ... The energy of the authorities, however, appears to have

> been directed primarily at restricting and chastising the press, rather than tackling the root problems reflected in the correspondents' reports. The authorities, it seems, are immensely concerned over Israel's image, especially abroad, as if the Uprising were primarily a public relations problem.[24]

This hostile attitude of the Israeli authorities fed, and to some extent reflected, the feeling amongst certain sectors of the Israeli public. However, one has to assume that the Israeli authorities had no part to play in the worst cases of intimidation of journalists. In March 1988 the CBS television network felt the need to hire security guards for one of its Israeli camera-men and its Tel Aviv office after receiving threatening telephone calls following the showing of their film of the soldiers beating two Nablus youths with rocks. They were not over-reacting. A month previously an extreme right-wing underground organisation called the Sicarii had attacked the home of Dan Margalit, a columnist with the daily newspaper *Ha 'aretz*. Taking their name from a band of Jews who used daggers to assassinate suspected collaborators in Roman- occupied Judea the Sicarii struck again in April 1989 with an arson attack on the Tel Aviv home of Amos Schoken, the publisher of *Ha 'aretz*. In a telephone call to the IDF radio station they explained that the attack was because 'Schoken is harming national morale', presumably a reference to the critical stance adopted by the newspaper with regard to Israeli policies in the occupied territories.[25] A year later the home of *Ma'ariv* correspondent Baruch Me'eri was targeted for an arson attack and threats were made against *Al-Ittihad*.[26]

However horrified the authorities might have been by such outrages, they were indicative of what Joel Greenberg depicted as 'a public atmosphere of hostility to the press, encouraged from time to time by official statements directed against journalists'.[27] As such, the authorities had to shoulder some of the responsibility for the extremism of so-called 'hot-heads'. It was one of the by-products of a third strand in their overall approach to controlling the media: the attempt to undermine the credibility of the sources of the damaging information, to discredit the media in the eyes of the public in Israel, overseas, and in the occupied territories themselves.

3. Disinformation and dirty tricks'

In Northern Ireland the British army made widespread use of 'psyops' (psychological operations) as part of their efforts to weaken the armed republican movement. Psyops were defined as 'the planned use of propaganda or other means, in support of our military action or presence, designed to influence to our advantage the opinions, emotions, attitudes and behaviour of enemy, neutral and friendly groups'.[28] Like their British counterparts the Israeli military and security forces used the media to send 'signals' aimed at undermining the unity and morale of the insurgent Palestinians, and to bolster public support at home and abroad. Most of the time these aims were pursued by attempting to control the flow of information directly, through the strategies outlined above. Blatant falsehoods were resorted to much less frequently. One of the main reasons for this was that when such untruths are revealed the overall credibility of the official public relations campaign can be seriously undermined. Indeed, what might appear to be deliberate deception on the part of official spokespersons can be the result of genuine human error, the failure to check the facts, and various chain of command problems. It can also reflect a form of military self-deception, whereby deceits and inaccuracies at each level of a bureaucratic process of news transmission add up to a complete distortion of the truth by the time the information is made public. Such would seem to have been the case with regard to an increasing proportion of IDF reports during the Intifada. In order to avoid the risk of being charged with violating army regulations concerning the treatment of 'rioters' and 'suspects' in the occupied territories, soldiers adopted the practice of 'whitewashing' their operational reports in an effort to camouflage their 'law enforcement' tactics. Thus, in one case concerning the killing of a Bethlehem youth shot by Border Policemen in December 1989, the evidence of a videotape filmed by the ABC TV network revealed that the IDF spokesperson's version, based on the account of the men involved, had been a tissue of lies. The police claimed they had fired warning shots in the air and that the youth and his companions had been threatening them with axes and metal bars. The film showed they had not been carrying weapons, and that no warning shots had been fired before the young man, Fadi Zabakly, was killed. As an IDF spokesperson remarked, the film posed a 'challenge to the army's credibility'.[29] Quite so - such are the potential costs of deception.

Moreover, it would seem that in the misrepresentation of events the soldiers in the field had the tacit support of their senior officers. Thus, at his trial, charged with ordering paratroopers to break the bones of West Bank villagers. Colonel Yehuda Meir alleged that a double standard was in operation. When senior officers spoke in public 'there was an attempt to say things which would appear all right', i.e. the official policy was to restrict beatings. But 'in the field they say other things', i.e. they advocate beatings as a punishment for stone-throwers and graffiti writers.[30] Meir accused his commanding officers, right up to the Defence Minister himself, of being a party to such subterfuge. It seemed as if dishonesty had become institutionalised ~ a part of everyday military life, with virtually everyone laundering reality to suit their own and what they presumed to be the military's best interests.

Whilst the institutionalisation of dishonesty and hypocrisy could have long-term deleterious consequences for the defence capability of Israel, in most cases the costs of disinformation campaigns could be far more immediate, depending on whether or not the deceit was uncovered. Moreover, even if the discovery of 'dirty tricks' caused public embarrassment and left official spokespersons with a credibility gap to bridge, this could seem a small price to pay for the damage inflicted on the enemy whilst the ploy is in operation. Thus, one of the more successful Israeli tactics for managing the media involved the impersonation of the press by Israeli security forces. Beyond gaining access to Palestinians for the purposes of information-gathering and arrest, the aim was clearly to plant the seeds of suspicion in the minds of the Palestinian community, to create a barrier between the information-givers and the disseminators of that information, and thereby help stem the flow of hostile news emanating from the 'other side'.

Rumours of Israeli security operatives masquerading as journalists had been rife since the start of the Uprising, but it was not until early July 1988 that the allegations entered the public domain when it transpired that Israeli civilians, posing as an ABC television film crew, had entered the West Bank village of Salfit, requested an interview with a youth, and then arrested him. Some nine months after this incident, on March 23 1989, a crew from the Visnews television network filmed two Israeli policemen using a car with foreign press signs while arresting a Palestinian girl in the Wadi Joz area of East Jerusalem. A few days later, on Land Day, there were reports of a Palestinian in Hebron being shot by settlers who were cruising the town in a van carrying 'press' signs. The result was that life for the non-Palestinian correspondents covering the Intifada became much more difficult. The incidence of Palestinians stoning press cars increased. Palestinians became much more reluctant to talk to the media, often insisting that journalists produce the press cards issued and accredited by the Arab Journalists Association in East Jerusalem before agreeing to be interviewed. As Glen Frankel, correspondent of the Washington Post, observed, 'The level of fear and hostility, if you could chart it, has gone up and up. ... Everyone seems to perceive that we are somehow part of the enemy.'[31]

Another form of deceit adopted by the Israelis was the publication of false communiqués and leaflets. For example, in July

1988 rival versions of Communiqué No.21 were published. Palestinians insisted that one was a fake, produced by the Shin Bet to create confusion and convey the impression that the leaders of the unified command were divided amongst themselves. Another example came to light during the battle of wills that took place between the Israeli authorities and the village of Beit Sahour over the non-payment of taxes in the autumn of 1989. As detailed in the previous chapter, for a few weeks this predominantly Christian village symbolised all that was laudable about the resistance struggle of the Palestinians against occupation: unarmed civilians facing up to military might by nonviolent means, making their stand on the democratic principle of 'no taxation without representation'. As a public relations exercise for the foreign media the civil disobedience campaign at Beit Sahour was a resounding success. It also did wonders for Palestinian morale at a time when it was sagging. As part of the attempt to break the will of the villagers, the Israeli intelligence sought to foment division by issuing a fake communiqué in the name of Hamas, attacking the 'wealthy Christians of Beit Sahour' for trying to 'ride the wave of the Intifada'.[32] The problem faced by the Israelis in such operations was that Palestinian society remained very small-scale, permeated by a whole web of communication networks. Given the widespread awareness of the Israeli strategy of trying to break the resistance by fracturing its unity, and given the intimate relationship between the leadership and the wider community, Palestinians were on their guard against such attempts to weaken their resolve.

On the other hand, as anyone who spent time in the occupied territories during the Intifada could bear witness, in a situation where open communication is severely restricted, Palestinian society was also particularly prone to rumour. There were occasions when the Israeli intelligence services tuned in to such rumours and sought to amplify them, raising allegations (not always false) about PLO officials abroad building themselves luxurious mansions with the money intended to support the victims of Israeli repression and the like. In a similar vein, the Israelis ensured that meetings between officials of the Israeli administration in the occupied territories and Palestinian community leaders received widespread publicity. According to Palestinians, such meetings were orchestrated to mislead international opinion that an Israeli-Palestinian dialogue was taking place. Reports of such gatherings also served to increase the concerns of Palestinians that some of their number were negotiating with the Israelis over the heads of their own community - thereby helping to create divisions in the Palestinian ranks within the territories, and between the leadership inside and the PLO leadership in Tunis.[33] On such occasions a huge responsibility fell on the shoulders of the Palestinian leaders who had to engage in considerable 'repair work' to mend the damage inflicted by such psychological operations. As for journalists (and researchers for that matter), caught in the midst of a miasma of rumour and hearsay, unable to check facts against stories, the situation could be a confusing and worrying one. After all, there was always the possibility that they themselves were being compromised, used by their 'special and confidential sources' (Israeli and Palestinian) as unwitting tools in the battle for the hearts and minds of publics and constituencies at home and abroad.

The power of the media in such a battle is often overemphasised. Occasionally one has the image of a hypodermic syringe that injects ready formed opinions and attitudes into those same hearts and minds. In fact, research seems to indicate that its power resides more in the area of setting public agendas, in selecting from the flow of events and occurrences those items to be elevated to the status of 'public issues', matters of concern and debate around and about which people adopt points of view and make judgements. It is in this area of public agenda-setting that the activities of the media advisers and spokespersons of both the Israeli and Palestinian camps were particularly active, with both sides doing their utmost to draw the attention of the media to those issues which they considered to be most deserving of interest, whether it was the latest example of 'Palestinian terrorism' or 'Israeli brutality', the most recent diplomatic statement of President Arafat or the rise of anti-semitism in Eastern Europe. Thus, in an interview shortly after his appointment as director of the GPO, Dr Yossi Olmeri expanded on how he saw his future task. One of his main priorities was 'to try and broaden the agenda of the foreign press in terms of emphasis on reporting matters from Israel', and he cited the incidence of 'inter-Arab murders' and the link between them and terrorism as examples of issues he would like to see covered. He continued:

> One gets the impression, especially in the West, that because of the emphasis on the Uprising, the Intifada is the only problem in the Middle East, or certainly the only problem confronting Israel in terms of security and strategic standing. This simply isn't true, especially when you bear in mind the arms race in the Middle East and the potential dangers posed to Israel by countries such as Syria, Iraq and Libya. The emphasis on the Uprising impacts unfavourably on Israel and international attitudes regarding the Palestinian issue. In this context, Israel appears much stronger than the Palestinians, and people therefore expect the stronger side to be conciliatory to the underdogs. The bottom line is that excessive coverage of the Uprising at the expense of any other issue is extremely damaging to Israel.[34]

A few months later, in March 1990, Israel imposed military censorship on reports about Soviet Jewish immigration to Israel. Although no official explanation for the move was given, it was assumed that it reflected growing concern at the possible American and Soviet response to the mounting Arab diplomatic offensive against the exodus, which was then running at somewhere in the region of 6000 a month. Whatever the reasons, it marked an about-turn on the part of the Israelis in terms of agenda-setting. As Ian Black of *The Guardian* commented:

> Ironically, the decision comes after several months in which the Israeli authorities have been encouraging the foreign press to cover all aspects of the wave of immigration. They have considered it an attractive alternative to the grim and often unflattering coverage of Israel's response to the Palestinian Uprising, until recently seen as one of the strongest stories in the Middle East.[35]

Sometimes, this public agenda-setting activity entailed the actual creation of an event around which it was hoped the media would flock. Thus, in March 1989 an International Jewish Solidarity Conference was held in Jerusalem. It was organised by the Israeli authorities as a public (and publicised) affirmation of their policies, in an effort to counter the mounting international isolation Israel was experiencing at that time in the light of her reluctance to make serious moves towards peace. More than 1000 Jewish leaders from around the world were invited to spend three days listening to speeches about education, the Israeli economy, immigration and international affairs. Very little time was allotted in the programme for discussion of such issues as talks with the PLO and the principle of exchanging territory for peace. The Jewish playwright, Harold Pinter, dismissed the conference as 'a public relations exercise where Jewish leaders will be instructed to endorse Mr Shamir's policies'.[36] Unfortunately for Prime Minister Shamir and the effort at news-management, while he was informing the assembly that peace with the terrorists of the PLO would only produce 'a peace of the graveyard' someone had leaked to the media an Israeli military intelligence report which warned that in the long run there was no alternative to dealing with the PLO - a reminder that no party or faction within either the Israeli or the Palestinian camp enjoyed a monopoly of power when it came to creating issues and setting agendas.[37]

Presentations of reality

By way of an illustration of the way in which pressures and affiliations can help determine a publication's perspective on what constitutes 'news', it is instructive to examine the relative prominence given to two crucial events that took place within a few days of each other in the early summer of 1990 by two partisan publications, the *Jerusalem Post International Edition (JPIE)* and *Al-Fajr Palestinian Weekly (AFPW)*. The *Jerusalem Post* general orientation was characterised by one commentator as 'a general endorsement of official state policy, except when the paper crusades for positions right of the Likud'.[38] By contrast, the English-language *Al-Fajr* was a Palestinian weekly published in East Jerusalem and closely aligned to the main stream of Fatah within the PLO.

On May 20 1990 seven Palestinian labourers were killed at Rishon Lezion by a lone Israeli civilian and a further seven Palestinians were killed in the subsequent demonstrations that convulsed the occupied territories. Ten days later, on May 30 Palestinian guerrillas affiliated to the Palestine Liberation Front launched an assault on a beach near Tel Aviv, four of them were killed and another seven were captured; there were no Israeli casualties. In the issue following the killings at Rishon Lezion, the *JPIE* (May 26 1990) devoted four column inches to the story at the bottom of the front page, under the headline, '7 Arab labourers slain, Jewish suspect held'. The *AFPW* (May 28 1990) placed the story in the middle of the front page, under the heading, 'Rishon massacre leads to widespread protests', and devoted a total of 138 column inches to the murder and the subsequent events, covering the reactions in the occupied territories, within Israel and in the United States and Jordan, in addition to an editorial leader on the outrage. By contrast, in the issue immediately following the Palestinian sea-borne raid on the Tel Aviv beach, *AFPW* (June 4 1990) made no reference to the event. Its lead story concerned the decision to boycott contacts with US officials taken by prominent Palestinians in protest against the United States veto of a UN Security Council resolution to despatch a commission of inquiry to the occupied territories. In the subsequent issue (June 11 1990) it devoted 57 column inches to the story, but most of the space was given over to consideration of the threat by the United States to break off its dialogue with the PLO as a consequence of the raid and the PLO's reluctance to dissociate itself unequivocally from the action. The *JPIE* of June 9 devoted virtually the whole of its front page to the story, including a full width photograph of the scene where the attack took place. In total, 67.5 column inches of text were devoted to the issue, including its impact on the United States - PLO dialogue and the condemnation of the raid from around the world.

In the respective space and prominence given over to the two events by these two avowedly partisan publications we can see the struggle being played out over what constituted a newsworthy event. It serves to remind us that the news, like social reality, is created and constructed - and in the context of the Intifada that process was never neutral, it was an integral part of the wider conflict. In their treatment of the two events, neither publication was involved in what one might consider to be deliberate distortion. What was involved was the partial presentation of reality, each viewing and portraying the world from their own perspective. In this regard it is important to emphasise that the Palestinian press and media were no 'cleaner' than their Israeli counterparts. Most of the Palestinian press within the occupied territories depended, more or less directly, upon funding and support from the PLO. They undoubtedly defined their role primarily in terms of the national struggle for liberation. Therefore they all engaged in various forms of self-censorship when it came to covering issues that might present the Uprising in a critical light.

This was particularly apparent with regard to the issue of violence in the Uprising, specifically in relation to the activities of the youth of the strike forces and the killings of alleged informers and collaborators. Most Palestinians in the occupied territories knew of instances where the strike forces had gone beyond the bounds of 'acceptable vigilance': like torching the shop of someone who dared to remonstrate with them for setting fire to tyres outside their home, like threatening to label as informers those teachers who dared to fail them in their school exams. Little of this appeared in the Palestinian press - nor was it reported by Palestinian human rights agencies.

Similarly, it was clear to many people that the killing of alleged collaborators had gotten out of hand during the third year of the Uprising - but it received only muted comment in the media. For example, on April 14 1991 the *Jerusalem Post*'s main editorial concerned the attempted slaying of a 40 year old advocate in Ramallah. A group of masked youths had reportedly attacked her with staves and axes in front of her ten year old son and left her for dead. Her 'crime' was to ignore the instructions of the leadership forbidding plea-bargaining with the Israeli authorities. According to the report in the *Jerusalem Post* several of her colleagues had planned to publish a condemnation of the assault, but withdrew it for fear of incurring the wrath of her attackers. This was at a time when the number of Palestinians killed as alleged collaborators was estimated to be in excess of 400. The reason the *Jerusalem Post* gave such prominence to the issue was clear - to show to the world that the revolt in the occupied territories was sustained only by terror and not popular support. However partial its interpretation, the basic facts of the case were true. To the best of my knowledge no Palestinian newspaper gave the story any prominence. To do so would have been deemed prejudicial to the national cause. By such sins of omission and commission the Palestinian media attempted to portray a particular version of the reality of the Uprising, and as such could never claim to be any more impartial than their Israeli counterparts.

The significance of language

The major tool that we have at our disposal when it comes to defining and interpreting the world about us is language. Where there are competing interpretations of that reality, then language itself becomes a subject of struggle, with both sides seeking to portray their own preferred image by means which involve the selective use of words and phrases. Should the occupied territories be referred to as 'Palestine' or as 'Judea, Samaria and the Gaza Strip'? Was the PLO 'the sole legitimate representative of the Palestinian people' or a 'terrorist organisation'? Was a stone-thrower a 'demonstrator' or a 'rioter'? Was a Palestinian killed by Israeli forces a 'martyr' or a 'casualty'? Was the killing at Rishon Lezion a 'slaying' or a 'massacre'? Were the subsequent events in the occupied territories 'massive protests' or 'stone-throwing incidents and other disturbances'? These are not questions of 'mere words', they were at the core of a struggle to impose particular definitions of reality upon the public. Just as the process whereby the 'news' is created is not neutral, neither are the words used to convey that news. As such, the lexicon becomes a crucial weapon in the armoury of psychological warfare.

With regard to the question of language and vocabulary, the state-run Israeli broadcasting authorities were subjected to almost as much pressure as the Palestinian media. Thus, following the Palestinian Declaration of Independence at the Algiers Conference of the PNC in November 1988 a meeting of the directorate of the Israeli Broadcasting Authority heard demands that the terms used on state radio and television should be changed: 'collaborators' should become 'Arabs who had contact with Israelis'; 'execution' should be replaced by 'murder'; 'the national leadership' should be 'the leaders of the rioters'; whilst the term 'Palestinian state' should be preceded by 'so-called'.[39] In protest against these and other restrictions an Israeli journalist resigned.

In his letter to the Broadcasting Authority he explained that he was 'not prepared to lend a hand in laundering reality, by using sterile words imposed from above'.[40] Frequently, however, journalists lent themselves unwittingly to partisan portrayals of reality, as the *Hadashot* correspondent Zvi Gilat acknowledged:

> Unable to confirm facts, not wishing to rile, attempting to remain neutral, the press unwittingly adopts the lexicon of the protagonists. The announcements of the IDF spokesman, a central source of information, often include not only a report of the incident, but the army's justification for it too. Here's a typical example: 'A Kalkilya youth met his demise last night in a clash with an IDF force. The soldiers were forced to open fire after identifying a youth who intended to throw a heavy stone and endanger their lives.' The 'youth' is sometimes a 13-year old. 'Met his demise' is a tender way of saying 'was shot and killed.' 'The soldiers were forced' - Really? Was there no other alternative? 'Intended to throw' - how do they know? Was there really a danger to their lives? 'A heavy stone' -- how much did it weigh? Journalistic language is sometimes corrupted, unawares, into a style whose purpose is to blur the facts ... The language of 'Arab sources' is no less one-sided and tendentious, and is at times an intentional perversion of the truth. In its reportage, the press unwittingly lends a hand to the corruption of language and the distortion of reality.[41]

Satisfying the thirst for news

The fact that the media was used by both sides to portray a particular image of the Intifada is in itself unremarkable. In my experience, however, correspondents who cover the Uprising were fully aware of their problematic status. Most of them had their own sources that they trusted. Such relationships were based on a kind of circumscribed reciprocity. On many occasions I sat in offices in East Jerusalem and elsewhere as a witness to such encounters. Both sides used the occasion to extract information from each other. The Palestinian would divulge his or her version of events and stories, and check it out with the information the journalist has gathered from other sources on both sides of the 'green line'. 'I'll tell you what I know, if you will tell me what you've heard' was the common pattern of proceedings. Of course, such relationships could only be founded upon trust established over time. Both parties knew that they are being 'used', but above and beyond that they also know that both could benefit from the exchange of information.

A responsible journalist should try and verify a story using more than one source. In similar fashion Palestinians grew accustomed to checking information from as many sources as possible. Like most people who have participated in some event or other that has become 'news', Palestinians were thirsty for feedback about what the world was saying about them, what reverberations their actions were having around the world. They also wanted to know what was happening in the Intifada itself. In a situation where there was censorship of the media and distorted communication through other channels, Palestinians had to get their news any way they could. A major source was the TV and radio. Most people on the West Bank checked out the coverage of Israeli TV against that of the Jordanian coverage. In the Gaza Strip the Egyptian channels could be received. When it came to radio the range of alternative sources was wider. The main Arabic stations from Israel, Jordan and Egypt were all acknowledged to be propaganda channels, likewise the PLO's *Voice of Palestine* broadcast from Baghdad which could only be heard late at night and was barely audible in the Gaza Strip. One Palestinian journalist dismissed the PLO station as 'full of rhetoric, for which people have little time', playing outdated military marches and anthems to armed struggle, and devoting half its airtime to the transmission of coded messages to activists in the occupied territories which, of course, most listeners are not meant to understand.[42] Radio Monte Carlo was considered to be a more authoritative source of information, whilst for those who spoke English, the World Service of the BBC was held in high regard until the Gulf war, when its broadcasts were perceived as little more than a mouthpiece of the coalition forces ranged against Iraq.

In the early months of the Intifada, the most popular radio station was *The Voice of Al-Quds*, which began broadcasting from southern Syria on January 1 1988. The station was run by Ahmed Jibril's Popular Front for the Liberation of Palestine - General Command, a faction in bitter dispute with the mainstream of the PLO. Despite its political affiliation the station was hugely popular with Palestinians throughout the occupied territories. The immediacy and accuracy of its reports on confrontations, strikes, and other Intifada-related events was a source of wonder and pride to Palestinians. As such it played an important role in maintaining morale amongst the population. Not surprisingly, the Israelis eventually decided to jam the broadcasts by the simple expedient of opening a new Arabic language channel on an adjacent wavelength. In the summer of 1989 the jamming stopped, a move which was widely assumed to reflect the Israeli desire to promote divisions within the Palestinian ranks by allowing a voice to Jibril. A few weeks later, in mid-September 1989, the station was jammed once again after it had begun broadcasting appeals to Palestinians to burn forests and fields inside Israel along with detailed instructions about how to set about such arson attacks. It remained a cause of concern to Palestinians that the PLO failed to establish a credible alternative station to that of *Al-Quds*, a concern that was barely assuaged by the proffered excuse that any truly autonomous Palestinian radio station would be vulnerable to Israeli attack.

Confronted by censorship of the press and the airwaves, Palestinians had to resort to other modes of communication. The underground press of leaflets and other literature was a vital means of communication and political debate. In addition to such 'semi-clandestine' methods of communication other channels became important. Perhaps the most important in such a small-scale society was face-to-face personal contact. As anyone who has spent any time in Palestinian society would be aware, Palestinians always have time for coffee and conversation. A lot of the most sensitive information was conveyed in this manner, by word of mouth. Moreover, most activists were linked into so many different social and political networks that the information would be quickly passed along. The telephone and fax machine were widely used, albeit with a certain degree of circumspection. Most activists assumed that any communication through such channels would be monitored by the security forces. For those who did have access to such equipment, however, they could be an important means of obtaining and delivering information, in the spirit of 'I know that they (the Israelis) know that I know that they are tapping this line ...'

In addition, the Palestinians had their own 'wall newspapers', in the form of the political graffiti that covered just about every vertical surface in the occupied territories. The Israelis, for their part, sought to censor the walls by having the slogans painted over, even resorting to spraying some of the walls of Gaza City with a black greasy substance. This 'battle of the walls' remained an on-going feature of the Intifada. Each morning the military would commandeer householders and passers-by to paint over the graffiti that had mushroomed overnight. Each night the wall artists returned to resume their craft. Layer upon layer, image upon image, slogan upon slogan - the walls of the occupied territories came to constitute a fundamental part of the popular culture of the Uprising.[43]

Ranking alongside the artwork of the walls as an expression of popular hope and struggle was the music of the Uprising. There was a burgeoning market of clandestine cassette tapes. Images of stones, children, soldiers, and burning tyres recurred in the lyrics of the songs. Much of the material produced was little more than a sloganising 'muzak' of the struggle - as one songwriter explained, 'When life itself is rich, you don't need creativity ... When someone is shot and killed in front of you, you don't need a newspaper to report it or a song to remember it'.[44] Whatever their artistic limitations, the songs and the music of the Intifada proved a potent force in expressing the emotions of the population, celebrating in particular the conquest of fear. The cassette was also the most common medium for avoiding the problems of the censor in the circulation of poetry and short stories during the Uprising, much of it written by detainees imprisoned in the Israeli detention camps.[45] With regard to other art forms, the Palestinian theatre was left with virtually no role to play because of the Israeli restrictions on performances throughout the occupied territories.[46] The public display of the work of Palestinian graphic artists was similarly circumscribed, although a number of paintings were reproduced and distributed clandestinely in the occupied territories. In addition a number of Palestinian artists established links with progressive artists in Israel and succeeded in having their work displayed in galleries in Tel Aviv and elsewhere in an effort to influence Israeli public opinion. However, the most potent symbol of their struggle for Palestinians, in 'fine art' as much as in 'popular art', remained the four colours of the Palestinian flag (red, green, white and black). These were displayed not just in the graphics on the walls, but also in the embroidery work of the village women, in the scarves and other items of apparel worn by women, and in the keffiyas worn by the men.

'Destructive ambiguity'

The wearing of the keffiya and the display of national colours in their dress by Palestinians was reminiscent of the actions of the Norwegians and Danes in their resistance to Nazi occupation during the Second World War. The Norwegians took to wearing paper clips whilst the Danes wore knitted hats of red, white and blue (the colours of the Royal Air Force) as symbols of their refusal to acquiesce to occupation. The target of such displays was more their fellow-countrymen than the Germans. It constituted a relatively low-risk manifestation of their sympathies that could be recognised by all who knew the 'code'. As such it was a significant statement of solidarity in struggle, and an important factor in maintaining morale. In similar fashion the Palestinians were sending signals of strength and steadfastness to each other by means of their apparel.

However, as the Intifada proceeded into its third year the main target of communication, according to leading spokespersons like Faisal Husseini, had become the Israeli public in an effort to sway opinion in favour of peace negotiations. In interviews with the media and at public meetings in Israel and elsewhere he and others did their utmost to convince the Israeli people that their long term interests resided in recognising the minimal demands of the Palestinians. As they extended the hand of friendship they sought to portray a future in which the two nations would live alongside each other in peace and cooperation. One of the major obstacles that hindered this initiative was the fact that there were a host of different communication channels emanating from the Palestinian camp – not all carrying the same message. The spokespersons of Islamic Jihad and Hamas proclaimed their goal of establishing their Islamic state between the river and the sea, whilst George Habash of the PFLP and others made no secret of their opposition (however 'loyal') to the historic concessions made by the PLO since the start of the Intifada. Meanwhile there were extremist factions from the PLO launching armed assaults on Israel and Israelis. The attack on the beach at Tel Aviv in May 1990, and Arafat's subsequent failure to condemn the raid, did little to assuage Israeli fears concerning the duplicity of the Palestinian leadership. As a journalist with the *Jerusalem Post* expressed it:

> The intended slaughter of bathers and vacationers on the Tel Aviv beach can hardly be called part of an 'armed struggle' against military or police targets, nor can it be blamed on fringe groups, Syrian controlled 'rejectionists' or Iranian fanatics. The operation is nothing short of 'smoking gun' evidence of Arafat's complicity in terrorism.[47]

The reports of Palestinians on their roofs cheering as the Scud missiles fell on Tel Aviv during the Gulf war was sufficient evidence for many Israelis that Palestinian talk of accepting the existence of Israel was just that -- talk and nothing more. In a similar way, the prominence given by the Israeli media to the killing of collaborators by Palestinians served to reinforce the old images of the Palestinian/Arab as blood-thirsty, authoritarian, prone to extremism and, above all, not to be trusted. The consequences of this fundamental ambiguity in the content of the messages that were communicated to the Israeli public by Palestinians will be returned to in the next chapter. At this point it is sufficient to emphasise the fact that if the Israeli 'folk-myth' of the Palestinians as terrorists seeking the destruction of Israel was to be 'de-demonised', then a fundamental prerequisite was a heightened degree of consistency in the content of the communications emanating from the Palestinian camp. No matter how emphatically Palestinian spokespersons denied that the incidents of armed attacks by Palestinians against Israelis had been part of the Intifada, no matter how strenuously they attempted to point out the disproportionality in the injuries inflicted and the casualties suffered, experience showed that one incident of 'terror' and its subsequent amplification by the Israeli media had a much greater impact on Israeli public opinion than any amount of Palestinian civil unarmed resistance and protestations of commitment to peace. As one Israeli woman retorted, when I tried to convince her of the sincerity of Palestinian protestations of their commitment to peaceful co-existence, 'It's alright for you,

you don't travel on the 405 bus each day between Tel Aviv and Jerusalem!' - a reference to the horror of July 1989 when 16 passengers were killed after a young Palestinian had caused the bus to crash down a hillside.

Conclusion

A Canadian supporter of Israel observed in 1989, 'Israel's moral standing is its strongest strategic asset, and the belief in the justice of its cause is the underpinning of its military prowess'.[48] Both the moral standing of Israel in the wider world, and the belief in the justice of its cause in relation to the Intifada within the country itself, suffered severe damage during the course of the Uprising. Although the external threat of Saddam Hussein and Israel's restrained response brought temporary respite during the early months of 1991 in the shape of national unity at home and prestige abroad, the burgeoning of restrictions on the press and the media in general continued to cause fears concerning the state of democracy within Israel. The fact that the restrictions on the media entering the occupied territories during the war were left in place after the cessation of hostilities seemed to indicate that the fog of war was being used to impose a thicker curtain between the outside world and events and developments in the occupied territories.

In a situation where the free activity of journalists was severely restricted, where reports were censored, and where many of the sources of information were avowedly partisan, a crucial role came to be played by human rights monitoring organisations such as the Ramallah-based Al-Haq, the Palestine Human Rights Information Centre, and the Israeli Information Centre for Human Rights in the Occupied Territories (B'Tselem). Relying upon the work of trained fieldworkers spread throughout the occupied territories, such groups maintained a steady supply of authoritative reports on every aspect of human rights abuse during the Uprising. From the Palestinian perspective the significance of the work of such groups increased in proportion to the decline in the media coverage of Intifada-related events. As the weeks and months of resistance turned into years, so there was a marked decline in the intensity and scope of media attention. The 1000 or more 'tourist-trade' journalists who flew in to cover the first months - and saturated the world's media with news, interviews, profiles and prognostications - had moved on by the first summer of the Intifada. This left the 300 or so permanent correspondents to continue the coverage. For a journalist a key determinant of what is considered to be 'news' is what their editor decides will interest their consumers, whether these be readers, listeners or viewers. There are only so many ways to report a curfew, a military siege, a beating, a gassing or a shooting. These were the most obvious manifestations of the Intifada which lent themselves to news reporting, and as time passed this currency became devalued as far as the media was concerned. Moreover by 1990, under the new Minister of Defence Moshe Arens, the Israeli forces had begun to avoid direct confrontations with the civilian population as much as possible, in an effort to overcome much of the negative publicity that such actions had brought upon their heads during the previous two years. The result of these developments was that the Intifada no longer occupied the same prominence and the same space in the world's media.

As items about the Intifada slipped from the TV screens and the pages of the press, so the feeling grew amongst Palestinians that the world had once again forgotten their suffering and their struggle. This sense that the world had grown accustomed to the level of violence within the occupied territories presented a serious dilemma to the leaders of the Uprising. By the summer of 1990 a powerful current of feeling had emerged within Palestinian circles that if they were to recapture the attention of the world, then they needed to heighten the drama of the Intifada. One way to achieve this, it was argued, was by the 'vertical escalation' of the resistance to embrace armed struggle. Critics of this argument urged the 'horizontal escalation' of the Intifada, advocating an approach which would draw more and more people into forms of civil disobedience, involving the construction of counter- institutional structures to meet the basic needs of the population. They urged modes of struggle that would increase and strengthen the Palestinian disengagement from the occupying forces, laying the basis for the future Palestinian state in the process of resistance to Israeli rule. A major problem with such a focus on the deep restructuring of Palestinian society, apart from the sheer enormity of the task in the light of the parlous state of Palestinian economic, educational, cultural, and health- related institutions, was that it would not lend itself to news reporting. What was being proposed was an on-going process rather than a series of events and encounters that would provide the drama and the immediacy necessary to capture the attention of the global media. But what was the alternative? Any recourse to armed struggle would undermine the legitimacy of the struggle in the eyes of the world, and it would play into the hands of right-wing politicians in Israel who saw a simple solution to the problem of the Palestinians: get rid of them, transfer them across the border into Jordan.

But this did not answer the core dilemma faced by advocates of continuing and deepening the unarmed resistance of the Intifada - how to devise a constructive mode of unarmed struggle that would generate enough news to satisfy the hunger of the media (and indirectly the morale of the Palestinians themselves), when the very means of struggle they were advocating was not in itself 'newsworthy', at least according to the criteria applied by the majority of media personnel around the world.

One of the great gifts of Gandhi as a political organiser was his ability to mobilise people around specific issues, to devise forms of resistance that confronted some of the worst evils of the British occupation of India in a constructive and dramatically 'newsworthy' manner. In his campaigns he focused on issues that were of immediate relevance to the people of India, and used these as a vehicle for mobilising people for the wider struggle to transform Indian society. Thus, in his resistance to the Salt Tax he sought to combine non-cooperation with an unjust law with the constructive practice of people making their own salt. Likewise, with the boycott of imported cloth: alongside the resistance campaign and the symbolic burning of British manufactured clothing, he also encouraged people to spin their own cotton and weave their own cloth, thereby helping to lay the foundations for a truly self-reliant India. Palestine was not India, but perhaps there were still lessons to be learned from one of the most famous practitioners of people power.[49]

---

[1] Brian Martin's study of 'backfire' is particularly relevant to this phenomena. See in particular B. Martin, *Backfire manual: Tactics against injustice,* Ed, Sweden: Irene Publishing, 2012.

[2] Quoted in *Reporting harassment*, Jerusalem: Jerusalem Media & Communication Centre, 1989, p. 33.

[3] *Reporting Harassment*, p. 3.

[4] Dina Goren, quoted in D. Mercer et al, *The fog of war*, London: Heinemann, 1987 p. 283.

[5] *The fog of war*, p. 265.

[6] *The fog of war*, p. 10.

[7] *Christian Science Monitor*, March 14 - 20, 1988.

[8] *The Guardian*, March 11, 1988.

[9] I. Black, 'Arabs upstage Israelis in media battle', *The Guardian*, April 8, 1988.

[10] Quoted by Jim Muir, *Middle East International,* May 14 1988, p. 6.

[11] Conversely, much of the news censored from the Arabic press appeared in the Israeli press.

[12] *Reporting harassment*, p. 5.

[13] *Reporting harassment*, p. 15.

[14] *Reporting harassment*, p. 17.

[15] *Reporting harassment*, p. 13.

[16] A Palestinian staff-member, Ribhi al-Aruri, was committed to a six month period of administrative detention and was later adopted by Amnesty International as a prisoner of conscience.

---

[17] It was estimated that during the early months of the Intifada there were up to 1,300 media personnel covering the story, compared to the normal figure of 2 - 300 foreign correspondents.

[18] Quoted in *Reporting harassment*, p. 27.

[19] *Al Fajr*, June 4, 1990, p. 6.

[20] On March 16 1988 all international telephone links from the West Bank and Gaza Strip were suspended. In August 1989 the military issued an order banning the sale, purchase or use of fax machines in the Gaza Strip in a further attempt to reduce the flow of information getting out.

[21] At a Tel Aviv University syrnposium on *Media coverage of the Intifada* an Israeli army spokesperson explained that army reports tended to be less accurate than Palestinian sources because there was normally 70 - 100 metres between the army and protesters and this made it difficult to know exactly how many people had been injured or killed. Reported in *Al Ittihad*, March 30, 1988 and cited in *Al Fajr*, April 3, 1988.

[22] *Al Fajr*, December 11, 1989, p. 5.

[23] *Al Fajr*, June 26, 1989, p. 16.

[24] *Jerusalem Post*, 24 June, 1988.

[25] *The Guardian*, April 26, 1989.

[26] Such threats and attacks were not confined to journalists; politicians were also targeted. The Sicarii were alleged to have been responsible for a bomb that was found in the car of Shimon Peres' wife. See *Al Fajr*, 7 May 1990, p. 9.

[27] *Jerusalem Post*, June 24, 1988.

[28] *Land operations Volume III – Counter revolutionary operations*, British Ministry of Defence, August 1969, quoted in L. Curtis, *Ireland and the Propaganda War*, London: Pluto Press, 1984, p. 229.

[29] *Jerusalem Post (International Edition)*, January 27, 1990, p. 5.

[30] *Jerusalem Post (International Edition)*, July 7, 1990, p. 7.

[31] Quoted in *Jerusalem Post*, April 3, 1989.

[32] D Kuttab, "Battle of wills at Bet Sahour", *Middle East International*, October 20, 1989, p. 10.
[33] See, for example, the report in *Al Fajr*, April 10, 1989, p. 3.
[34] *Jerusalem Post (International Edition)*, November 11, 1989, p. 9.
[35] *The Guardian,* March 3, 1990.
[36] Quoted in *The Guardian*, March 21, 1989.
[37] *The Guardian*, March 23, 1989.
[38] D. Leon, *New Outlook*, May-June 1990, p. 7.
[39] *Hadashot,* November 17, 1988, quoted in *Al Fajr*, November 28, 1988, p. 11.
[40] David Grossman, quoted in *Ha'aretz*, November 18, 1988.
[41] Z. Gilat, 'The Intifada and the Israeli press', *New Outlook*, November-December 1989, p. 39.
[42] D. Kuttab, *Mideast Mirror*, August 24, 1989, p. 10.
[43] See P. Sternberg and A. Oliver, *The graffiti of the Intifada*, East Jerusalem: PASSIA, 1990.
[44] H. Barghouti, quoted in *The Guardian*, July 11, 1988.
[45] See P. Kidron, *Middle East International,* October 20, 1989, p. 9.
[46] In East Jerusalem where the censorship rules were more relaxed the theatre group of Al-Hakawati were able to stage some public performances.
[47] *Jerusalem Post*, May 31, 1990.
[48] Irwin Coder, *Jerusalem Post*, April 2, 1989.
[49] I remain deeply indebted to Bob Overy for these insights into Gandhi's method. See B. Overy, *Gandhi as Political Organiser: An Analysis of Local and National Campaigns in India 1915–1922'*, unpublished Ph.D. thesis, University of Bradford, 1982. Accessible at http://tinyurl.com/omeuz24 (January 14 2015).

Andrew Rigby

8

LINKS IN THE CHAIN – THE RESPONSE OF THE ISRAELI PEACE MOVEMENT

Introduction: 'the great chain of nonviolence'

In his advocacy of nonviolent resistance to oppression, Gandhi laid particular emphasis on the transforming power of self-suffering in the struggle for justice. Through their preparedness to suffer for the cause of truth, he argued, nonviolent activists could convert the oppressor, revealing to them the error of their ways, offering them the possibility of joining in the creative struggle towards a better future from which both sides might benefit. More recent advocates such as Gene Sharp have taken a rather less 'starry-eyed' approach, arguing that nonviolence is an efficient means of waging power-politics, its strength lying in its capacity to erode such sources of an oppressor's power as the morale of the troops and public support at home.

Despite such attempts to wean nonviolence from the embrace of pacifist idealists, it still remains difficult for all but the 'true believers' to accept that nonviolent methods on their own can be an effective means of waging a resistance struggle to a successful conclusion. After all, we have witnessed the terrifying and awesomely repressive powers of totalitarian regimes. We know that state control of the instruments of communication and education can foster a world view that appears to render its subjects immune to any appeals to morality and conscience, denying any claim the victim/opponent might make to a common humanity and, indeed, blaming the victim for whatever horrors are visited upon them. We know that soldiers can go on obeying morally unjustifiable orders - so long as they define their victims as 'other', separate from themselves and thereby less than fully human. It follows from this that there is very little chance of the nonviolence of the dehumanised stirring the consciences of oppressors.

As a general rule the degree of 'shame power' exercised by nonviolent resisters is directly related to the social distance between the parties to the struggle. The shorter the distance, the more likely are the oppressors to perceive their victims as human, recognising them as fellow members of a common humanity. On the basis of such insights Johan Galtung sketched a model of a 'great chain of nonviolence'. The image he presented was of nonviolence communicating its message from group to group, social layer to social layer, until it reached the nucleus of the political structure that was being challenged by civil disobedience and other resistance activities. Thus, in the case of the Israeli-Palestinian conflict, Galtung argued that whilst nonviolent resistance by Palestinians themselves might only exercise a limited degree of shame power, solidarity and support actions by Israeli sympathisers would heighten and multiply the impact upon the morale of the occupying forces and upon Israeli public opinion in general.[1] From this perspective the role of Israeli peace and protest groups opposed to the continued occupation of the West Bank and Gaza Strip becomes a crucial factor effecting the outcome of the struggle. Acting as the conscience of Israeli society, they could point out to their fellow citizens the costs incurred by the routine transgression of those values to which they claimed adherence, raising the spectre of social and political division within the society and state, presenting to the wider international community an alternative vision of the future than that adhered to by the political establishment, working to undermine the claims to legitimacy advanced by those who rejected any possibility of exchanging land for peace. Insofar as they constituted a bridge between the two sides of the struggle, as members of Israeli society and yet feeling some degree of sympathy and even solidarity with the Palestinian cause, the position of such dissidents could never be an easy one. It is the purpose of this chapter to examine their role during the Intifada.

Background

Throughout the history of Zionist immigration to Palestine there was a minority current of opinion that warned of the bitter consequences of discriminating against the Arab population. Brit Shalom (Covenant of Peace), founded in 1925, was Palestine's first recognised peace group. Dominated by Ashkenazi intellectuals, many of them faculty members at the Hebrew University in Jerusalem, they urged that Palestine be recognised as the national home of two peoples with equal rights. The group never had more than a hundred members. It stayed in existence until 1933 but, like its successor in the 1940s Ichud (Unity), it never succeeded in gaining significant public support for its binationalist stance, and had serious problems coming up with practical political proposals that were equally acceptable to both Jews and Arabs. Jews rejected any proposal to limit immigration, whilst the Arabs saw no reason to make any concessions and were profoundly sceptical of a group that had amongst its leading figures individuals who were responsible for purchasing Arab land for Zionist settlement.[2] Generally speaking the fate of Brit Shalom was typical of all the pre-1967 peace groups. They remained small, failed to command much public attention or to attract any significant support.

However, following the 1967 war and the occupation of the West Bank and Gaza Strip the debate about the character of the Israeli society and state took on a new tenor, marked by a basic shift in the approach of most Israeli 'doves'. From advocating a bi-national solution based on equality between the two peoples within a unified state, support emerged for the division of the land. There was little consensus concerning the amount of land to be relinquished in the cause of peace, however, and the different peace groups remained divided amongst themselves, with the Zionist groups split along party political lines and the anti-Zionists, such as the Israeli Socialist Organisation known as Matzpen (Compass), retaining a commitment to their own versions of a bi-nationalist state and thereby rendering themselves exceedingly marginal to mainstream Israeli debate. In fact it was Matzpen and the communists who were the first to begin campaigning for a withdrawal from the newly occupied territories. They remained lone voices for the first decade of occupation as the Zionist doves as a whole did little to arouse public interest in the question of withdrawal. There was still a widespread belief that the Labour-led government was actively pursuing the path of peace, whilst for most Israelis these were years of general satisfaction - there was employment, Israel was powerful, the Arab world was divided, and things were looking good. Far more prominent than any peace movement in the arena of extra-parliamentary activity during these years was the burgeoning Land of Israel Movement, which laid claim to the whole of Palestine as the land of Israel.

The sense of well-being began to crumble rapidly following the October 1973 Yom Kippur War. The feeling of security generated by the occupation of the territories had proved itself ill-founded. The Labour government had shown itself to be incompetent as well as corrupt, both in its lack of preparedness for the war and in its failure to deal with inflation, industrial unrest and the associated social conflicts that came in its wake. As a result the level of public protest around all these issues grew between 1973 and 1977, although it remained predominantly bound within the confines of parliamentary party politics. Thus, many erstwhile supporters of the Labour alignment channelled their activities into the formation of new political parties. Katz (Citizens Rights Movement) was launched in 1973 and

Dash (Democratic Movement for Change) in 1976. They both helped contribute to Labour's electoral defeat in 1977.

In 1977, President Sadat of Egypt broke ranks with the Arab world and visited Jerusalem. The price he demanded for his signature to a peace treaty was the complete withdrawal of Israel from the Sinai and the opening of negotiations on the future of the occupied territories. Whilst the negotiations were taking place the Likud-led government drew up plans to extend the settlement of the West Bank and Gaza Strip in order to ensure permanent Israeli rule over these biblical lands. Appalled at what they saw as a threat to the prospects for peace and seeking to mobilise public pressure, 350 reserve officers and soldiers sent Prime Minister Begin a letter in the spring of 1978 which was published as a petition and eventually obtained some 250,000 signatures. In what became known as 'the officers' letter' they warned:

> A government that prefers the existence of Israel in borders of the greater Israel to its existence in peace in the context of good neighbourly relations will arouse in us grave misgivings. A government that prefers the establishment of settlements across the Green Line to the ending of the historic conflict and to the establishment of a system of normal relations raises questions about the justice of our course. A government policy that leads to the continued rule over one million Arabs is liable to damage the Jewish democratic character of the State, and will make it difficult for us to identify with the basic direction of the State of Israel ... we know that true security will be achieved only with the advent of peace. The strength of the Israeli Defense Forces lies in the identification of its soldiers with the course of the State of Israel.[3]

The publication of the letter created a groundswell of support for what became Shalom Achshav (Peace Now), the most important movement in the Israeli peace camp. At one of its first demonstrations in Tel Aviv in March 1978 some 30,000 participated, unprecedented numbers for Israel, and new adherents continued to swell its ranks. They were urged to form local groups and engage in any activity that was in keeping with the spirit of the letter and the slogans 'Peace is greater than Greater Israel', 'Occupation corrupts', and 'Settlements: an obstacle to peace'. This was as near to a programme that Peace Now went. No positive steps were proposed and the aim, right from the start, was to appeal to as wide a section of the Israeli public as possible. It was an approach that was depicted as trying to move the mainstream of Israeli public opinion 'half a step' at a time, so that eventually the national consensus would come into alignment with Peace Now.

An early indication of the determination not to step beyond the bounds of the 'centre ground' within the Israeli political spectrum came in August 1978, when Peace Now denounced 'The Letter of the Hundred' sent by reserve soldiers to the Minister of Defence declaring that they would refuse to defend Israeli settlements, which they considered to be 'an expression of annexationist aims and of the rejectionist policy of the government' which thwarted peace efforts and endangered 'the Zionist endeavour'.[4] Although Peace Now was prepared to organise demonstrations against such obstacles to the peace process as new settlements, the solidly middle class professional Ashkenazis that constituted the bulk of its adherents were reluctant to endorse any form of action or civil disobedience that could be construed as disloyal to the state of Israel and its democratically elected government. This disavowal by Peace Now of any form of civil disobedience, and its refusal to support any kind of conscientious objection to military service (a particularly controversial step in the Israeli context), continued throughout the Lebanon War. What Peace Now did instead was to hold a series of protest demonstrations urging the withdrawal of Israeli troops from Lebanon, culminating in the mammoth demonstration in Tel Aviv on September 25 1982 when a reported 400,000 people, 20 percent of Israel's adult population, protested together against the massacres in Sabra and Chatila. The event has passed into the folk-memory of Peace Now supporters as the high-point of the movement.

Due to its overriding concern to remain within the mainstream of Israeli political culture and the priority placed on loyalty to the state, Peace Now left considerable space for the emergence of a plurality of more particularistic organisations and groups oriented to specific sections of the Israeli public. One such group that pre-dated the formation of Peace Now, Oz ve Shalom (Courage and Peace), was targeted at religious Jews. Formed in 1975, its main aim was to counter the claims of the Gush Emunim (Bloc of the Faithful) settlers concerning their religious right to the whole of the land of Eretz Israel. In 1982 it joined forces with another group of religious Zionists, Netivot le Shalom (Pathways to Peace). They argued that whatever historical and biblical claim the Jews might have to the whole of the land, the Palestinian desire for national self-determination precluded the fulfilment of this goal and that withdrawal from the occupied territories was essential if Israel was to fulfil its prophetic vocation to be a moral 'light unto the nations'.[5]

Another 'special interest' peace group was formed in 1983. This was East for Peace, and the constituency towards which it was targeted was the Sephardic community of Jews in Israel. It was established as part of an attempt to counter the stereotypical image of the Oriental Jews that had become current amongst the bulk of Peace Now's supporters who came from pre- dominantly European and North American backgrounds. Their essentially racist view of the Jews who had come to Israel from North Africa and the Arab world depicted them as authoritarian, rejectionist hawks who threatened not only the peace process but the future of democracy in Israel itself. Believing that

Peace Now was too 'European-oriented', the small group of Sephardi intellectuals and academics that constituted the core membership of East for Peace tried to link the issue of peace with that of social justice for Israel's poor, amongst whose ranks the Sephardi were disproportionately represented. They argued that the way to peace lay through Israel's integration into the Arab world. - without, it has to be said, achieving much public impact.

A group which had considerably more public and political impact was Yesh Gvul (There is a limit/border). This was founded at the outset of the war in Lebanon by a group of reservists who published a letter declaring their reluctance to perform their military duty beyond the borders of the state of Israel on Lebanese land. During the course of the war some 2,500 reserve soldiers signed the petition, and about 160 of them were tried and sentenced for their refusal to take part in the invasion. When the war in Lebanon ended Yesh Gvul lost much of its impetus, although a small number of activists kept the organisation alive as a support group for those few individuals who refused to serve in the occupied territories. The refusal to perform one's military service because of moral and political concerns was totally abhorrent to Peace Now, which had always stressed the primacy of obeying the legal government of the day, however distasteful its policies. In this Peace Now was completely at one with majority opinion, for whom the IDF constituted one of the few unifying institutions that symbolised both the state and the society of Israel. As such, the refuse-niks of Yesh Gvul defied not only the law but also a very powerful social taboo.

In defending the right to refuse military service, the members of Yesh Gvul stressed that they were not objecting to military duty per se. Rather, they were exercising their moral obligation to refuse to serve in an army that exceeded its legitimate purpose as the Israeli *Defence* Force. As such, theirs was a selective form of conscientious objection. The number of 'absolute objectors' in Israel, people who refused to participate in any form of military activity because of their humanitarian, religious or political principles, had always been minuscule. Such people remained a minority amongst the ranks of dissenters within the Israeli peace and protest movements. And yet, despite their marginality, these few 'wise fools' somehow retained their commitment to the pursuance of peace and reconciliation between the Israeli Jews and the Palestinian Arabs on both sides of the Green Line.

By contrast. Peace Now refrained from sharing its platform with Palestinians sympathetic to the PLO until 1986, when it organised a demonstration in Hebron. In 1981, however, a protest group had been formed that was not exclusively Jewish in composition and which organised demonstrations with Palestinian participation, confronting the occupation authorities in the West Bank in a far more determined manner than Peace Now was prepared to contemplate. This was the Birzeit Solidarity Committee (BSC) which was formed to protest against the closure of the West Bank university in November of that year. Following the reopening of the university the Committee, drawn primarily from the ranks of radical students and faculty at the Hebrew University, decided to widen its focus to the occupation as a whole. It became the first Israeli peace group to move its political activity beyond the Green Line into the territories themselves. As one of the founder members recalled,

> We wanted to show the Palestinians that some Israelis are willing to risk beating and tear-gassing. The army would not kill us because we are Jews ... But our presence on the West Bank stirred a lot of enthusiasm among the local population. We went to Ramallah, Hebron, Dheisha refugee camp - wherever repression took place - and put a spotlight on many dark corners of the occupation which the Israeli public would have preferred to pretend did not exist.[6]

Critical of Peace Now's vagueness concerning the future status of the occupied territories and accusing it of opposing the occupation for the purely selfish reasons of the damage it inflicted upon Israeli society, the BSC was unequivocal in its call for total withdrawal from the territories and the evacuation of all Jewish settlers, accompanied by negotiations with the PLO leading to the formation of an independent Palestinian state with East Jerusalem as its capital. Not surprisingly, such a radical stance was complete anathema to Peace Now, who prohibited the participation of the BSC in any of its demonstrations.

With the Israeli invasion of Lebanon in 1982 the BSC changed its name to the Committee Against the War in Lebanon (CAWL) and on June 8 broke the Israeli taboo on staging protests whilst fighting was still going on by organising the first anti-war demonstration. At a later demonstration many adherents of Peace Now attended, frustrated at the silence of their own leadership - thereby prompting Peace Now to organise its own anti-war rally a few weeks later. This also set a pattern that was to be repeated in the future whereby Peace Now would leave it to one or more of the smaller peace groups to organise protests around controversial issues, and only after the mood of public opinion had been tested would they mobilise their own resources.

Early in 1985 the BSC spawned another committee - the Committee Confronting the Iron Fist (CCIF). Unlike the BSC the membership was predominantly Palestinian, but it also included some of the Israeli members of the original grouping. They organised demonstrations and other actions aimed at drawing attention to the deportations, administrative detentions, collective punishments and all the other facets of the 'iron fist' policy. An interesting feature of the CCIF was the feet that whilst the Israeli and Palestinian members failed to agree on a common political platform, both sides were prepared to work together to protest against the occupation, as an exercise to further dialogue and mutual understanding. A similar motivation lay behind the formation of an avowedly nonviolent grouping that went under the name of Palestinians and Israelis for Non-violence. Affiliated to the International Fellowship of Reconciliation, this group worked primarily as a support network for the Palestinian Centre for the Study of Nonviolence (PCSN) which had been established in East Jerusalem by Mubarak Awad in 1985.[7]

Born in Jerusalem, Awad had spent the bulk of his adult life in the United States where he had come across the writings of Gandhi, Martin Luther King and Gene Sharp amongst others. He became convinced that nonviolent methods were the most effective means of resisting the Israeli occupation, and he outlined the key features of such a strategy in an article in the Journal of Palestine Studies in 1984. After his return to Jerusalem Awad tried to interest Palestinians in nonviolent methods of resistance, holding seminars and workshops, urging people to boycott Israeli products, offering assistance to villagers whose land had been expropriated, running a small mobile library, and publishing Arabic translations of some of the classic works on nonviolence. One of the most widely publicised of the Centre's actions was the attempt to plant olive tree seedlings near the village of Quattanyah to replace the original trees that had been uprooted by the Israelis. The action took place on January 25 1986, Israel's national tree-planting day! In Awad's own words:

> On the day of the planting, over a hundred Israelis and foreigners joined with the villagers. We began to plant the seedlings. Israeli soldiers arrived too and began to pull them up, but the planters outnumbered the soldiers. We planted seedlings faster than they could be uprooted. We sat by the plants, protecting them with a nonviolent presence. Then the major came and said, 'OK, hold on. The trees can stay and you go to court to resolve the problem.' We agreed. But the next day, when we came back with an Israeli TV producer who was filming a story

> about the trees, we found they had been uprooted. The story was on Israeli television. The result was that we lost those seedlings, but our action and the military response publicised what was happening all the time to the Palestinians - their land being confiscated, their lives destroyed. So the villagers had proved that, in a nonviolent way, they could confront the authorities and their guns.[8]

This account is indicative of the ebullience and optimism that Awad displayed. In fact the Centre faced many problems, not the least of which concerned finding an appropriate Arabic term for nonviolence that did not carry with it connotations of passivity and acceptance. Awad was further handicapped by his organisational isolation within the Palestinian community. He lacked the sponsorship of any of the key political personalities or factions. He was a United States citizen with an American passport, and he was a Christian. Moreover, his Arabic was not very good - when Palestinians heard him calling for the formation of a nonviolent organisation suspicions were aroused that he planned to launch an alternative to the existing organisation i.e. the PLO. In fact during the pre-intifada period it seemed that Mubarak Awad received a more sympathetic hearing from Israelis than from Palestinians, which did little to allay the doubts in some quarters about his nationalist credentials.

Similar suspicions were entertained on the Israeli side of the divide concerning those who insisted on engaging in dialogue with the 'enemy'. Meetings between Israelis and the PLO had begun on a more or less regular basis early in the 1970s. Most of these involved anti-Zionist Israelis, however, and had little impact on the Israeli public or political establishment. By the mid-1970s the pace had quickened, a trend marked by the formation in 1975 of the Israeli Council for Israel-Palestine Peace, whose members affirmed their readiness to take part in a dialogue 'with all Palestinian elements who are ready to promote contacts between the two peoples of this country'.[9] At the heart of this development was Uri Avnery who, from that date, kept the Israeli government fully informed of his meetings with senior PLO representatives. Indeed, by the 1980s increasing numbers of Israeli peace activists had proven themselves willing to sit down with the PLO. In order to forestall what it feared was a growing public readiness to accept the 'terrorist organisation' as a partner in talks concerning territorial compromise, the National Unity government responded in August 1986 by passing legislation that outlawed such meetings, thereby creating the opportunity for peace movement activists to court political martyrdom by defying the law.

In summary, by the outbreak of the Intifada the extra-parliamentary protest wing of the Israeli peace camp could be characterised as a loosely structured movement composed of a number of separate organisations. At the hub was Peace Now, an umbrella movement targeted at the mainstream of Israeli public opinion. Lacking any clear organisational structure, having no formal members as such and few full-time officials, vague concerning practical peace proposals and eager to avoid confrontation with the government, especially when the Labour Alignment was in power - Peace Now still remained the only organisation capable of mobilising people on a mass scale. Around it was arrayed a variety of more particularistic groups aiming their message at different sections of Israeli society and reflecting a range of political stances, from the religious Zionism of Oz ve Shalom through to anti-Zionist advocates of a democratic secular state.

Peace Now had always predicated its approach on the democratic nature of the Israeli state, believing that if sufficient people could be convinced of the need to recognise the Palestinians' right to some form of self-determination, then this would impact on policy-makers. Their prime target was that sizeable proportion of the population which was ambivalent about the issue of the territories, with a genuine yearning for peace but a lack of any clear notion of how this might be achieved. In trying to arrive at some assessment of its performance during the years prior to the Intifada there were a number of criteria by which it could be adjudged to have been successful. It had proven itself capable of mobilising large numbers of people on its occasional mass demonstrations. In the process it had succeeded in attracting media attention and forcing the government to take its views into account, particularly with regard to the institution of a commission of inquiry into the Sabra and Chatila massacres and the subsequent withdrawal, albeit partial, from Lebanon. On the central issue of the Israeli-Palestinian conflict however its efforts seemed to have borne less fruit. Whereas public opinion polls in 1968 revealed a solid majority of Israelis (around 70 percent) expressing a preparedness to return the recently acquired territories (apart from East Jerusalem) to Arab sovereignty for the sake of peace, by 1986 this figure had dropped to 41 percent, with 50 percent opposed and nine percent unsure.[10]

In seeking to explain this relative failure to shift the scales of public opinion in favour of territorial compromise Peace Now activists tended to blame the Oriental Jews who provided the bulk of the support for the Likud bloc. However, looking beyond such scapegoats, Mordechai Bar-On identified five factors underpinning this apparent shift towards a more hawkish posture.

1. The strong emotional attachment felt by Israeli Jews for the land of the occupied territories where so much of Biblical history took place.
2. That element in Zionist thinking that believed in the sovereignty of collective will-power, whatever the obstacles. This enabled Israelis to ignore realities such as the existence of the Palestinians living under occupation.
3. That contradictory mix in the Israeli psyche which others have referred to as the 'national siege syndrome'. This combined a deep sense of fear, based on the conviction that the outside world was basically hostile and antagonistic, with a

belief that the maintenance of a significant deterrent strength would be sufficient to counter all dangers.

4. An increasing lack of faith in the possibility of peace.
5. The incidence of Arab violence against Israelis and Jews which, according to Bar-On, constituted the most immediate and apparent factor contributing to Israel's intransigence in relation to the Palestinians.[11]

It was these factors that fed into the emergence of a 'New Zionism' in the situation created by the occupation of the West Bank and Gaza Strip. The standard-bearers of this creed, which had its antecedents with Jabotinsky and the Revisionist Zionists, were the members of the Land of Israel Movement and the religious-nationalists of Gush Emunim. These were the new 'pioneers" charged with the sacred task of 'redeeming the promised land' and rejuvenating the Jewish nation in the process. The defeat of Labour and the election of Begin's Likud government in 1977 gave these new pioneers a new legitimacy. It was the disquiet of the adherents of the old Labour Zionism with this new trend, coupled with the emergence of more extreme groups such as Kahane's Kach, who advocated the expulsion of all Arabs from the Land of Israel, which provided the impetus behind the formation of Peace Now. In an effort to counterbalance the appeal of this 'New Zionism', the ideologues of Peace Now consistently advocated a 'sane Zionism', which, they argued, could not be reconciled with the domination by force of some 1.5 million Palestinians. It was in this sense that Peace Now affirmed that the 'Palestinian problem' was in essence an 'Israeli problem' and they saw themselves as leading a moral crusade for the soul of Zionism, reflecting the conviction of Martin Buber that 'Independence of one's own must not be gained at the expense of another's independence'. The vision was of a democratic, tolerant, pluralistic Zionist state and society, with security resting upon harmonious co-existence with its neighbours in the region - quite how this was to be achieved was never spelled out with any clarity.

The mushrooming of Israeli peace and protest groups

At the outbreak of the Intifada the Israeli peace movement lay relatively dormant, and Peace Now was slow to respond to the new situation. Whereas its vagueness with regard to the conflict with the Palestinians presented no great problem so long as the major political issues in Israel were matters of 'foreign policy' such as peace with Egypt and withdrawal from Lebanon, its reluctance to step beyond the bounds of national consensus with regard to the occupied territories (occasionally expressed as the 'Three no's': No withdrawal from the 1967 borders, No Palestinian state, and No negotiations with the PLO) immobilised the organisation during the early weeks of the Uprising. Its failure to call out its supporters in protest or to issue any statement of outrage or dissent from government attempts to suppress the Uprising by force was attributed by some observers to the close links that many Peace Now activists had with the Labour Party, one of whose senior leaders was the Minister of Defence and as such a major architect of that policy.

Into the vacuum thereby created a proliferation of groups and initiatives emerged. The majority of these were segmental groupings representing particular sections of Israeli society, lacking any clear programmatic prescriptions for action beyond a general commitment to urge a political rather than a military solution. A second category consisted of specific task-oriented groups which also eschewed any firm attachment to any particular platform or political stand-point, but expressed their commitment to a peace agenda by organising their activities around particular aspects of the occupation. A third category of groups aspired to operate nationally, with definite political programmes aimed at bringing the occupation to an end and leading to a peace settlement. Alongside all these new groups, Yesh Gvul rose once more into the limelight, seeking to advise and support the increasing numbers of reservists with doubts about serving in the occupied territories. What follows is a brief overview of the range of groups that mushroomed into the public domain in the context of the Intifada.

1. Professional groups

Amongst the protest groups that drew their participants from particular sections of Israeli society, there emerged a surprisingly large number of 'professional' organisations and committees. Their activity might consist of little more than sending occasional letters to the press or publishing statements expressing their concern, but more often it went beyond that. Thus, medical doctors organised a group called Physicians Against the Occupation, working as a pressure group in solidarity with Palestinian colleagues to draw attention to the state of health facilities in the occupied territories. Mental health workers including psychiatrists, psychologists, social workers and the like formed Mental Health Workers for the Advancement of Peace, issuing petitions and organising conferences and meetings to warn about the implications of the occupation on the mental health of the young soldiers and their victims. Academics in Tel Aviv formed Ad Caan (Thus Far and No Further), inviting guest lecturers from the West Bank and Gaza Strip, holding seminars, teach-ins and sit-ins, protesting in particular against the closure of Palestinian universities, seeking to draw upon their professional status and expertise to add weight to their political interventions. Creative writers and artists organised themselves into a joint Israeli-Palestinian committee - one with the longest name of them all: Israeli and Palestinian Writers, Artists and Academics Committee Against the Occupation and for Peace and Freedom to Create! On June 13 1988 they signed what they claimed to be the first peace treaty between Israelis and Palestinians, thereby illustrating in the words of one of their number, 'that it was possible to reach a compromise, with pain and gritted teeth ... for the sake of the future of the two peoples, whose common interest was to live together and not die together'.[12]

In drawing up a peace treaty, the committee had to confront the difficult issues of the future of Jerusalem and the Palestinian right of return. Most groups avoided such specifics for the sake of maintaining unity within their ranks, confining their positive political proposals to the demand that peace negotiations with the Palestinians be commenced as a matter of urgency to end the occupation. This was particularly the case with groupings that sought to appeal to whole strata of Israeli society such as the youth, with groups like Youth Against the Occupation and Youth for Refusal being formed.

2. Women's groups

More remarkable than the emergence of youth groups was the prominent role quickly taken by women in the protest activities. On December 2 1988 150 women participated in a women's peace gathering to mark one year of the Intifada. Linking the oppression of women to that of the Palestinians, the organisers affirmed:

> We, as feminists who daily wage war against oppression in our society, are especially sensitive to the oppression of other groups and peoples, men and women alike. We believe that the rules of this game, which divide the world into victims and oppressors, the victorious and the vanquished, are not the ones which will bring a just solution to all sides in the Israeli-Palestinian conflict.[13]

The gathering led to the formation of Reshet (The Women's Network for Peace). Amongst the affiliates was one of the earliest women's groups to be founded in response to the Intifada, Shani (Israeli Women Against the Occupation). Shani was started in Jerusalem in January 1988 with the aim of helping women develop a more informed political basis to the emotions aroused by the outrages being perpetrated in the occupied territories. Discussion meetings, seminars, public lectures, fact-finding trips and solidarity visits to the West Bank constituted its programme, complemented by the occasional nonviolent training session in preparation for demonstrations and other actions.

Undoubtedly the best known and most highly publicised women's nonviolent protest action in which members of Shani and other groups participated was that known as Women in Black. Each Friday lunchtime at major intersections in Jerusalem, Tel Aviv and Haifa women dressed in black stood in silent vigil, holding placards in the shape of a hand signalling 'Stop!' with the slogan 'End the Occupation'. They would stand together for an hour or so, enduring verbal abuse and harassment from vehicle drivers passing by and from counter-demonstrators. The protests, which had started in January 1988, constituted a visibly powerful and politically impressive form of witness. Its origins lay with a group of Jerusalemite women who decided to hold a demonstration in protest against the murder of women and children in the Gaza Strip. On that first Friday in France Square in West Jerusalem they decided they should return the following week. The regular Women in Black became a familiar sight, and in June 1988 similar weekly pickets were started in Tel Aviv and Haifa. As one of the initiators explained:

> For women it is easier to express themselves as women rather than just as people. Women are also more persistent in fulfilling their commitments, which explains why these demonstrations have lasted for such a long time. We avoid any attempt to define political programmes for ourselves - there are many other structures for this - so as to keep those things which unite us, and to continue to identify ourselves as women, without a political identification.[14]

Another project launched by women was the Peace Quilt. Some 5000 Israeli women participated in the creation of a cloth made up of individual squares - each embodying a personal statement about peace. The quilt, about 200 metres in length, was started in January 1988 and was eventually displayed in front of the Knesset in June of that year as a symbolic peace cloth for the negotiating table.

3. Ad hoc groups

Parents Against Moral Erosion was established as a mutual support and pressure group by parents of IDF soldiers, concerned about what they considered to be the impossible dilemmas faced by their children serving in the occupied territories and the impact this was having upon them. Alongside the opening of a 'Hotline for Soldiers' Parents', they also added their voices to those calling upon the government to start negotiations for a political settlement.

A group representing a somewhat smaller section of the community was Israelis by Choice/ Olim (new immigrants) against the Occupation. This was formed by a group of American immigrants at the time when Mubarak Awad was fighting against his deportation order. They sought to highlight the cruel paradox that they, as Jews born in North America, enjoyed the right to live and be politically active in Jerusalem; a right denied to someone such as Awad who was actually born in the city. Following his eventual deportation in June 1988 they organised a daily picket outside the Prime Minister's official residence in Jerusalem for a couple of hours each afternoon calling for an end to the occupation.

Another group which established a regular pattern of protest during 1989 was Runners for Peace. Most Fridays a group of Israelis from Jerusalem joined with some Palestinians from the Bethlehem area for an afternoon run, wearing T-shirts bearing the slogan 'We want peace between Palestine and Israel, both free and secure'. Like other groups that sought to engage in joint protest activity with Palestinians, these political sportsmen encountered selective harassment from the military who tended to focus their attentions on the Palestinian participants - including the detention of one 19 year old runner from Aida refugee camp.

4. Task groups

Few of the protest groups had any kind of formal membership and most of the activists participated in the activities of more than one group. Thus, many of those who regularly devoted a portion of their time to standing on a picket-line or helped to draft petitions and letters of protest would also be likely to be involved in one or other of the task-oriented groups that had been formed. These organised their actions around a specific aspect of the occupation, with the purpose of extending relief, solidarity and support to those Palestinians who suffered as a consequence of their resistance activities. Thus, amongst the women who participate in the weekly vigils of Women in Black one could find members of the Women's Organisation for Political Prisoners (WOPP). Formed in May 1988 in response to the harassment of Palestinian women by the security forces, the group's aim was to support women who had been imprisoned in Israeli jails for their social and political resistance activity and whom WOPP considered to be 'political prisoners'. Its work developed on a number of fronts. At one level it acted as a relief agency: visiting prisoners, collecting and distributing food and clothing for their families, and engaging in other forms of welfare activity. It also worked to arouse Israeli and international opinion against the denial of prisoners' basic rights: illegal arrests and administrative detentions; lack of proper medical care - particularly for pregnant women; the refusal of the authorities to allow breast-feeding women to keep their child with them in prison ; using women prisoners as hostages to bring pressure to bear on their family and friends.

WOPP was typical of other task groups insofar as the participants did not share a political platform or ideology. What united them was their opposition to the occupation, and their commitment to struggling against it by working around a particular issue, in this case the plight of women political prisoners. In similar fashion, the Committee for Beita was formed in April 1988, following the military reprisals against the village which resulted in the deportation of twelve of the villagers and the destruction of sixteen houses and the subsequent campaign by settlers to have the entire village destroyed. A group of about 30 Israeli men and women took it upon themselves to assist in the rehabilitation of the village. Builders and architects offered their services to repair the damaged homes and replace those that had been demolished, whilst lawyers launched a legal campaign to obtain compensation for the villagers and arranged legal aid for those who were prosecuted for their involvement in defending themselves from the settlers on that day in April 1988 when two of their number and a young Israeli woman were shot dead.[15]

Other groups that came into existence during the Intifada with a similar focus upon a particular dimension of the occupation, without requiring of its members any firm commitment to any single political programme, included Shomer Achiv (His Brother's Keeper - the Rabbinic Human Rights Watch). An exceedingly rare phenomenon in Israel, the group consisted of a coalition of rabbis from orthodox, reform and conservative streams who got together early in 1989 to stress the moral imperatives of Judaism and to 'cry out against the growing acts of humiliation, degradation and abasement against the Palestinian people'.[16] It concentrated primarily on the paucity of medical facilities in the occupied territories and the attempts to use health care as an instrument of control and suppression. In acting as a pressure group to bring about changes in Israeli policy, its members would draw upon their religious credentials to add weight and legitimacy to their task. In similar manner, the Committee Against Torture in Israel, which was formed in April 1990, included amongst its members lawyers, psychiatrists, criminologists and physicians who could lay claim to relevant expertise in their efforts to publicise cases of torture and press for its abolition as a means of interrogation in Israel.

The best known of the human rights organisations was B'Tselem ('In the image'), the Israeli Information Centre for Human Rights in the Occupied Territories. Established in December 1988, it received (in association with its Palestinian equivalent, Al Haq) a Jimmy Carter Award for 'profound commitment to human decency and the protection of human rights' in 1989. Its aim was to provide an authoritative monitoring and publicising of human rights abuses in the territories by means of monthly bulletins, special reports, and parliamentary questions placed by some of the Knesset members who were on its board. As its director explained, 'Our main aim is to tell the Israeli public what is going on. Our geographical area is the territories; but our target is the Israeli citizen'.[17] On a more personal level, she confessed, 'I don't want to be the conscience of this country, but if my children ask me in the future what I did during the Intifada, I'll at least be able to say: "I did my bit. I was one of those who warned."'[18]

Whilst B'tselem acted primarily as a documentation centre and refrained from taking up individual cases, this became the focus of another human rights group, Hotline for the Victims of Violence, staffed by Israelis and Palestinians. It started out primarily as an agency to assist Palestinian victims of military and settler violence, helping them to file complaints with the appropriate authorities. Increasingly, however, it came to operate as a missing persons bureau. Almost half the requests for help during 1989 came from people trying to locate friends and relatives who had been arrested, 20 percent of cases concerned physical violence, 16 percent damage to property, and 18 percent other abuses.[19]

One of the human rights abuses which particularly concerned Palestinians during 1989 was the deportation of those lacking the proper residency permits required by the Israeli authorities. By the end of that year some 250 Palestinians, mainly wives and children, had been deported to Jordan because they did not have the necessary 'legal' status for permanent residence according to the military government. A number of Israeli organisations joined the campaign around this issue, including the Association for Civil Rights in Israel, and in June 1990 it was announced that the 250 expellees would be allowed to return. However, this still left a considerable number of Palestinian families whose spouses remained separated because one or other of them lacked the necessary documentation to reside permanently in the West Bank or Gaza Strip. A voluntary group, Israelis for Family Reunification, was formed to work alongside the Palestinian Centre for the Study of Nonviolence in a joint campaign around this issue of 'invisible transfer', the idea being that an Israeli family would 'adopt' a Palestinian family and take up their case with the appropriate authorities. The initiative for the formation of the group came from members of The Twenty-First Year, one of the few Israeli peace groups that had come into existence in response to the Intifada with some kind of political programme and set of proposals of how Israelis should act to advance the peace process.

5. Political groups

The label 'political groups' is applied in this context to those groups within the extra-parliamentary Israeli peace camp that laid claim to a more defined political identity than the sectional and task-oriented groups. They included The Twenty-First Year, Dai la Kibbush (End the Occupation), and Hala ha-Kibbush (Down with the Occupation). Discerning the exact nature of their political identities and the differences that existed between them could be a rather tortuous task for those unfamiliar with the history and sectarian practices of non-Zionist political factions in Israel. Indeed one activist advised me that the key factor distinguishing each of these three groups was their geographical base: Hala ha-Kibbush was strongest in Tel Aviv and Haifa, Dai la Kibbush in Jerusalem, and (according to some cynics) The Twenty-First Year was strongest in the Hebrew University, particularly amongst the associate professors!

The Twenty First Year was launched in December 1987 on the initiative of a lecturer in Philosophy at the Hebrew University in Jerusalem. Its founding statement committed the signatories to 'refuse to collaborate with the system of occupation in all of its manifestations'. They argued that the occupation was total, embracing the cultural, economic and political life within the territories and within Israel - deforming Israelis as well as Palestinians. As the occupation was total in its effects, so resistance needed to be total and wide-ranging. They called for a boycott of goods produced by settlers, they urged Israeli Jews not to go to the occupied territories, they supported those who refused to do military service within the territories, and encouraged members to examine the curricula of their local schools and to challenge any content that presented a distorted version of the occupation. The Twenty-First Year also organised solidarity and fact-finding visits to the occupied territories, frequently arranged in coordination with other groups such as Dai la Kibbush.

Dai la Kibbush traced its origins to the original 'Committees' (BSC/CAWL/CCIF). Shortly before the outbreak of the Intifada a few surviving members of the original groupings formed Dai la Kibbush For Israeli-Palestinian Peace. Its platform contained the unconditional demand to end the occupation and called for the recognition of the PLO and the commencement of negotiations at an international peace conference leading to the establishment of a Palestinian state alongside Israel. Its activists were drawn from a range of left-wing and non-Zionist parties - their historical rivalries seemingly irrelevant in the context of the Intifada. However, it had no formal membership list and tried to practise the experiment of having a revolving executive with new people taking over coordinating functions each month. Weekly meetings were to plan such activities as demonstrations and leafleting, house meetings for dialogue between Israelis and Palestinians, and the regular Saturday solidarity visits to a village or refugee camp in the occupied territories

The structure and functioning of Hala ha Kibbush followed a similar pattern. It was formed in 1985 with a membership drawn primarily from the left wing of the Israeli Communist Party whose members had also been active in the 'Committees'. It initiated a number of protest actions but its level of activity increased dramatically with the outbreak of the Intifada. Seeking to appeal to activists with a variety of political positions who were united in their opposition to the occupation and willing to express concrete solidarity with the Palestinian struggle in the West Bank and Gaza Strip, the organisation eschewed any detailed political solution to the conflict - confining itself to an affirmation of unconditional support for the Intifada and the demand for immediate withdrawal from the occupied territories.[20] As was remarked above, Hala ha Kibbush was particularly active in Tel Aviv and Haifa. It was instrumental in organising the first food convoy to the Gaza Strip in January 1988 and held regular collections of toys and learning materials for the children of Jabaliya Camp, alongside its regular pickets, vigils, leafleting, solidarity visits, house meetings, and participation in joint actions and demonstrations with other groups.

There is a well-known saying about Israelis to the effect that whenever six of them are gathered together you will hear seven different opinions - the peace camp provided little evidence to doubt the veracity of this observation! However, the different groupings made efforts to coordinate their activities by means of occasional national gatherings. At the city level, such as in West Jerusalem, coordinating meetings were held much more frequently with each group reporting on their planned actions and seeking the cooperation of the others. The result was that the dangers of stultification occasioned by the dominance of a single organisation were minimised, and whilst outsiders might have found the range of groups confusing and the duplication of effort wasteful - the activists themselves seemed quite happy to live with such a fluid and flexible infrastructure.

6. Yesh Gvul

The massive deployment of troops in the occupied territories in order to suppress the Intifada led to that much remarked upon phenomenon - 'shooting and weeping'. Protest songs exploring the themes of guilt and responsibility became popular during the Intifada. One of them, 'Shooting and Crying' by Si Hyman, contained the refrain:

> Boys play with lead, girls with steel dolls;
> Life looks different in the shadow of filth.
> Shooting and crying, burning and laughing,
> When did we ever learn to bury people alive?
> Shooting and crying, burning and laughing.
> When did we ever forget that our children too
> have been killed?[21]

In another, 'Chad Gadya' by Chava Alberstein, the questions were asked:

> Till when will the circle of horror continue?
> The prosecutor and the prosecuted
> The one who beats and the one who is beaten
> When will this madness end?
> I was once a peaceful lamb and kid
> Today I am a preying tiger and wolf
> I've already been a dove and I have been a deer
> Today I don't know what I am any more.[22]

This was the kind of refrain one could hear again and again from those who were opposed to the occupation, but felt that they must meet their obligations to the state by fulfilling their military duty and serving in the army, even an army of occupation. They argued that during their tour of duty they could act as a restraining influence upon the 'Rambos' in their unit - humane agents of civilisation in the brutal world of occupier and occupied. These were the people like the restaurateur, a Peace Now sympathiser, who was serving his journalist friends a meal one week and angrily confronting them with a rifle the next, as he prevented them from entering a closed military area. They were the people like the man I accompanied on a 'peace convoy" to the West Bank in the late spring of 1989. The aim was for members of the Israeli peace camp to visit Palestinian communities as friends, rather than as occupiers. Our contingent visited a village a few miles north west of Hebron. After a couple of hours sitting and talking in the sun, my companion indicated he wanted to leave. As we walked down the road to his car he was obviously in some distress as he confessed:

> I'm bored. It achieves nothing. Why do I still continue in this kind of activity? OK - the media were here and we may influence Israeli public opinion. But next month I know I will be driving down these same roads in a jeep, wearing my uniform! Do you realise that I spend one twelfth of my life here - just trying to get through my thirty days reserve duty without being injured and not hurting anyone else!

A minority of Israelis tried to resolve their dilemma by refusing to serve as agents of occupation. The overall number of 'refuseniks" during the Intifada is unknown. More than a hundred soldiers, over 90 percent of them reservists, were jailed, some of them repeatedly. But hundreds more avoided prison sentences due to the action of their commanding officers who assigned them to duties that did not clash with their consciences regarding the occupation and the treatment of Palestinians - a solution that suited both sides insofar as it kept the objectors out of the headlines as well as out of jail.[23] Yesh Gvul was the movement to which all these people turned for advice, support and counselling.

Yesh Gvul was a strange entity, a soldiers' movement that was a part of the wider peace movement. It tried to steer a difficult path between the law and morality, refraining from urging disaffection upon reservists and soldiers, whilst pointing out that they had a duty to disobey illegal orders; reluctant to adopt specific political positions in order to avoid division within its ranks, yet participating with other organisations and groups in peace demonstrations and related actions. Very few of the people associated with Yesh Gvul were what one would term 'absolutist' in their objection to military service. Theirs was a selective objection to service in the occupied territories rather than to military service *per se.* A very few moved beyond this boundary and adopted the stance of the total resister, either because of pacifist conviction or through the realisation that the performance of any role within the IDF involved participation, however indirectly, in the occupation.

One of those who came to this conclusion was Adam Keller. In April 1988 he had been arrested whilst on reserve duty. Not content with putting up 'Stop the Occupation' stickers around the base near Tel Aviv where he was stationed, he had spray-painted peace slogans on 117 parked tanks, armoured personnel carriers and trucks! He was fined, demoted from corporal to private and sentenced to nine months imprisonment, with six months suspended. Early in 1990 this one man graffiti commando was drafted for reserve duty once again. This time he refused even to don the uniform, arguing 'The IDF was founded as the Israeli Defence Forces, but it has become the Israeli occupation forces, an instrument to oppress another people. I refuse to be a smoothly working cog in that machine.'[24] Sentenced to 28 days in prison, he began a hunger strike after being forced to wear military uniform. On his release he was exempted from future reserve service for 'psychiatric reasons'. As far as he was concerned 'If such an army calls me 'crazy', then crazy I am proud to be'.[25]

7. *Peace Now*

There can be little doubt that most of the leading figures in Peace Now would endorse the use of such an epithet to describe the stance of activists such as Keller. As far as Peace Now was concerned, those who refused military service placed themselves beyond the parameters of the national consensus and thereby rendered themselves politically irrelevant. Indeed, Peace Now (along with the relatively conservative pressure group Council for Peace and Security) prided itself on the prominent role played by senior reserve officers in its activities as a means of securing legitimacy for its pronouncements.[26] As already noted it consistently refused to endorse any confrontation with the authorities or any form of civil disobedience for fear of alienating public opinion. Its leaders likened it to a train, moving slowly towards its destination - people could get on and off the 'peace train' whenever they wanted, according to the extent of their identification with its speed and direction. The secret of its ability to mobilise thousands of people lay, so it was argued, in its ability to deliver a sophisticated and balanced phrasing of its political positions which 'advanced the consensus by half a step and have drawn it gradually to our side'.[27] Thus, whilst reservists were refusing to serve in the occupied territories and members of the more marginal anti-occupation groups were getting themselves arrested in pickets and demonstrations of solidarity with the Palestinians, Peace Now continued to plough its centrist furrow. The problem was that, under the impact of the Intifada, this notional middle ground became narrower and narrower.

It is generally agreed that one of the most significant consequences of the Intifada with regard to Israeli public opinion was an increasing polarisation of political opinion, with a corresponding intrusion into mainstream political debate of viewpoints that had previously been considered beyond the pale. Thus, on the right, the extremist views advocating the 'transfer' of the Palestinians, which had previously been the preserve of Kahane and Kach, had become a legitimate policy preference endorsed by significant sections of the electorate. Likewise, at the other pole, the need to recognise the PLO as a partner in talks leading to the formation of a Palestinian state alongside Israel had become an increasingly commonplace assumption amongst sectors of the population. The result was that the national consensus based on the Three No's disintegrated. To some observers it seemed as if a situation had been created whereby no one in Israel could afford the luxury of being neutral about the Intifada. The occupation and the Intifada could not be separated, and could not be ignored. Peace Now could not remain untouched by this process and by the summer of 1988 some of its leading figures, particularly some of those from the Tel Aviv area, were talking in private of the need to recognise the PLO following King Hussein's relinquishment of his claim to the West Bank. The subsequent failure of the Labour Alignment to make any substantial gains in the general election created the conditions necessary for the leadership of Peace Now to take the decisive step of launching a campaign under the slogan 'There is a Partner for Discussion. Speak with the PLO', calling for direct negotiations on the basis of mutual recognition and the cessation of violence. A month later, on December 24 somewhere in the region of 10 - 15,000 marchers participated in the first demonstration organised by Peace Now against the government's refusal to talk to the PLO. None of the other groups could dream of getting so many people out on the streets on a wet Saturday evening, and hopes began to rise that this was a harbinger of a mass mobilisation against the government's intransigence.

1990: Time for peace

The truth of the matter is that Peace Now failed to mobilise anything like the numbers that came out onto the streets to protest against the invasion of Lebanon in 1982. Indeed, by the early months of 1989 the activity of the peace camp in general had reached a plateau as Peace Now followed the lead established by the smaller protest groups in organising peace convoys and solidarity visits to the neighbours across the Green Line.

Whilst still refusing to support the refuse-niks of Yesh Gvul, by 1989 its members were beginning to adopt slightly more confrontational approaches in their pursuance of peace. In May

1988 Peace Now had planned a motorcade to Nablus to distribute leaflets expressing comradeship with the Palestinians. The symbolism of the event was somewhat diluted by their acceptance of the restrictions imposed by the military authorities who insisted on providing an escort, forbade the handing out of leaflets and the display of banners, and stipulated that there were to be no meetings with Palestinians. The final rally was held on the rifle-range of a military camp outside Nablus! By September 1989 Peace Now activists were prepared to try and break the curfew imposed on Beit Sahour and, as a further expression of solidarity announced their intention of purchasing items confiscated by the Israeli tax gatherers when they came up for auction, with the aim of 'leasing' the goods back to the villagers in order to prevent their subsequent confiscation.

Despite the undoubted radicalisation of Peace Now, it was still wary in its dealings with other protest groups, as was revealed by the delicate negotiations that preceded the 1990:Time for Peace international peace rally that took place in Jerusalem at the end of December 1989. The original initiative had come from the Associazione per la Pace (Italian Peace Association) and was taken up by the UN - affiliated International Coordinating Committee for Non-Governmental Organisations on the Question of Palestine (ICCP). In September 1989 a delegation went to Israel/Palestine to discuss the proposed event. In taking this initiative the European peace movement was building on the experience gained at a joint Palestinian-Israeli gathering at Amersfoort in Holland in 1986 convened by the Dutch Pax Christi group. A significant number of representatives from European peace organisations had also participated in the ill-fated Al Awda 'Boat of Return' initiative of February 1988, when they joined Palestinian deportees in an attempt to sail from Athens to Israel in an effort to draw world attention to Israel's violations of international law and human rights whilst expressing solidarity with the Intifada. The Israel authorities sabotaged the planned voyage by sabotaging the ship in a Cyprus harbour.[28]

The original idea behind the action for January 1990 was to mobilise Palestinian nationalist organisations and Israeli peace organisations, with the participation of a sizeable international contingent, in a joint nonviolent demonstration of support for Palestinian rights and the cause of a just peace. Peace Now, however, was very reluctant to cooperate with the more radical wing of the Israeli protest movement and considered the ICCP to be too pro-Palestinian. Eventually a formula was found that satisfied all parties - the responsibility for different events over a three day period would be divided between the different participating organisations. Thus it was that on December 29 1989 the streets of Jerusalem were taken over by women - Israelis, Palestinians, and overseas participants. Following a congress attended by around 1,500, a gathering of around 3,000 women joined the traditional Friday vigil of the Women in Black. This was followed by a Women's Peace March from West to East Jerusalem in which somewhere in the region of 5,000 women participated. It was an impressive display as the women marched down the hill alongside the walls of the Old City singing and shouting their slogans of 'Peace Yes! Occupation No!', 'Two States for Two People!'. Amongst the foreign participants the Italians were to the fore, singing their own versions of 'Bella Ciao' and making an attempt at 'Occupation No' in Hebrew which sounded suspiciously like 'Kibbutz No' rather than 'Kibbush No'! The celebratory atmosphere was shattered somewhat when they reached their final destination in East Jerusalem when the police moved in with clubs and tear-gas, later claiming that some youngsters had unfurled a Palestinian flag and chanted nationalist slogans.

The next day some 30,000 people formed a Human Peace Chain around the walls of the Old City, including a surprisingly large number of Palestinians, considering the fact that the Israelis had been trying to prevent them from entering the city from the

West Bank for some time prior to the event. Surrounding the demonstrators was a second chain of some 2,000 police and border guards armed with clubs, rifles, tear-gas and water cannon. They began to practise their crowd-control methods some time before the official start of the event by letting off a few rounds of tear-gas outside the Damascus Gate, followed by a trial drenching of demonstrators who had the temerity to be chanting 'We Want Peace' alongside Herod's Gate. Whilst the majority of Palestinians, Israelis and foreigners held their ground, one or two Palestinian youths managed to throw a few stones before being stopped by fellow demonstrators. Others began singing the Palestinian national anthem 'Biladi, Biladi'. This was all that the police needed by way of an excuse to start launching tear-gas canisters and rubber bullets into the crowd. By the end of the day some 50 demonstrators had been arrested, another fifty had been quite seriously injured, and hundreds suffered from the effects of tear-gas.

For the Israelis in the crowd this kind of unprovoked action came as a profound shock. They were witnessing at first hand and for the first time the kind of brutality routinely inflicted upon the Palestinians during the Intifada. There was a rush of theories to explain the police attack as Peace Now demanded an independent investigation into the police behaviour.[29] If it was meant as a warning to Israelis against holding any further joint protest ventures with Palestinians, then it failed as Peace Now announced its preparedness to participate in future events. A common theory amongst Israeli leftists was that the brutality was part of an attempt to provoke the Palestinians to violence, in order to show the Israeli public and the wider international community that these so-called 'nonviolent' Palestinians were in fact as violent and unreasonable in their behaviour as any other gang of terrorists and as such were not fit people with whom to negotiate.[30] Another possible explanation was that following the controversial visit of Archbishop Tutu the previous week, when he had compared events in the occupied territories to the situation in South Africa, added to the unprecedented influx of foreign peace activists, the security authorities were very tense and over-reacted to the situation in the only way they knew how - with violence.

Whatever the reason, the police violence gave to the event a level of publicity that it would otherwise never have achieved. It served to convince the bulk of the Israeli participants that the need to change government policy was more urgent than ever. If the authorities were prepared to behave in such an outrageous manner in Jerusalem, when the world media was there to film and record it, then what must their behaviour be like in the occupied territories where they were shielded from the public gaze? What was the future of civil and political rights within Israel if the security forces were so willing to bring the Intifada home - by beating and intimidating Israeli citizens who had the temerity to engage in public protest? What about the damage done to Israel's standing in the international community as pictures of police running amok were broadcast around the world? The need for an alternative Zionism, a sane Zionism, was never greater.

Conclusion

A considerable amount of time during the Time for Peace rally was devoted to small group meetings and workshops, where a natural focus of discussion was an evaluation of the Intifada as it entered its third year. The consensus amongst Palestinians was that their main target should become Israeli public opinion, to convince them of the wisdom of withdrawal. When people like Faisal Husseini talked about Israeli public opinion it was clear that he was thinking of the Likud voters rather than the dissidents of the protest groups and the doves of Peace Now. They were cast in the role of go-betweens, links in the chain of communication.

Palestinian participants also expressed their disappointment with the performance of the Israeli peace movement. It had failed to mobilise the tens of thousands that had filled the streets following the invasion of Lebanon. Moreover, Palestinians were beginning to tire of the repeated meetings with Israeli doves who flocked over the Green Line at weekends to meet with Palestinians. Whereas many of the Israeli women's groups and professional groupings had established strong working relationships with their Palestinian counterparts around issues of mutual concern, it seemed to many Palestinians that the majority of Israelis participated in the peace convoys and solidarity visits for reasons which had more to do with their own personal and political needs rather than with supporting the Intifada. To understand this phenomenon it is important to realise that prior to the Intifada the majority of Israelis never met with Palestinians - except as labourers or as hawkers on the streets of Tel Aviv or perhaps as the people they stopped at road blocs during their reserve duty. They never met as everyday human beings. Under the changed circumstances of the Intifada there emerged a genuine desire to meet with these people who, far from being objects of contempt or pity depending on one's political persuasion, had revealed themselves capable of standing up to privation, hardship and repression. At first Palestinians were enthusiastic about welcoming these people into their midst. Gradually, however, the feeling began to spread that what was taking place was a dialogue between unequal partners in which they, the Palestinians, were being cast in the image that the Israelis felt was necessary in order to further their own campaign to sway the Israeli public. Thus, at one meeting at Beita the Israelis decided they ought to leave after objecting to the nationalist slogans chanted by some of their hosts. One of their number, a member of the Knesset, complained as he left, 'After all I've done for them, they should show some consideration for the sensitivity of the Israeli public.'[31]

Palestinians began to feel as if they were being cast in the role of therapists, engaging in dialogue in order to assuage the fears and ease the consciences of Israeli doves. At one such encounter session in which I participated I eavesdropped on the conversations taking place. The dominant theme to which the Israeli participants kept returning was that of fear. 'How can we trust someone like Arafat who was responsible for terrorist attacks on innocent civilians on buses and children in schools? Can you understand the deep need we feel - even though we have all the weapons and tanks - the deeply felt need for security?' The people from whom they were seeking reassurance were the villagers of Nahalin who, one month earlier, had buried five of their young men killed by Border Police. Despite such frustrations the Palestinian advocates of dialogue with the Israelis realised that such fears were real. Fear was the dominant emotion in Israel. It was this fear that Palestinians, with the aid of the Israeli peace movement, sought to address. The complexity and difficulties associated with this task were compounded by the fact that the Palestinian issue touched the very heart of that fear. For Israelis the conflict with the Palestinians was not a foreign policy issue like the invasion of Lebanon, it raised far deeper problems. Most of them could not forget that the PLO was formed in the 1960s with the proclaimed aim of destroying Israel. As such, the Intifada, when viewed through the prism of old suspicions, continued to raise questions about the whole future existence of Israel as a society and a state. Is it any wonder that the peace movement failed to mobilise the same numbers as it did over Lebanon? In the context of the Israeli peace groups acting as links in a great chain of nonviolence, communicating to their fellow citizens a vision of a cooperative future with the Palestinians based on two states for two peoples, the depth of this fear of the other - the Palestinians - continued to represent a virtually insurmountable obstacle.

In a conflict where one of the parties defines the issue at stake as entailing their very survival and existence, then any attempt by the other party to convince them otherwise requires, at the very least, an exceptionally high degree of consistency in the content of the reassurances being communicated. When one starts to consider the nature of the Intifada, the heterogeneous composition of the Palestinian nationalist camp, and the fact that the struggle took place within the context of a changing regional and international arena rather than in some hermetically sealed capsule - then one starts to grasp the scale of the problem with which the Palestinians and the Israeli peace camp had to grapple. How to explain the scale of the challenge?

First of all there is the need to recognise that the medium by which a message is communicated is as vital as the content. The Intifada was not a nonviolent struggle in the sense of refraining from inflicting physical harm and injury upon the Israelis. It was, for the most part, an unarmed struggle during which the use of lethal weapons had been eschewed by the Palestinians. However, under certain circumstances stones could kill, as can firebombs and Molotov Cocktails. Even when they do not kill they can create fear and panic - and reinforce the image of the other as fundamentally threatening. Likewise, the image presented by the youths responsible for throwing the stones and the petrol bombs, with the keffiyas wrapped round their faces. They might be shouting 'Down with the occupation', but their appearance conveys a deeper message - that of the 'masked terrorist'. For Palestinian youths in the Intifada, wearing the keffiyah as a mask became tantamount to a fashion, a symbol of commitment to the struggle. For the Israeli public, dependent on their own media for their images, the mask became synonymous with 'mindless violence', best illustrated by the brutal killing of collaborators. Not an image conducive to accepting at face value the reassuring words of Palestinian political leaders and intellectuals about peace and cooperation, particularly when the Palestinian camp contained within its ranks factions which had declared their intention of establishing an Islamic state in the whole of historic Palestine.

Despite the essentially 'non-life threatening' forms of unarmed struggle that became the routine of the Intifada, I was assured by one leading figure in Peace Now that what stayed in the psyche were the 'atrocities' - the stabbing of an old man in Jaffa Street, the murder of Israeli hitch-hikers, the tragedy of the Jerusalem-bound bus which was forced over a precipice by a young Palestinian in July 1989 causing the death of 16 passengers. As he remarked, 'We are not talking about whether this is rational or not - this is the popular perception'. This sense of outrage and fear reached an unprecedented level in the weeks following the slaughter on October 8 1990 at the al-Aqsa Mosque, as individual Palestinians sought revenge by knife attacks on Israeli Jews.

The burden borne by the spokespersons of the Intifada when trying to convince their allies in the Israeli peace camp, and through them the Israeli public in general, of the sincerity of their commitment to peace was made even weightier by the intervention of Palestinians from outside the occupied territories. As has been remarked, Israelis viewed the Palestinians through the lens of old suspicions, based in part on their experience of past examples of Palestinian terrorism. Thus, when the Iraqi-sponsored Palestine Liberation Front launched its disastrous sea-borne raid on a Tel Aviv beach at the end of May 1990, all the old fears and nightmares returned, fuelled by Arafat's failure to condemn the assault. Palestinian protestations about the imbalance between the violence perpetrated by their guerrillas and the human suffering caused by Israeli state terrorism fell on deaf ears in such circumstances. The raid of May 30 1990 took place at a time when relationships between Israeli doves and Palestinian nationalists had become strained by the question of the mass immigration of Soviet Jews, and the fear that they would be settled in the occupied territories sparked by Prime Minister Shamir's declaration that 'a large country is needed for a large migration'. The question of migration thereby became inextricably linked in the Palestinian mind with their worst nightmare - the annexation of the occupied territories and the expulsion of the Palestinian population. In Israel at the time, however, there was a kind of euphoria shared by all shades of

Zionist political opinion at the prospect of the mass immigration of Soviet Jews. For such people, any attempt to halt the exodus of Jews from the Soviet Union was tantamount to questioning Israel's right to be sovereign within its own borders, and to question Israel's sovereignty was to question its right to exist.

In August 1990 another external factor intruded to deal a crippling blow to the joint efforts of Palestinians and Israelis to sway Israeli public opinion. Iraq invaded Kuwait. Palestinians in the occupied territories applauded Saddam Hussein, whilst the PLO appeared equivocal in its attitude towards the Iraqi action. For the Israeli peace movement this all came as a terrible blow: how could they possibly convince their fellow citizens to trust people who were prepared to applaud a tyrant like Saddam Hussein? With the outbreak of war in January 1991, and the Scud missile attacks on civilian targets in Israel, the Israeli population joined together in a display of national unity in the face of external threat. Prime Minister Shamir enjoyed an unprecedented degree of national support, and notable Israeli 'doves' such as the novelist Amos Oz criticised their Western counterparts for demonstrating against the war. Thoughts of dialogue with Palestinians were superseded by more immediate concerns. However, Peace Now displayed a degree of political maturity by maintaining its commitment to the on-going dialogue with Palestinians. Its leaders followed a 'twin-track' approach: acknowledging the difficulties and differences over the Gulf Crisis, but recognising that this was a more transient phenomenon than the Palestinian question, which they continued to address at meetings with Palestinians. However, in the context of the war there was no chance of Israeli peace activists persuading their fellow citizens to see the Palestinians as trustworthy peace-partners – particularly amidst reports of Palestinians cheering as Iraqi missiles flew overhead to strike at Israeli population centres.

[1] See J. Galtung, *Non-violence and Israel/Palestine,* Honolulu: University of Hawaii, 1989, p. 19.

---

[2] See D. Hall-Cathala, *The peace movement in Israel, 1967-87,* Basingstoke: Macmillan, 1990, p. 28.
[3] Quoted in Adam Keller, *Terrible Days*, Amstelveen: Cypres, 1987, pp. 167 - 68.
[4] *Jerusalem Post*, August 23, 1978.
[5] Oz ve Shalom, *English Bulletin*, no 1, p. 2. (n.d)
[6] E. Farjoun, quoted in I. Ertugrul, 'Working together for peace', *Middle East International,* January 9, 1987, pp. 15 -16.
[7] One of the principles of Palestinians and Israelis for Non-violence was to organise actions in which Palestinians, Israelis and international visitors participated. In this way, one of the founder members claimed they anticipated the 1990: Time for Peace Rally. (Interview with Amos Gvurtz, January 1990.)
[8] Quoted in Tom Keene, 'Mubarak Awad: Behind the Intifada', *Peace Media Service*, nd. (1990)
[9] Uri Avnery, *My friend the enemy*, London: Zed Books, 1986, p. 72.
[10] Figures quoted in Mordechai Bar-On, 'Trends in the political psychology of Israeli Jews, 1967 - 86', *Journal of Palestine Studies*, v. 17, n. 1, Autumn 1987, p. 24.
[11] 'Trends in the political psychology of Israeli Jews, 1967 - 86'.
[12] Y. Kaniuk, *New Outlook*, September 1988, p. 26.
[13] *The Other Front*, n. I5, December 8, 1988, p. 5.
[14] *The Other Front*, n. 1, August 8, 1988, p. 2.
[15] One of the main problems faced by the Beita Committee was that every time the volunteers went to the village to work, the army would declare the area a closed military zone and deny them entry.
[16] Quoted in D. Gavron, 'The fight for civil rights', *Jerusalem Post (International Edition),* January 13, 1990, p. 17.
[17] Quoted in Gavron, 'The fight for civil rights'.
[18] Quoted in *The Guardian* February 5, 1990.
[19] Gavron, 'The fight for civil rights.'

[20] The central theme of its platform had been support for the fourteen demands made by Palestinian personalities in January 1988.

[21] Translation from *News from Nowhere*, v. 4, n. 6, May 31 1988, p. 11.

[22] Translation from *The Other Front*, no 36, May 10, 1989.

[23] One estimate was that there were approximately ten 'grey refusals' for every 'refuse-nik' sentenced.

[24] *Al Fajr*, February 26 1990, p. 3.

[25] See *The Other Israel*, no 41, April-May 1990, p 11.

[26] The Council for Peace and Security was founded by Moshe Amirav, one-time member of Likud. Composed primarily of high-ranking reserve officers, it urged the exchange of territory for peace on the grounds that Israel no longer needed the whole of the occupied territories for security purposes.

[27] Yossi Ben Artzy, *The Other Front*, n. 24, February 9, 1989.

[28] See A Rigby, 'Alawda: the PLO Boat of Return that never sailed', WRI Newsletter, February/March 1988, p. 3.

[29] Subsequent investigations led to the removal of the East Jerusalem police chief and disciplinary procedures were initiated against other officers.

[30] See, for example, *The Other Front*, n. 58, January 2, 1990.

[31] Quoted in *The Other Front*, n. 31, March 29, 1989.

9

CONCLUSION

The basic aim of the Intifada had been to bring an end to the Israeli occupation of the West Bank and Gaza Strip as a necessary precondition for the establishment of a Palestinian state alongside Israel. Despite all the years of struggle the occupation continued. Judged from such a perspective, the Uprising did not succeed in its political aim. However, to focus solely upon the single political goal of ending the occupation would be to ignore all the other achievements of the Uprising, the various manifestations of the 'shaking off' process that have been the main focus of this book. In a very real sense the Intifada succeeded in transforming the relationship between Palestinians and the Israeli state and society – at least for a time.

One of the key features of the Intifada, like other examples of civilian resistance, was the refusal of the Palestinians to cooperate with the occupier, the rejection of their position as subjects and the assertion of their status as active citizens. This spirit of revolt and self-assertion spread throughout all elements of Palestinian society, and it was this process of self-transformation at the individual and collective level that had been the driving force for political transformation. As such, whilst the intensity of the confrontations might ebb and flow, so long as that spirit remains the Intifada cannot be said to have ended or to have failed.

Despite such observations, it must still be acknowledged that the efforts of the Palestinians since the Uprising began in December 1987 failed to produce the dramatic results achieved by other expressions of people power such as in Eastern and Central Europe in 1989. In trying to come to some understanding of this 'relative failure' attention needs to be directed at three crucial factors: 1) The limitations of the Intifada as a movement of non-cooperation and disengagement, 2) the contradictions that lie at the heart of an unarmed civilian-based resistance movement and 3) the role of external third parties to the conflict.

The limitations of the Intifada as a movement of non-cooperation and disengagement

Advocates of nonviolent forms of resistance have placed particular emphasis upon the power of mass non-cooperation. The argument focuses upon the social sources of power, the thesis being that in the final analysis tyranny rests upon the cooperation, forced or otherwise, of the oppressed. The withdrawal of such cooperation, it is claimed, removes the social sources of the oppressor's power. All that is required is that sufficient numbers of people, including those in strategic institutional positions, summon the courage to say 'No' and are prepared to suffer the consequences of their defiance. This is the power of the powerless who, by their non-cooperation and defiance, can render a society ungovernable.

This approach to the challenge of confronting an alien power influenced the strategic thinking behind the Intifada. However, in the lived history of the Intifada, as I have tried to show in this book, a number of factors became apparent which revealed some of the limitations of nonviolent resistance in the case of the Palestinian struggle against the Israeli occupation. Any analysis of the relative failure of the Intifada has to start with the unusual degree of intransigence displayed by the Israeli government. It was – and remains - so committed to holding on to the occupied territories that it was prepared to pay an exceptionally high price to sustain its rule. The converse of this is that Palestinians were unable to raise the costs of continued occupation to a level necessary to cause the Israeli authorities to withdraw. Why was this the case?

An important element in the equation has been the fact that Israel has sought dominion over the land of Palestine, it has never wanted the people. Indeed, Israel would dearly love to see the back of the Palestinians. Therefore it had been prepared to live with non-cooperation and defiance, using the battle of the Intifada to tighten the screws of oppression and intensify the costs of resistance borne by the Palestinian community. The hope being that increasing numbers of Palestinians would lose confidence in their national struggle, and seek their personal destinies elsewhere, leaving more and more of the land free for Israeli settlement.

A further factor which must be considered is that since 1967 Israel's dependency upon the Palestinians of the occupied territories had been primarily as a source of labour and as a captive market for its products. Due to the influx of new immigrants from the Soviet Union, the dependency upon the Palestinian workforce had been radically reduced whilst over this same period the dependency of the Palestinians upon Israel as a source of employment actually increased. The economic base of Palestinian society, seriously underdeveloped at the commencement of the Uprising after 20 years of occupation, had been further undermined by Israel since 1987 as part of the punitive response to the Uprising. Not only had this prevented the Palestinian economy from developing to a level where it could provide employment for Palestinians in need of work, but it also seriously limited the impact of any efforts to boycott Israeli-produced goods within the occupied territories. The fact is that Israel remained the only source of many of the basic necessities of life for Palestinians within the occupied territories.

This fragility of the economic base of Palestinian society, coupled with the generally weak infrastructure, particularly in the fields of education, health and welfare services, meant that the Palestinians had to bear an exceptionally heavy cost for their resistance. After nearly four years of active defiance, it would appear that a civilian-based resistance movement such as the Intifada could only succeed in dislodging the Israelis if it was backed up by a sufficiently strong infrastructure of institutional supports. These are necessary so that the basic needs of the people could be met in the process of struggle. Only in this way could resistance itself become institutionalised, embedded as a dimension of 'normal life', and as such become sustainable against an opponent as determined and intransigent as Israel. In summary, then, it would appear that Palestinian efforts to impose intolerable costs on Israel through rendering the occupied territories ungovernable were seriously hampered by the weakness of the indigenous support systems necessary to sustain such a struggle, and the relative immunity achieved by Israel in relation to the sanctions that the Palestinians sought to impose in the process of their unarmed insurrection.

The contradictions of unarmed civilian resistance

In addressing the limitations of the Palestinian attempts to disengage from Israel, attention has so far been focused on the relative weakness of the sanctions that were brought to bear in the effort to coerce the Israelis into bringing the occupation to an end. Non-cooperation with tyranny also seeks to inject another kind of transformative dimension into the arena of struggle in addition to that of coercion. This is the power of conversion and persuasion. By standing firm in the face of injustice, it is argued, nonviolent activists seek to display their preparedness to undergo the utmost penalties for the sake of their ideals. They thereby seek to confront their opponents, the instruments of injustice, with the fundamental evils for which they are responsible. In Gandhian terms, by the firm holding onto Truth (satyagraha), and refraining from inflicting physical harm upon one's opponents, it is believed that they will be won over eventually to a new understanding of the conflict situation and an appreciation of the justice of the cause for which the activists are struggling and suffering. These are the two hands of nonviolence. The one beckons towards a new vision of a cooperative future, seeking to engage the Israeli public and their political leaders in dialogue, using the moral vocabulary of what ought to be. The other condemns the intolerable present and seeks to impose such a heavy cost upon the occupiers as to force them to withdraw. There is an inevitable tension between the two: the one involves an attempt to 'embrace' the opponent, the other entails an absolute rejection of the evil for which they are responsible. What gives to that tension its dynamic and creative aspect, it is argued by advocates of nonviolence, is nonviolence itself: the refusal to inflict physical hurt upon the other in the process of struggle. Only through nonviolence, it is believed, can compassion for one's opponent be held in dynamic tension with the anger at the evil for which they are responsible.

However, the Intifada had not been a nonviolent Uprising, but rather a predominantly unarmed one. As a consequence the twin dimensions of conversion and coercion tended to work in opposition to each other. In other words, when efforts at coercion go beyond the admittedly hazy boundary of nonviolent action to include modes of resistance which are intended to inflict physical injury upon the opponent, then the counter-productivity of such activity, in relation to the efforts to sway the hearts and minds of the other, becomes all the more acute. The Israeli who was moved by the image of Palestinians refusing to submit to the dictates of a brutally repressive regime, and whose sympathies for fellow human beings pursuing a patently just cause was thereby aroused, could also be moved to anger and resentment against the 'other' who, directly or indirectly, could be deemed responsible for the injury and death inflicted on his or her fellow-citizens. When one takes account of the siege mentality of the bulk of the Israeli public, their paramount concern with security, their fear of the perceived threat to their existence posed by the Palestinians and the Arab nations as a whole, then the negative impact of trying to force them to withdraw from the occupied territories by means of physical coercion becomes all the more apparent, particularly if one recognises that the key determinant of such a withdrawal taking place must come from the Israeli people themselves. If one accepts that the dominant emotion in Israeli society is fear, then it is clear that this fear has to be confronted and transcended if the two peoples are ever to live in peace together. But it seems equally apparent that any attempt to coerce the Israelis into submission, by means that have the effect of reinforcing their over-riding concern with security, will only heighten that fear and intensify their determination not to give ground. It will only serve to convince them that any future imposed upon them under duress is bound to be worse, from a security point of view, than the current state of affairs, however unsatisfactory the status quo might be.

Of course it is easy for outside observers like myself to make such judgements when we are far removed from the humiliations and the hardships that have been (and continue to be) an integral part of everyday life for Palestinians under occupation. On my visits I could be moved to tears and to blind anger by what I witnessed - but I was always able to leave it behind with a sigh of relief, having once again survived that last intimidatory experience of leaving Israel from Tel Aviv airport. I knew something of what it was like to live under an 'iron fist', however vicarious my experience might have been. I therefore had some idea of what it was like to be treated with contempt, to have one's very humanity denied, let alone one's basic rights as a citizen. In such situations it is all too easy to give way to the desire for revenge, to hit back with whatever weapons come to hand. If nothing else, it gives one a feeling of 'doing something'. This is completely understandable, and few would dispute that it is better to resist by violent means than to do nothing in the face of injustice. But, however beneficial the throwing of stones and fire-bombs might be from the point of view of the individual assailant's therapeutic needs, it has to be adjudged counterproductive from the wider political perspective of getting the Israelis out. In the context of the occasional life-threatening interventions of Palestinian guerrillas from outside, the increasingly frequent knifings of Israelis by deranged Palestinians, and the calls by extremists for the recovery of the whole of historic Palestine, such actions help to perpetuate the Israeli image of the Palestinians as fundamentally threatening. As such they militate against any effort to convince them that the best road to true security lies in acknowledging the collective and individual rights of the Palestinians.

The failure of third parties

In observing that Palestinian efforts to obtain the withdrawal of the Israeli occupation by means of physical, albeit non-lethal, force have militated against efforts to persuade them to withdraw, I am not suggesting that force and coercion have no part to play in the dynamic. Not for a single moment can one imagine some kind of mass Israeli conversion process whereby they come to love their Palestinian cousins. Appeals to the heart might work with some people, but for the mass of folk it is their perceived individual and collective self-interest that tends to rule the day. The fact is that most Israelis would be a lot happier if there were no such people as the Palestinians (and vice versa). Even amongst the doves in the peace camp one would get the feeling that they were stricken by the fear that behind the human being that they acknowledged when in dialogue with Palestinians, they could not dismiss the suspicion that there remained another level, a darker and perhaps more powerful 'other' behind the facade that was fundamentally threatening. What is clear to most observers is that the Israelis, public and politicians alike, will only be persuaded to sit down and talk peace with the Palestinians if they can be convinced that this is the least hurtful and threatening of the available options.

It is by influencing the range and the nature of the options open to Israel that the Palestinians have exercised their power in the struggle for peace. After four years of the Intifada the status quo was no longer quite so attractive to Israelis, insofar as the Uprising and its associated costs could not be separated from the occupation itself. At the same time the Palestinians sought to make the prospect of negotiation more appealing by unequivocally recognising Israel's right to exist and limiting their own demands to the establishment of a Palestinian state in the West Bank and Gaza Strip.

However, in this struggle to influence options the Palestinians and the Israelis have never been the only players. There have always been a host of third parties with an interest in the outcome of the conflict who have played a determining role in effecting the range of possible choices open to both parties. Thus, when King Hussein relinquished his claim to the West Bank he eliminated one option. By conceding responsibility for the West Bank to the PLO, not only did he appear to be putting an end to the so-called 'Jordanian option', he was also endorsing the claims of the PLO as the legitimate representatives of the Palestinians in the occupied territories. In the process he was also announcing, in effect, that 'Jordan is not Palestine', as part of his effort to forestall any Israeli plans to transfer the population of the West Bank to the East Bank of the River Jordan.

Washington, of course, has been a key target of Palestinian attention. The United States has the leverage necessary to vitally affect the available options open to Israel, the capacity to create the conditions whereby accommodation with the Palestinians becomes the 'least unattractive choice' facing the Israelis. Its failure to do so remains a key factor in enabling Israel to persist in its intransigent stance. Third parties to any conflict are rarely moved by appeals for their sympathy. Expressions of sympathy, after all, cost rather little. Particularly when the third parties are nation states, they are influenced far more by considerations of self-interest than by feelings of moral outrage, despite the rhetoric that politicians are so adept at mouthing. The plain fact of the matter is that the Palestinians historically have lacked the resources to vitally affect the self-interest of the United States. This was brought into sharp relief in August 1990. Iraq's invasion of Kuwait appeared to threaten the stability of the Gulf and the continued supply of oil to the industrialised world in general, and to the United States in particular. Within days the build-up of American troops in Saudi Arabia was under way, to be followed by contingents from her Western allies and elsewhere. Iraq's contravention of all the rules of international behaviour could not be tolerated. At the very minimum Saddam Hussein must be forced to withdraw from the territory he had occupied by force. If the UN sanctions proved ineffective, then force of arms would have to be used. And so it was.

Few can be so naive as to believe that such a stance came about as a result of international sympathy for the plight of the Kuwaitis. It was clearly to defend the supply of oil, upon which depended not only the profits of companies but a whole way of life built around cheap oil and petroleum-based products. Is it any wonder that the Palestinians were so outraged by the blatant hypocrisy of the international response to Iraq's occupation of Kuwait? The world had seemed perfectly able to live with the Israeli occupation of the West Bank and Gaza Strip for over 20 years. The lesson was clear – the Palestinians would have to discover oil before they could hope to arouse the active intervention of external powers such as the USA.

The United States was not the only 'third party" which failed to exercise its influence in the interests of peace between the Palestinians and the Israelis. The various domestic crises within the Soviet Union undermined her influence in the Middle Eastern arena. As for the European Community, it failed to show itself willing to use its undoubted economic power to its full potential in relation to the conflict, although there was a growing recognition that Israel's choice of options could be seriously affected by the move to full economic union within the community. There was mounting concern within Israel that her access to this market might be restricted in the light of her rejectionist stance with regard to the peace process. When one turns the spotlight towards the Middle East itself, it is hard to dispel the belief that for the majority of Arab regimes the prospect of the Palestinians achieving their statehood through the exercise of people power represented a nightmare scenario. Who knows what lessons their own subject peoples might absorb from such an outcome?

For as long as these third parties fail to exercise their ability to affect the options available to Israel by increasing the relative cost of her intransigence, then there seems little prospect of any way out of the current impasse. For Israel the Intifada became something akin to a chronic disease, it is debilitating in all kinds of ways but it is not 'life-threatening'. So long as she can keep on drawing sustenance from her various external support-systems, and so long as she is not torn asunder by internal social and political divisions, there seems to be little reason why she should be swayed from her present stance.

From civilian resistance to social transformation

All this reflects a scepticism of the intellect, and it needs to be balanced by an optimism of the will. As an academic who has spent some of his time teaching about the Palestinian-Israeli conflict, one of the points I used to try and get across to my students is that if they are ever to get to grips with the complexities of the conflict, then it is important to appreciate something of the emotions and the psychoses that both parties bring to the fight: the fear of the Israelis, their fatalism about the prospects for a true and lasting peace, their paranoia about their neighbours (which, like most forms of paranoia, has a basis in reality); the unreal dreams of the Palestinians, their sense of time and history which gives substance to the dream, however far off in the distant future it might be located - after all, how many centuries did it take before Saladin came along and drove the Crusaders from the land?

When one thinks about this conflict, it is always possible to come up with nightmare futures, but it is also possible to envisage a scenario of hope if one's faith in the future is sufficiently strong - and what else have the Palestinians had to sustain them except their hope for the future?

The question of 'linkage' between the question of Palestine and the Iraqi occupation of Kuwait came to the fore in the aftermath of the Israeli slaying of unarmed Palestinians on Temple Mount in early October 1990. It served to remind the world that so long as the issue of Palestine is left unresolved there can be no peace in the Middle East. In this sense, the Gulf crisis could not be separated from the Arab-Israeli conflict. Indeed, the linkage between the disputes goes back to the early decades of this century when the colonial powers of Britain and France divided up the region into respective spheres of influence and penned in the artificial boundaries upon which the present day state structure of the Middle East is based, with Britain promising a homeland for the Jews in Palestine and separating Kuwait off from Iraq, whilst France carved out the state of Lebanon from Greater Syria in response to the pleas of the Christian Maronites.

The linkage was cemented over the years by the conflict between Israel and the Arab world. It was this core dispute that has led to the militarisation of the whole region, with over 25 percent of government expenditure throughout the area devoted to military purposes. It was this conflict, and the accompanying militarisation, that allowed authoritarian tyrants such as Saddam Hussein in Iraq and President Assad in Syria to rise to power and hold on to it by the most brutal of means. Furthermore, it was the security fears that haunted the Israeli public that led to the political ascendancy of the irredentists that have continued to hold the balance of power within Israel.

It is clear that any long-term hopes for peace in the Middle East depend upon a comprehensive settlement that addresses the aspirations of the Palestinians. A fundamental component of any such process must involve the demilitarisation of the region.

Only then will the space be created that can encompass the yearnings of the Israelis for security, the demands of the Palestinians for justice, and the dreams of the Arab people as a whole for a new democratic order in the Middle East. Of course, for such a dream to become a reality, it requires the principle protagonists to give up their own maximalist dreams for the sake of peace. Palestinians, of course, have had more than three years' experience of resisting occupation by means that have been primarily unarmed. As such it is possible to identify a direct linkage between the means adopted to resist Israel's occupation of Palestinian land during the Intifada and the future defence policy of a Palestinian state. But, beyond the experience gained in the methods of unarmed struggle and resistance, the Palestinians of the West Bank and Gaza Strip experienced a far deeper educational process during the course of the Uprising - an education in active citizenry.

It has already been remarked that one of the most vital aspects of the whole Uprising had been the involvement of virtually the entire society in some aspect or other of the resistance. This involvement in the fight for political change reflected a deeper transformation, a process of self-re- generation whereby a people traditionally cast as subjects transformed themselves into active citizens, a people who began to grow accustomed to direct action. Direct action refers to far more than the demonstrations and street confrontations with the occupier which were the surface events of the Intifada. The practice of direct action involves the exercise of the capacity for self-management and mutual care in all spheres of life, unprompted by any external state-like coercive agency. As such, Palestinians initiated in the Uprising a process of self-change every bit as significant as the project to restructure the political domain. It is upon such a bedrock of active citizenry that a new society and polity could be constructed, by people prepared to take upon themselves the responsibility for developing and managing their own communities and institutions for the collective good of the whole society.

ANNEX

PALESTINIANS IN ISRAEL

Contributed by Marwan Darweish

The Intifada shocked both the Palestinian people and the rest of the world. The scenes of Palestinian youth confronting the Israeli army with stones and the exceptionally harsh Israeli reaction to this had a powerful effect on public opinion throughout the world, with the result that Israel's image as a vulnerable state fighting to defend its very existence was seriously undermined. The Arabs in Israel, as a part of the Palestinian people and at the same time citizens of Israel, were the first to express their clear support for the Intifada. This support, combined with the physical closeness to the occupied territories, had a significant effect on the Arab community in Israel.[1] The purpose of this chapter is to examine the different forms this support has taken, the way in which the Intifada has impacted upon the Arab community within Israel, and the Israeli reaction toward its Arab citizens when they showed their solidarity with the Intifada.[2]

Palestinians in Israel: the background

The first Arab-Israeli war broke out in 1948 and was followed by the establishment of the state of Israel. The immediate effect upon the Palestinian population was twofold. First, the exodus of a large proportion of the Palestinians, who became refugees. Second, the transformation in the status of those Palestinians who remained. They became a minority in their own homeland, cut off from the rest of their people.

Mari has depicted the situation of those 120,000 who remained within the boundaries of Israel:

> ... emotionally wounded, socially rural, politically lost, economically poverty-stricken and nationally hurt,... it was an agonising experience. ... Arabs in Israel were left without political leadership and an educated elite.[3]

They continued to live under the heavy hand of military rule from 1948 until 1966. By the 1980s the Arab minority within Israel had grown to 700,000, constituting around 16 percent of the total Israeli population, the majority of them living in villages. Although they were promised equality in the state's Declaration of Independence, they continued to suffer from deprivation and discrimination after 42 years. The confiscation of the majority of their land rendered them economically dependent upon the Jewish sector, which in turn caused a transformation in the class structure of the Arab population from a predominantly peasant society to one where the majority of males became part of the unskilled working class.[4] The scale of dependency remained so great that even by the late 1980s there were still only somewhere in the region of 8,000 Arab workers employed in manufacturing facilities within the Arab sector.[5] With regard to access to public services and amenities such as health, education and the like, Jewish local authorities enjoyed a budget up to three times higher than those in the Arab sector.[6] The result can be seen clearly in the inadequacy of the basic services provided by the Arab local authorities.

The national curriculum which Arab students were required to follow reflected the values and assumptions of the dominant Jewish culture and Zionism. Arab culture in general, and anything that hinted of Palestinian nationalism was excluded. Furthermore, the impoverishment of the Arab local authorities meant that the physical condition of the majority of schools remained very poor. Overcrowded and underequipped, many classes were held in rented rooms lacking adequate facilities.[7]

Despite these handicaps, by the time the Intifada broke out there had been significant developments in the political consciousness and organisation of Arabs in Israel. The Committee to follow up the Concerns of Arab Citizens in Israel (CFCAC) was formed in 1987. It soon became the most representative and powerful body established within the Arab community since 1948, the chief forum for Arabs in Israel, with representatives from a whole range of voluntary organisations and from all the different political groups, including the Islamic movement and Arabs associated with Zionist parties. This virtual parliament of Arabs in Israel had agreed on two principle demands: equality for Arabs in Israel and the establishment of a Palestinian state in the occupied territories. The twin foci reflecting the fact that by the outbreak of the Uprising Israeli Arabs had started to become politically significant within Israel and within the Palestinian national movement. This in turn reflected the duality of their identity as Israelis and as Palestinians: their civic identity as citizens of the state of Israel and their sense of national identity as Palestinians. They had become Palestinian-Israelis.

Solidarity with the Intifada

The different types and displays of support carried out by the Arabs in Israel can be divided into three main categories: political support, material support, and moral support.

1. Political support

Taken unawares like everyone else, the first political reaction by Arabs in Israel to the Intifada took place on December 21 1987 with a total general strike of the Arab community on 'Peace day'. In their leaflet, the organizers expressed the concern and solidarity of the Arab population in Israel with the Intifada.

> The events in the occupied territories directly concern the Arabs in Israel as an inseparable part of the Palestinian people and as citizens of the State of Israel. We perceive the Intifada as

> a people's struggle for its freedom and independence. We proclaim our full solidarity with the struggle of this people, our people, against the Israeli occupation.[8]

It is significant that from this first collective display of solidarity the Palestinian-Israelis made a clear distinction between the occupied territories and Israel, between the Palestinians on the two sides of the Green Line. On the one hand the organising committee emphasised the fact that Arabs in Israel were an integral part of the Palestinian people with whose struggle they identified. On the other hand the differences between the two communities were acknowledged: the Arabs of Israel were citizens of that state. Ian Lustick underlined this point when he observed:

> The Israeli Arabs are taking an active and integral part, not in the uprising in the occupied territories, but in the general political life in Israel, specifically on the debate about the future of the occupied territories.[9]

The 'Peace Day' marked the point when Arabs in Israel as a community began to actively identify with the Intifada. The strike was total in all Arab villages and towns and throughout all spheres of life. There were demonstrations and marches organised throughout the localities, which occasioned a number of confrontations with the authorities when tear-gas was used and over 100 people were arrested.[10] Individual incidents on the day of action included Molotov cocktails and stones being thrown at Israeli cars. A number of roads were also blocked, in particular the Wadi Ara road running through the Arab villages in the area known as the Triangle between Tel Aviv and the north of Israel. An observer described the confrontations with the Israeli authorities on the strike day as follows:

> In Nazareth, in Jaffa, in Um el Fahem, in Lod, and only a shade less fervently than the Pales-

> tinians in Ramallah, Balata, Gaza city and Jabaliya - Israeli Arabs blocked roads, threw rocks, burned tyres and shouted religious and nationalist slogans. Israel itself got a taste of civil war.[11]

More than anything else it seemed as if the Intifada had united all Palestinians in Israel behind one goal: unconditional support for the Intifada. An agreement based on three principles was forged between all political forces, from the left radicals to those affiliated with Zionist parties: the establishment of a Palestinian State in the West Bank and Gaza Strip alongside Israel, recognition .of the PLO as the sole legitimate representative of the Palestinian people, and full equality for the Arab citizens of Israel.

'Land Day' of 1988 was marked by another general strike in solidarity with the Intifada and against the continuation of Arab land confiscation. In addition to the annual 'Land Day' demonstrations there were a number of other general strikes. Thus, the strike in November 1988 in protest against the demolition of Arab homes took on an added dimension in the context of the Palestinian National Council Meeting in Algiers and the declaration of the independence of the State of Palestine. Both Palestinians in Israel and the occupied territories declared a general strike on May 21 1990 to mourn and protest against the killing of eight Palestinian workers by an Israeli gunman the previous day in Rishon Le'Zion. Demonstrations swept the Arab community in Israel and large scale clashes with the police occurred in Nazareth and other locations.

It is worth noting at this point that following the outbreak of the Intifada, the Arab leadership in Israel became far more prepared to use strikes as a form of protest than in previous years. Indeed, 1988 marked the first time that the Arab community had struck for more than one day in a year. This increase was inevitably perceived as a negative development by Alex Bile, the

Deputy Adviser to the Prime Minister for Arab Affairs when he observed in May 1989:

> From the beginning of the Intifada there was an increase in political activity by Israeli Arabs, on both the level of political institutions and of the individual. There have been four days of strikes whereas in the past there was only one a year. The general strike weapon has increased.[12]

Rouhana estimated that between December 1987 and June 1989 the Arabs in Israel held 35 regional and national strikes and demonstrations in support of the Intifada.[13] The largest took place in Nazareth on January 23 1988 when an estimated 50,000 gathered to demonstrate their solidarity with their compatriots in the occupied territories.[14] Alongside these, there were a number of local strikes and demonstrations. Many of these occurred spontaneously in reaction to events and without any encouragement from the established political groups and parties. As such they were indicative of the pressure that was put on the political leadership within the Arab community to take firm and radical actions in support of the Intifada.

A massive demonstration did take place on June 3 1989. This was designated 'Palestinian-Israeli Peace Day'. Palestinians in Israel and members of Israeli-Jewish democratic and peace groups joined together in a day of action. Workshops, meetings and discussion groups were organised where Palestinian families, students, ex-prisoners, women and artists from the occupied territories met with Arab and Jewish citizens of Israel. This event illustrated a significant feature of the response to the Intifada in Israel: the substantial increase in the level of cooperation between the Arab and Jewish citizens of Israel and the Palestinians of the occupied territories. Even the religious leaders of the Arab community in Israel, who had traditionally worked closely with the Israeli authorities, participated in this process. Thus, at a meeting in Nazareth on February 2 1988, about 50 Muslim and Christian figures gathered to express solidarity with the Intifada. This group also included three Rabbis who were planning a 'solidarity visit to the holy places in Jerusalem and prayers for peace in the Middle East'.[15]

Apart from the general strike days and the demonstration in Nazareth in January 1988 the Arab political parties and groups in Israel proved themselves hesitant to participate in the coordinated planning necessary to organise such large-scale events. A key reason for this failure was the fact that each party was more interested in promoting its own campaign, trying to 'use the Intifada' for election purposes. Thus, during the election campaign of 1988 in the Arab community the candidates competed with each other to display their support for the PLO and the Intifada, using the jargon, symbols and slogans associated with the PLO and the Intifada in their search for votes. As one candidate proclaimed: 'First we must insist that we are Palestinians. We must support the Palestinian cause as Israeli citizens by contacts with the PLO and support for the Intifada.[16] In similar vein, it was noticeable that the leadership of political groupings repeatedly sought to attract support by meeting with PLO officials and the Palestinian national leadership in the occupied territories.[17]

2. *Material support*

The cooperation between Palestinians on both sides of the Green Line went far beyond political point-scoring and superficial dialogue. There were reports that some of the leaflets distributed in the occupied territories and signed by the UNC were printed in one of Israel's universities and some Arab villages. Printing businesses in the Galilee and Triangle were raided by Israeli police and some people were arrested. A more widespread form of cooperation and expression of solidarity, however, was evidenced by the emergence of popular relief committees to organise the provision of direct material support to the Palestinians in the occupied territories.

In considering the role of these relief committees it is important to realise the geographical proximity of the two communities. The distance between Arab villages in the Triangle region of Israel and the West Bank was only a very few miles. In two cases the villages actually straddled the Green Line. There is no doubt that this proximity and ease of access provided a unique opportunity for Palestinians in Israel to organise relief campaigns in support of the Intifada. This local activity undoubtedly spurred on the CFCAC to call for the establishment of Popular Relief Committees in all Arab locations when it met on January 19 1988. The committees that were established represented a broad range of political parties, social organisations, professionals, students and community groups in the channelling of food, clothing, medical supplies and money to the Palestinians in the occupied territories. By way of a contrast, the Islamic political movement in Israel did not cooperate in this project but continued to work through its own organisations and networks.

In general the work of the relief committees fell into two main categories: the supply of food and money, and the provision of medical supplies.

Right from the early days of the Intifada local committees emerged in each village to collect food, money and clothing from the residents to support the Intifada. Members of the committees would go round shops and from house to house asking for donations. This campaign took on added urgency as a result of the curfews and other forms of collective punishment imposed by the Israeli forces on villages and refugee camps in the occupied territories. The first few months of the Intifada witnessed a high level of generosity – people donated rice, lentils, flour, olive oil, olives, canned food and so on. During January 1988 it was estimated that more than 100,000 tons of food were sent to the occupied territories. Almost everybody who was asked for a donation responded positively.[18] There was a profound feeling among people that this was the least they could do to contribute while people were sacrificing their lives in the

West Bank and Gaza Strip - according to one account the equivalent of about £15,000 was collected in two days from two small Arab villages in the Triangle area.

A significant feature of the relief activities was the participation of Israelis, both Zionist and non-Zionist. In similar fashion, the Popular Relief Committees facilitated the bringing together of political opponents in the Arab sector. Thus, in May 1989 more than twenty political groups and peace organisations from both sectors joined in a campaign to send food to Rafah refugee camp in the Gaza Strip. Also noteworthy was the participation in the relief activities by Bedouin villages from the Negev, whilst Arab student committees in Israeli universities were particularly active in fund-raising. More significant however was the central role played by high-school students with pupils in each village organising campaigns to raise funds.

From the beginning, in tandem with the food campaign, local committees requested medical supplies from pharmacies. Some of the supplies were purchased with the money donated by people. In February 1988 there was the first direct appeal from the West Bank and Gaza Strip to the 'Committee to follow up the Health Concern in the Arab sector'. It came as a result of the large number of casualties, and called on 'the popular relief committees, the owners of chemists, medical traders and companies to help our brothers in the occupied territories. We urge you all to donate medicine and first aid material'.

Unfortunately a key feature of the medical supply campaign was its relatively poor organisation - largely operating without professional advice, and often with little coordination between the local committees and the health organisations in the occupied territories. As a result it was very difficult to estimate its effectiveness and worth. The limitations of the medical campaign could be attributed in part to both the decentralised nature of the campaign and the lack of any serious initiative from Arab medical personnel in Israel. But whatever the reasons the general response, particularly with regard to the donation of blood, was poor. Exceptions included the Arab university students, especially those at the Hebrew University in Jerusalem, who organised supplies in coordination with El Makassed Hospital in Jerusalem. As the head of the Arab students committee proudly remarked: 'We did not expect such a wide and positive assent from the students. They had to queue for hours to be able to give blood'.[19] Another exception was the Druze Initiative Committee which arranged visits to the West Bank to donate blood and visit injured people as acts of solidarity with the population.[20]

It is very difficult to give exact figures about the material and medical support given to the Intifada. Some observers have estimated its value as having reached somewhere in the region of £2 million by March 1990. However, there was a strong feeling among the Arab population that they had not demonstrated sufficient support. Indeed, it was only in December 1989, two years after the outbreak of the Intifada, that a 'national higher committee" was established to coordinate the activities of the local popular committees and arrange visits to identify the needs in the occupied territories.

3. Moral Support

At the outbreak of the Intifada the wide media coverage of the confrontations between Palestinians and the Israeli army inspired Palestinians in Israel to express deep concern and moral support for their fellow nationals. The Intifada prompted much discussion among people and became the major news in the Arabic press in Israel. On the one hand, people expressed a profound feeling of moral support, pride and admiration for the 'children of the stones', but on the other hand there was a growing feeling of anger, resentment and frustration towards the Israeli authorities. As one Um el Fahem resident commented in May 1989, 'Watching the news promotes discussion and anger against Israel. The Intifada is in our minds and hearts. In the streets, cafés, schools, the Intifada is the first topic we talk about.'[21]

The popular relief committees organised regular visits to villages and refugee camps in the occupied territories to express sympathy and solidarity with the struggle. There is no doubt that such visits had a deep impact on the Palestinian visitors from Israel. They could witness at first hand the circumstances of those living under occupation and their struggle to free themselves. The visits encouraged people to organise various activities in support of the Intifada when they returned home to their villages. This in turn strengthened the bonds between the two communities of Palestinians. The head of one local relief committee explained in an interview how the visits had reinforced the relationships:

> We think we can encourage them; it is our role to do that, but they encourage us as well. They see the end of this dark time. They are full of hope and believe that the day will come when their struggle will succeed in overcoming the occupation.

A Disappointing Effort?

Although there was consensus amongst all shades of political opinion within the Arab community concerning the importance of supporting the Intifada, there was considerable controversy over the actual level of that support. Thus, it would appear that after the Land Day strike of 1988 the level of solidarity action dropped. Even though political parties proclaimed the importance of developing further means of supporting the struggle, few of them invested the necessary effort to translate their words into action. In fact it became clear that the political groups had not even exploited to the full all the legal possibilities for extending support, let alone engaging in any forms of civil disobedience. As one Arab activist remarked:

> I am not satisfied with the moral and material support that Palestinians in Israel have given to their brothers in the State of Palestine. The re-

> lief campaign has become 'seasonal' and sometimes only for propaganda. Our voice inside has not reached its maximum effect and power.[22]

Evidence to support this view emerged from Rouhana's interviews with sixty Arab leaders from all points on the political spectrum who agreed that 'the absolute value of the support is minimal and fell below that which their community could and should be offering'.[23]

This sense of disappointment came to be shared by the Palestinians in the occupied territories. This was in sharp contrast to the admiration expressed for the support shown during the first months of the uprising when a Palestinian lecturer at the Islamic University in Gaza was moved to bear witness that 'the donations of the first months of the Intifada had helped to stop a siege on the refugee camps in Gaza Strip. We did not expect Palestinians in Israel to play any role or to give any help'.[24]

Effects of the Intifada on Palestinians in Israel

1. *A sense of solidarity and unity*

One result of the 1967 war was that it brought together two parts of the Palestinian people after twenty years of separation. A major consequence of the Intifada was to strengthen this sense of a common bond between the two communities, a shared awareness of their identity as Palestinians. The Intifada became a part of the political awareness of Arabs in Israel and contributed to a strengthening of their self-confidence and political determination. As one Arab activist remarked: 'The Intifada has become a model for us, how we should face the occupation. We now see a possibility of ending our own oppression.'[25]

It seems clear that the 'national unity" established between the different factions within the occupied territories during the Intifada also had an effect on political life in the Arab community in Israel. Thus, the Committee to Follow Up the Concerns of Arab Citizens became the forum in which major decisions were made and for a while it took on the mantle of a legitimate national leadership. As Rouhana observed:

> The committee gained the respect of the Arab public through its show of unity, despite deep political divisions within its ranks. The committee has earned the status of national leadership because it represents daily concerns, national needs, and the consensual political views of the Arabs in Israel. No other authority, including the Israeli Government, enjoys such status within the Arab community.[26]

2. *A sense of difference*

In the years prior to the Intifada the main political agenda of the Arabs in Israel had been twofold: to seek equal rights within Israel and to campaign for the establishment of a Palestinian state. In a paradoxical manner, whilst the Intifada strengthened the sense of solidarity and actual support for the establishment of a Palestinian state amongst Arab citizens of Israel, it also heightened their sense of separateness, the awareness that the actual differences between the two communities had increased. Palestinians in the occupied territories were engaged in a national struggle for liberation and were denying the legitimacy of Israeli rule. The Arabs in Israel, in contrast, were a part of Israeli society and citizens of the Israeli state. However disadvantaged they might be, they were an undeniable part of the socio-political and economic life of Israel. As Majid al-Haj remarked, 'The orientation of Israeli Arabs is different from that of the Palestinians in the territories. The Israeli Arabs want to adapt, the Palestinians want to secede.'[27] From this perspective it becomes possible to argue that far from 'crossing the Green Line', the Intifada reinforced the boundary separating not just the Israeli Jews but also the Arab citizens of Israel from the Palestinians of the West Bank and Gaza Strip.

3. Double marginality

As noted Palestinians in Israel continued to see their main political struggle as encompassing the two goals of equal rights within Israel and an independent Palestinian state. In relation to both the Israeli state and the anticipated Palestinian state, they occupied a marginal position on the periphery of both entities. To this day they have not been fully integrated into Israeli society, they are still discriminated against and still constitute a disadvantaged sector of that society. Furthermore, they have remained marginal to the struggle for a Palestinian state, they played a supporting role in the Intifada but were never central to the struggle, whilst the dreamed of Palestinian state in the West Bank and Gaza Strip remained the goal of the Palestinians and was never intended for them.

The Uprising had the effect of heightening this sense and experience of 'double marginality'. The Intifada remained the struggle of the Palestinians in the occupied territories, not that of the Palestinian citizens of Israel. Moreover, as a result of the clashes between Palestinians and Israeli Jews in the occupied territories and the open support for the Intifada amongst the Arabs of Israel, the tensions between the Arab and Jewish citizens of Israel were intensified during the Intifada, with feelings of bitterness and anger, mistrust and fear characterising relationships between the majority and minority communities within Israel.

The Israeli Reaction

1. Threats and sanctions

From the start the response of the Israeli authorities to Arab expressions of solidarity with the Intifada was harsh. In particular the Peace Day general strike on December 21 1987 met with a severe reaction from politicians across the political spectrum and led to calls for 'tough measures' to be taken against the Arab population. President Chaim Herzog was quoted as saying that 'the demonstrations could lead to another chapter in the Palestinian tragedy'.[28] This was interpreted by many as a sinister reference to 1948 and the exodus of the majority of the Palestinians from their homeland. In similar vein Defence Minister Rabin advised Arab Knesset members that 'you have known tragedy in the distant past, and it would be better for you and for us that you not return to that tragedy'.[29] Prime Minister Shamir expressed his belief that 'Arabs do not know the meaning of democracy', and warned them that their stand with regard to the Intifada would eventually determine their status in the country. He offered them a stark choice: 'They could follow the PLO or remain loyal citizens of Israel. But if they chose the path of the PLO, there would be dire consequences'.[30] The then deputy minister responsible for Arab affairs urged that government offices should cease all dealing with the Committee of Local Arab Council Heads, whilst the leader of the Likud party in the Knesset advocated the re-imposition of military rule over the Arab population in Israel and the cutting off of all financial aid to Arab councils that supported the strike.[31] Other Knesset members demanded the dismissal of all Arab workers who supported the PLO and/or participated in the strike, and their replacement by Jewish or foreign workers.

The attacks on the Arab population from the Israeli extreme right-wing, although more predictable, were vicious. The Tehiya Party presented a proposal to the Knesset that suggested revoking the Israeli citizenship of Arab citizens who were involved in any incitement to oppose the state or who cooperated with 'terrorist organizations'.[32] Such demands and warnings made it very clear to the Arab population that they were not equal citizens of the state and they did not have the same right to protest against government policy as the rest of the population. It became apparent to many Arabs that not only were they 'second-class' citizens, but they were also 'conditional citizens' - their citizenship being dependent upon 'good" political behaviour.

If one of the aims of these threats was to intimidate the Palestinian citizens of Israel and deter them from engaging in any further displays of solidarity with the Intifada, then the tactic met with some success. As one commentator confirmed:

> For older people the government's reaction to initial support of the Intifada was strong enough a message to stop any further expressions of support. The reaction of Israeli officials to these expressions of support, including that of Shamir, was so mean and threatening at the time, as to have left many observers shocked and bewildered.[33]

2. *New measures*

It was clear that the traditional perception of the Arabs in Israel as an internal security threat came once more to the fore during the Intifada. There were claims that the Intifada had crossed the Green Line, that the threats to the very existence of Israel came not just from the Arabs outside but also from the Arabs inside the country. This all helped to justify and explain the need for new measures to monitor and control the enemy within.

In addition to the formation of new intelligence and police units, new legislation was introduced with the aim of halting the flow of cash from abroad to Palestinians in Israel and the occupied territories. The Third Amendment to the Prevention of Terror Ordinance (1984) came into force on May 23 1989. It made it an offence to receive or bring into the country property known by the recipient to be connected with a terrorist organisation; permitted the foreclosure on property received directly or indirectly from a terrorist organisation or property that was thought to be used for the purposes of such an organisation; permitted the registration corporations to refuse to register a company or association suspected of being an illegal corporation.[34] Furthermore the new law was retroactive so existing associations also became liable to foreclosure.[35] In conjunction with these legislative and policy changes police officers were given new wide ranging powers to seize property from individuals, associations and any premises used by them, including the right to enter such premises without a search warrant.

Palestinians in both Israel and the occupied territories expressed deep concern about the new measures. It was obvious that the measures had been brought into effect to stop the flow of financial assistance to the Intifada from abroad, and a major conduit for this support was believed to have been channelled through the 70 or so non-profit making associations operating in the fields of education, culture, health, economic development and human rights within the Arab sector of Israel. Accordingly the direct targets of the new legislation were the Palestinian organizations in Israel.

3. Racism

The Intifada, and the reaction it unleashed in Israeli society provided fertile ground for the growth of racist attitudes. The result was the emergence of a political and social climate within which groups and individuals felt free to express their prejudices against the Arab population resident within Israel. The incitement campaign led by top Israeli officials against the Palestinian community in Israel a few weeks after the outbreak of the Intifada had the effect of encouraging others to engage in hostile and racist attacks. One result was that the ethnic cleansing of Israel through the 'transfer' of the Arab population from one part of the country to another, or even outside the country altogether, became a legitimate topic of political debate, along with increasing demands to limit the rights of Arabs in Israel.

At a meeting of the Israeli government held in mid-1988 the situation of the Arabs in Israel was discussed. One Likud member of the government likened them to the 'sharp edge of the javelin' at the head of all the 'enemies of Israel', including the PLO The proposals discussed to control this threat from within included the suggestion that every citizen should be required to swear allegiance to the state flag, laws should be introduced to deal with Arab nationalism, and Arabs should be required to serve in the Israeli army with a maximum penalty of loss of citizenship and expulsion from the country for refusal.[36] Furthermore, a number of public and political figures came out in favour of some form of 'transfer' of the Palestinian population within Israel. The minister for agriculture, Katz Aoz, declared in May 1989, during a visit to a Jewish settlement in the Galilee, that his aim was to create an: 'internal transfer of the Arab population'. He suggested there be a mass transfer of Arabs from the Galilee to other parts of the country to ensure a Jewish majority there.[37] The President of Beersheva University made the astonishing admission that he opposed the transfer of Arabs - not because of moral considerations but on practical grounds alone![38]

The Jewish mayors of mixed towns, with Arabs and Jewish populations were to the fore in advocating the relocation of Arab inhabitants. The mayor of Acre expressed his desire to see Arabs move out of the old city, maintaining that: 'I want to help them with their housing problem. Those who do not agree will not be forced to leave. But if they do not want to leave they should not complain.'[39] In a similar vein the Mayor of Naharya, to the north of Acre, described the presence of 250 Arab families living in the town as

> … a dangerous phenomenon that we have to put an end to, because we do not want the town to be an Arab Jewish mixed town like Acre. Arabs can work in the town but they need not live here.[40]

Zri Bar, a former commander of the paramilitary Border Guards and Likud mayor of Bamat Gan, a town adjacent to Tel Aviv, called upon Jewish municipal heads to hire Jews in place of the thousands of Arabs employed by the municipalities. He justified his plea by charging that 80 percent of the murders, rapes and homosexual assaults in Tel Aviv were perpetrated by the Arabs! As he spoke hundreds of Jews were scouring the streets of Ashdod beating up Arab workers after the discovery of the body of a paratrooper who had gone missing three months previously.[41]

The growth of racist attitudes within Israel was reflected in opinion polls. In 1988 a survey of 1,152 Israelis that excluded Arabs, kibbutz members and settlers from the occupied territories revealed that 41 percent of the respondents supported the transfer of the Arab population in Israel, 45 percent thought that Israel was too democratic, and 51 percent opposed granting equal rights to Arab citizens of Israel.[42] In a survey of 1,200 Israeli Jews carried out in April 1988 Professor Smooha of Haifa University discovered that 68 percent agreed that the right to vote should be denied to 'Israelis who support a Palestinian state in the West Bank and Gaza under the leadership of the PLO'. 57 percent favoured the denial of the right to vote in national elections to Israeli Arab citizens.[43]

4. Attacks against Arabs

One of the consequences of the Intifada was a heightening of the demonization and dehumanisation of the Palestinians in the eyes of the Jewish citizens of Israel. This was evidenced most clearly by the increase in the numbers of physical attacks on Arabs. Prime Minister Shamir seemed to endorse such assaults when, in response to the killing of two Israelis in Jerusalem in May 1989, he urged citizens to be prepared to defend themselves against such attacks and to make sure that assailants 'do not get away unharmed'. One of the earliest examples of the lynch-mob atmosphere occurred in the summer of 1988 in Or Yahoda, near Tel Aviv, when three workers from the Gaza Strip were burned to death while they were sleeping in their hut. Later, in September of the same year, a flat in Jaffa used by Arab workers was burned down, in this case without injuring the occupiers. There were also a number of stabbing attacks on Arab workers, one of which resulted in the death of a worker from the Galilee during his work in the market of the old city of Acre.[44]

For Arabs in Israel the result of such attacks was an increasing sense of insecurity and fear. They felt vulnerable and largely unprotected. Some even began to avoid speaking Arabic in public when they were in the cities, so as to avoid drawing attention to themselves. This fear became all the deeper after the murder of eight Palestinians by an Israeli gunman on May 21 1990. In such an atmosphere the Arab media in Israel became the target of special attention. During the first two years of the Intifada two Arab weeklies, *Al-Raya* and *Al-Jamaheer*, were closed down on the grounds that they had links with terrorist organisations. *Derech Hanitzotz*, a weekly published in Arabic and Hebrew, was closed down on the same grounds. *Al-Ittihad*, the only Arabic language daily in Israel, was closed by the Israeli authorities for a week in March 1989. This closure, which took effect just before Land Day, came as a consequence of the paper publishing 'provocative articles and news which identified with the uprising in the occupied territories and which threatened public security'. In June 1990 *Sawt-al-Haq Will Hurriya*, a weekly associated with the Islamic movement, was closed for three months on the orders of the minister of the interior.

Political activists within the Palestinian community of Israel were also targeted by the security forces. By June 1988 it had been estimated that 663 arrests had been made for activities related to solidarity and support for the Intifada. Amongst their number were several detained without trial, whilst many of them were activists in the popular relief committees. During 1989 Palestinian activists in Israel began to experience an intensification of this 'hard-line' approach. Whereas the authorities had shown a degree of tolerance towards slogans identifying with the Palestinian struggle in the occupied territories, by mid-1990 this attitude had toughened. People participating in legal demonstrations were now arrested for shouting slogans considered by the Israelis to be an 'incitement to violence'.

Conclusion

With the outbreak of the Intifada Palestinians in Israel began expressing heart-felt feelings of solidarity and identification with the Palestinian struggle in the occupied territories. They showed this solidarity by organising general strikes and demonstrations. Popular relief committees were also established to provide food, money and medical supplies to the population of the occupied territories. However the harsh Israeli reaction and the fractures between the different Arab political groupings brought about a gradual decline in the level of active support after the first few months of the Uprising.

Under the impact of the Intifada the tension between the twin dimensions of the identity of Arabs in Israel has mounted. They were Palestinians, but they were also citizens of the state of Israel. This duality had been reflected in the political struggle of the Arab community within Israel, which developed along twin paths and was sharpened under the impact of the uprising. The 'twin-track' nature of their political programme reflected their structural location on the periphery of both the Palestinian nationalist movement and Israeli society itself. They were not fully integrated into the struggle of the Palestinians of the West Bank and Gaza Strip, neither were they fully integrated as equal citizens of Israel. Whilst some observers felt that this position of being on a 'double periphery', with a foot in both camps, so to speak, made the Palestinian citizens of Israel a potential bridge between the two sides in the ongoing conflict around the continuing occupation of the Palestinian territories, the years that have intervened since the end of the first Intifada have provided little or no evidence that such a space exists for them to fulfil such a peace-making role. Indeed, with the passage of time the Palestinians inside Israel have found themselves in an increasingly sensitive and vulnerable position, particularly in the context of the increasing racism in Israel and the continuing attempts by the state to suppress any political manifestations of the Palestinian national identity.

[1] Throughout this chapter such terms as 'Arabs in Israel' , 'Palestinian citizens of Israel', 'Arab sector', 'Arab community' will be used as labels for the communities that have grown up from the Palestinian population that remained in the country after 1948. These terms are highly political and contested, and have been used in the text as seemed appropriate

[2] Much of this chapter is based on interviews carried out by Marwan Darweish during 1989.

[3] Sami Mari, *Arab education in Israel*, Syracuse, NY: Syracuse University Press, 1978, p. 18.

[4] A detailed account of the land confiscation can be found in Sabri Jiriys, *The Arabs In Israel*, London: Monthly Review Press, 1976.

[5] Sarah Kreimer, 'Entrepreneurialism in Israel's Arab communities', *New Outlook*, July-August 1987, p. 9. See also Elia Zureik, *The Palestinians in Israel; A study in internal colonialism*, London: Routledge & Kegan Paul, 1979.

[6] *Jerusalem Post*, May 5 1988, May 13 1988 & December 21, 1988.

[7] See *Arab education in Israel* and S. Graham-Brown, *Education, repression and liberation*, London: World University Service, 1984.

[8] Quoted in *Al-Itihad*, December 20, 1987.

[9] Quoted in *Davar*, March 16, 1988.

[10] It was significant that there was full participation of the Arab minority from both the 'mixed towns' and from Bedouin villages where political involvement in Arab political activity had been relatively weak prior to the Intifada.

[11] *Present Tense*, April-May, 1988. It was noticeable that the Hebrew press (in contrast with the Arabic press) presented a very dramatic picture of the events. See *Ha'aretz*, *Maariv*, *Yediot-Ahnanot*, December 22, 1987.

[12] Interview, May 16, 1989.

[13] Nadim Rouhana, "The Intifada and the Palestinians of Israel: Resurrecting the Green Line', Journal of Palestine Studies, v. 19/3, no. 75, 1990, p. 64.

[14] Interview, May 16, 1989.
[15] *Al-Ittihad*, February 2, 1988.
[16] Quoted in *Jerusalem Post (International edition)*, June 24, 1989.
[17] See *Ha'aretz*, April 25, 1989.
[18] Personal experience collecting donations in Umm Al Fahem.
[19] Interview, May 1989.
[20] The Druze Initiative Committee was established in 1975 to support members of the Druze community in Israel who refused to serve in the Israeli military.
[21] Interview, May 1989.
[22] Quoted in *Kul-al-Arab*, February 27, 1989.
[23] 'The Intifada and the Palestinians of Israel', p. 64.
[24] Personal communication.
[25] Personal communication.
[26] N. Rouhana, 'The political transformation of the Palestinians in Israel: From acquiescence to challenge', *Journal of Palestine Studies*, v. 18, n. 3, Spring 1989, p. 45.
[27] *Present Tense*, April-May 1988.
[28] *Jerusalem Post*, December 25, 1987.
[29] Quoted in *Jerusalem Post,* December 22, 1987.
[30] Quoted in *Jewish Herald* (New York), January 8, 1988.
[31] *Ha'aretz*, December 21, 1987.
[32] *Hatsofeh*, December 22, 1987.
[33] Ghassan Bishara, *Al Fajr*, September 4, 1989, p. 5.
[34] *Al Fajr*, July 10, 1989, p. 9.
[35] *Middle East International,* June 23, 1989, pp. 8 -9.
[36] Reported in *Bi-Aritz*, n. 189, September 4, 1988, p. 32.
[37] Quoted in *Davar*, May 18, 1989.
[38] *Hadashot*, February 24, 1988.
[39] *Jerusalem Post*, February 24, 1989.
[40] *Al-Ittihad*, May 19, 1989.
[41] *Middle East International*, May 12, 1989, p. 7.
[42] *Ha'aretz*, May 8, 1988.
[43] *Al Fajr*, June 11, 1990, p. 3.
[44] *Maariv*, September 15, 1988.

POSTSCRIPT

PALESTINIAN POPULAR RESISTANCE SINCE THE FIRST INTIFADA

The aim of this chapter is to review the waves of popular unarmed resistance that have taken place in the occupied Palestinian territories since the first Intifada. Before engaging with the analysis, however, the historical context needs to be set.

'Oslo Accords'

In June 1992 a Labour-led coalition came to power in Israel that was publicly committed to 'land for peace', whilst the PLO was feeling diplomatically isolated on the world stage and feared the growing influence of *Hamas* within the occupied territories. This was the context for the 'track two' negotiations facilitated by Norway that came to be known as the Oslo Process, and which resulted in the joint Israeli-Palestinian Declaration of Principles that was signed at the White House in Washington on September 3, 1993. In the preamble to the Declaration both sides agreed:

> … it is time to put an end to decades of confrontation and conflict, recognize their mutual legitimate and political rights, and strive to live in peaceful coexistence and mutual dignity and security and achieve a just, lasting and comprehensive peace settlement and historic reconciliation through the agreed political process.

There was widespread euphoria at the announcement, which we now know to have been tragically misplaced. Israel continued to negotiate from its position of strength, imposing its demands on its weaker partner.

'Oslo II' and the fragmentation of the Palestinian territories[1]

In July 1994 Arafat set up office in Gaza City but whilst the Palestinian flag was flying in the Gaza Strip and in Jericho Israel continued to control the borders of these small pockets of land and thereby dictated security policy and to a very large extent controlled the economic life of the autonomous cantons. What unfolded in the subsequent years was a cycle of violence driven on the Palestinian side by a growing sense of frustration at the lack of any peace dividend. It was also fuelled by Islamist political groups who, in an effort to challenge the Oslo Accords which they deemed to be a betrayal of the Palestinian patrimony, recruited suicide bombers to target civilians within Israel. The Israelis responded with targeted assassinations, collective sanctions (particularly the closure policy that prevented movement of Palestinians within the occupied territories), new expropriations of land for settlements, the suspension of negotiations, and renewed pressure on the Palestinian Authority (PA) to deal with the 'terrorists'. The impact of the closures was particularly harsh, resulting in escalating unemployment and levels of poverty, whilst enforcing the separation of the West Bank from the Gaza Strip, with Israel controlling all movement between the two territories. Meantime Israel continued to construct and expand the settlements along with a large network of connecting roads to serve them. In effect the territories were being divided into separate segments by these new 'facts on the ground', a situation that was formalised by the second 'Interim Agreement' signed on September 28 1995.

'Oslo II', as it came to be known, divided the West Bank into three administrative divisions categorised as Areas A, B and C, each to enjoy a different degree of Palestinian self-government until a final peace agreement was established. [2] Area A covered three percent of the West Bank encompassing the main Palestinian population centres but excluding East Jerusalem. This was to be under the full civil and security control of the PA. Area B covered 23 – 25 percent of the West Bank and included those rural areas where there were no Israeli settlements. Within this area the PA would exercise civil control but security would be the joint responsibility of the Israeli and Palestinian authorities. Area C covered the remainder of the West Bank, approximately 73 percent of the territory and here Israel was to continue to exercise complete civil and security control. It was widely presumed that once the interim agreement was in place and progress towards a final settlement underway then Israel would gradually transfer increasing tracts of territory over to Palestinian control. The presumption was that over a period the Palestinians would move towards self-government over expanding stretches of contiguous territory rather than in the separate pockets separated from the others by territory over which Israel retained control as established under the interim agreement. In 1995 there might have been grounds for such an optimistic scenario, but as events unfolded it became increasingly clear that Israel had no intention of transferring territory of any significant scale over to the PA. At the time of writing Area C, over which Israel exercises complete control, covers over 60 percent of the West Bank.

The combined impact of these developments was to bring about a set of conditions that undermined any possibility of launching any new mass-based unarmed civilian resistance movement against the occupation.

1. First of all, any initiative had to deal with the PA that had been tasked by Israel and its international backers with controlling dissent within the Palestinian community. From the start the PA displayed a marked suspicion and antipathy towards any civil society organisation that evidenced signs of

independence of thought, action and funding.[3] Moreover, the PA had rapidly developed a track record for corruption and nepotism rather than respect for human rights and democratic processes.

2. Secondly, for the majority of the Palestinians within the population centres designated as Area A the occupation was experienced 'at a distance'. The Israeli soldiers were no longer entering the streets of the towns and villages on a daily basis, they were manning the check-points that controlled the movement of Palestinians between their zones of relative autonomy. Moreover, the settlers now travelled along highways specially designated for them from which Palestinians were banned. As a consequence there were no immediate sites of contention at which Palestinian protestors might confront the agents of the occupation, except at the growing number of checkpoints and road-blocs.
3. The leverage power over the Israelis that could be exerted by Palestinian non-cooperation was virtually nil. Drawing the lessons from the Intifada, Israel had attracted guest-workers from around the globe to take the place of the Palestinian labour upon which significant sectors of the Israeli economy had once depended.
4. There was a lack of potential leaders of any coordinated unarmed popular resistance movement. The cadres from the Intifada followed different trajectories, but two career paths were common. Some joined the new PA, whilst others founded or joined non-governmental organisations concerned with themes like democratisation and peace-building, a trend encouraged by foreign donors who directed funds towards the promotion of warmer relationships between Palestinians and Israelis through 'people-to-people' dialogue projects. Such programmes often included conflict resolution training and capacity-building components, but they did not include training for unarmed civil resistance.[4]

As a consequence of these factors, by the summer of 2000 the occupation seemed more firmly entrenched than ever. The confiscation of land and the expansion of settlements had continued at an accelerated pace since the signing of the Declaration of Principles. The West Bank and Gaza Strip had been divided into cantons separated from each other by Israeli controlled territory. Innumerable check-points and barriers had been set up throughout the territories controlling the movement of Palestinians and enabling the Israelis to confine them within their particular enclaves, with disastrous consequences for economic activity and general living standards. Moreover, as Sarah Roy observed, 'In these policies Israel relied on the Palestinian Authority and its vast security apparatus to maintain control of the population, suppress any visible forms of opposition, and provide protection for Israeli actions.' [5]

The second (Al Aqsa) Intifada

The second (Al Aqsa) Intifada began in September 2000, occasioned by Ariel Sharon's provocative entry into the Temple Mount/ al-Haram al-Sharif area. But the deeper cause was the build-up of resentment and anger resulting from seven years of a peace process that had served to deepen Palestinian dispossession and deprivation whilst strengthening the Israeli occupation, a situation made worse by the malfunctioning of the Palestinian Administration and its leadership. The rapid militarisation of the uprising effectively side-lined any significant role for civil society groups in the struggle. A younger generation of cadres came to the fore who were influenced to a significant degree by the example of Hezbollah in Southern Lebanon whose guerrilla tactics had succeeded in forcing Israel to withdraw in May 2000.

Within a short while every Palestinian faction, secular and Islamic, had spawned its own armed militia. Armed struggle was back on the agenda. Particularly significant was the re-emergence of the armed wing of *Hamas* which took the fight beyond the borders into Israel itself. The suicide bombings inevitably brought about massive Israeli retaliation. Following the murder of 30 Israeli Jews in a suicide bombing at a restaurant in Netanya on March 27 2002 the Israelis launched Operation Defensive Shield

Table 1

1st Intifada	2nd Intifada
Predominantly unarmed resistance.	Predominantly armed/violent resistance.
Mass civilian involvement.	Civilians confined to 'support' functions.
Cohesion & unity via popular committees.	Fragmentation with power to local militias.
Predominantly secular.	Enhanced confessional character.
Attempts to influence Israeli publics through dialogue of words and actions, shame power etc.	Attempts to influence Israeli publics through intimidation and fear.
Active support from Israeli peace groups.	Limited role for Israeli peace groups in context of suicide bombings/terror attacks.
Significant international support & third party pressure for peace settlement.	Particularly after September 11, 2001 resistance viewed through the lens of 'war on terror'.

and re-occupied the Palestinian enclaves from which they had withdrawn under the terms of the 'Interim Agreement' of September 1995. They then intensified their domination of every aspect of Palestinian life - enforcing curfews and closures, demolishing dwellings and forcing people out of their homes, effecting mass arrests, assassinating alleged militants and other 'terrorists'. Amidst the violence and the associated destruction of the socio-economic fabric of Palestinian society, there was little space for any large-scale unarmed resistance. Indeed, sometimes it seemed as if the prime role of Palestinian civilians was to act, like their Israeli counterparts, as vehicles for propaganda in their capacity as 'innocent victims' of the barbaric outrages of the 'other'.

The second Intifada thus stood in stark contrast to the first, its violent character limiting both internal participation and external third party involvement and support. The main points of contrast are summarised in table 1.

Construction of the separation barrier and the re-emergence of unarmed popular resistance

Some people did issue repeated calls for a turn towards civilian-based popular resistance along the lines of the first Intifada, but the necessary conditions for this were no longer present. Since Oslo there had been an increase in social, economic, geographical and political divisions within Palestinian society which had undermined the level of social solidarity and trust necessary for large-scale civilian mobilisation. Moreover, in place of the dense network of civil society organisations that had been one of the seed-beds of the first Intifada, Palestinian society was now dominated by foreign-funded NGOs with relatively tenuous links with the grass-roots. Furthermore the weakness of the PA and the debilitating impact of the *Fatah - Hamas* political rivalry meant that there was not the political coordination necessary for mass mobilisation. As one veteran of the first Intifada observed,

> There is no unified command, no programme, no real coordination between the different political forces. ... The 1987 Intifada was a complete system, which ruled our lives. And the

> objective of the movement was clear. Today nobody knows what we want.[6]

The result was that throughout the second Intifada unarmed civilian resistance remained localised and overshadowed by the violence of the militias. However, by 2003 the instances of popular unarmed resistance had begun to multiply, sparked by the Israeli decision to construct a Wall to act as a physical barrier between the West Bank and Israel. They commenced construction in the spring of 2002 and within a very short while its impact was being felt by villagers who were denied access to their fields, saw their trees destroyed and their land expropriated. It was this new challenge to their well-being and way of life that sparked a wave of protest. As the Separation Wall extended and more villages organised to resist its advance, so other communities who were threatened by the expansion of settlements threatening the expropriation of their land began to organise and protest. As the number of sites of contestation increased many of the local organisers, who were drawn mainly from the generation of the first Intifada activists, allowed themselves to dream that they might be initiating a new unarmed Uprising. As one leader of a local popular committee expressed it, 'We came alive in the first Intifada. Then we died in the second. Maybe now we are being reborn.'

Overview of popular resistance, 2003 – 2014

Looking back over this period what we saw was the emergence of a series of localised centres of active popular resistance against the construction of the Wall or the threat of land expropriation from local settlements. At no stage was there anything comparable to a mass movement of protest – at the height of the popular resistance during 2010-11 there was a maximum of 40 - 50 villages and neighbourhoods where there was some form of organised unarmed resistance against the ongoing occupation. Some of these pockets of resistance, such as Budrus and Bil'in, gained an international profile during the peak of their resistance but this declined with the passage of time. Despite the difference in scale compared with the period of the first Intifada there have been some notable features of the more contemporary wave of popular resistance that are worthy of note.

1. Most village-level campaigns were launched after people saw the bulldozers approaching their lands or settlers setting up fences in preparation for land expropriations. There was virtually no advance planning – in most locations it was a case of reacting to a new development initiated by the Israeli state or settlers.
2. In the first Intifada the main international presence had been the flood of journalists who covered the first months of the Uprising. One of the significant aspects of the more recent wave of popular resistance has been the involvement of international and Israeli solidarity activists. Palestinians in the main welcomed this involvement as a sign that they were not alone, and because the Israeli occupation forces and settlers seemed to moderate their violence when internationals and Israelis were present. In this manner the internationals acted as a kind of protective shield for the Palestinian protesters.
3. Another significant role played by international and Israeli activists has been as long-term accompaniers of those Palestinians particularly at risk of violence from Israeli occupation forces and settlers, particularly those Palestinians living in zones designated as Area C such as the Jordan Valley, the South Hebron Hills and Hebron city itself where they have remained under constant pressure as a consequence of Israel's ethnic cleansing policies in areas. For example, in the South Hebron Hills activists from the Israeli solidarity group *Ta'ayush* and from *Rabbis for Human Rights* have acted as a protective presence in the area since 2000. In 2004 they were joined by international volunteers with the Italian project *Operation Dove* who have been accompanying local children on their route to school that passes close to an Israeli

settlement. In the old city of Hebron a Christian Peacemakers Team has been present since 1995.[7] More recently, in 2002, the World Council of Churches established The Ecumenical Accompaniment Programme in Palestine and Israel (EAPPI) in response to a call from the local Heads of Churches in Jerusalem. By 2015 this programme had brought over 1500 volunteers to act as accompaniers for periods of three months in different locations in the West Bank.[8] The prime goal of such activists has been to work with local communities in order to strengthen their steadfastness and resilience (*sumud)* in the face of unceasing assaults on their way of life and attempts to undermine their resolve. For much of the time this support has been expressed through accompaniment and associated documentation and dissemination of reports of the human rights abuses perpetrated against them. But there have also been more direct and constructive forms of support, such as rebuilding dwelling places that have been destroyed, building schools and kindergartens, constructing play areas for children, trying to ensure the supply of basic amenities such as clean water.

4. Another feature of the more recent wave of popular resistance compared with earlier periods has been the increased use of new forms of communication and technology to monitor and record abuses perpetrated by Israeli occupation forces and settlers, with footage uploaded to websites within minutes of their being recorded, and thereby made available to networks across the globe.
5. Whilst demonstrations and confrontations have been important as a way of challenging particular threats to Palestinian interests, Palestinians have had most success reclaiming land threatened with confiscation by resorting to the Israeli legal system. One case that attracted international attention was that initiated by activists from Bil'in . The Wall was constructed initially such that a significant area of village land was left on the Israeli side of the barrier. Alongside the

regular protest actions local activists with the assistance of Israeli solidarity groups such as *Yesh Din (There is law)* took the matter to the Israeli courts. The villagers' claim to the land was recognised and on September 4 2007 the Israeli Supreme Court ordered the Wall to be rerouted.

6. One of the most notable features of the post-second Intifada popular resistance has been that it has been confined largely to various pockets of resistance within the West Bank, with little or no civilian-based resistance within the Gaza Strip. Israel withdrew from the Gaza Strip in 2005, and in June 2007 Hamas seized control following months of clashes between Fatah and Hamas militias. The immediate outcome was international condemnation of the coup and the new Gaza-based administration and widespread support for the Israeli blockade. As a consequence the Gazan population were forced to survive in a 365 square kilometre prison compound. In such circumstances resentment against the Israeli gaolers grew, as did the desperate rhetoric of the Hamas administration. Militant groups took to launching rockets at Israeli population centres, which provided the Israelis with the pretext for launching the three wars that have taken place since 2008.[9]

In such a context there has been very little space for civilian - based resistance apart from constructive work to provide for the basic needs of the population. International activists have tried to play a supporting role both on the ground and through various efforts to challenge the Israeli blockade by attempts to deliver humanitarian aid by sea.[10] However, in January 2011 a group of young Gazans, inspired by the events of the 'Arab Spring' in Tunisia and Egypt, issued their own heart-felt cry for change. It concluded with the following words:

> We want three things. We want to be free. We want to be able to live a normal life. We want peace. Is that too much to ask? We are a peace movement consisting of young people in Gaza

> and supporters elsewhere that will not rest until the truth about Gaza is known by everybody in this whole world and in such a degree that no more silent consent or loud indifference will be accepted.
> This is the Gazan youth's manifesto for change!
> We will start by destroying the occupation that surrounds ourselves, we will break free from this mental incarceration and regain our dignity and self-respect. We will carry our heads high even though we will face resistance. We will work day and night in order to change these miserable conditions we are living under. We will build dreams where we meet walls.[11]

They liaised with contemporaries in the West Bank and farther afield, and planned a day of demonstrations to take place in Gaza and the West Bank demanding political unity and an end to the split between Hamas and Fatah. On March 15 2011 thousands of predominantly young people marched in different locations. They were met by Fatah thugs in the West Bank and Hamas thugs in the Gaza Strip who attempted to hijack the protests and disperse the marchers. An indication of how both regimes could feel threatened by manifestations of popular protest – a far cry from the first Intifada.

The challenges facing popular resistance in the occupied Palestinian territories

It is clear that whilst the first Intifada succeeded in shaking Israeli decision-makers and touching significant sections of the Israeli public, the more recent waves of popular unarmed resistance – particularly the resistance to the construction of the Separation Wall and associated expansion of settlements – have failed to impose sufficient cost on Israel to cause any significant re-assessment of the wisdom of continued occupation of Palestinian territory. At the same time this does not mean that the popular resistance has been pointless and futile. The resistance has been significant as an ongoing symbol of the Palestinian refusal to acquiesce to the status quo of occupation and as a means of communicating that refusal – and the justness of their cause – to wider constituencies globally. As such direct comparisons can be made between the popular unarmed resistance of the Palestinians and the nonviolent resistance to Nazi occupation in occupied Europe during the Second World War. Europeans who engaged in different forms of unarmed resistance against German occupation never thought that their activities would somehow drive out the enemy. Liberation, they knew, would have to come through outside intervention in the guise of the military might of the allied forces.The significance of their resistance lay in the way the different acts of dissidence and defiance evidenced the fact that significant sections of the subject population refused to accept the legitimacy of the occupiers' regime. As Jacques Semelin noted, the goal of such activities was 'to preserve the collective identity of the attacked societies; that is to say, their fundamental values. ... civilian resistance consisted primarily of a clash of wills, expressing above all a fight for values.'[12]

This point – and the nature of the outside intervention that Palestinians might anticipate in their struggle to end the occupation – will be returned to later. For now, though, the question remains: Why have the Palestinians been unable to launch a mass movement of popular resistance against occupation? Why is it that the popular resistance has been confined to particular pockets and has never looked like developing into a mass movement?

When you discuss this matter with members of the popular resistance committees that were formed to coordinate resistance in villages and neighbourhoods they point to a number of challenges that they face in mobilising people. They point to the deepening sense of resignation amongst people – 'We fought against the construction and the routing of the Wall and we lost, so why continue with a futile resistance that only imposes extra burdens on us?' There is also the political fracture between Fatah and Hamas that has been so debilitating and damaging to the Palestinian cause. There is the widespread distrust of anyone seeking to set themselves up as a leader, even at the grassroots level – there is the presumption that such people are serving their own interests whatever they might say about the common good. And underpinning all this is the profound privatisation of people's focus and concern – the concentration on the fortunes and well-being of the family above any wider concern – which has been manifested by a reluctance to carry the burden of resistance so that others might reap the reward.

As I write this I am reminded of an experience several years ago, in September 2004. With a friend we were driving from East Jerusalem to Ramallah when we got caught in a chaotic traffic jam as we approached the Qalandia checkpoint. It was a Hobbesian nightmare of a war of all against all, as drivers inched and fought their way towards the checkpoint. My friend who was driving turned to me at one point and remarked with such great sadness, 'You see what they have turned us into … fighting against each other in this manner!' This epitomised for

me the collapse of that spirit of social solidarity that the two of us had known during the years of the first Intifada. To explain this we need to look at some of the structural changes that have taken place since the Oslo 'peace process' and how they have impacted on people's sense of identity and community.

1. Geographical fracturing of the West Bank

At the time of writing the West Bank has been divided into separate cantons as a consequence of the Oslo II Agreement dividing the territory into Areas A, B and C. This has meant that people cannot travel easily from one part of the West Bank to another without having to face the humiliation and the stress of negotiating road blocs and check-points.

2. The separation of the West Bank from the Gaza Strip

Israel controls access to the Gaza Strip and no-one, particularly residents from the Wes Bank can gain entry without specific permission from the Israeli authorities. This has resulted in a deepening gulf between the two populations.

3. The political fracture between Fatah and Hamas

The geographical or spatial separation between the Gaza Strip and he West Bank has been mirrored (and exacerbated) by the political rivalry between Fatah and Hamas, with each of them enjoying their own fiefdom within the territory that they control.[13]

4. Corruption and cronyism within the Palestinian Administration

Over the years since the Oslo Agreements public disillusionment with the corruption, cronyism and malpractice that permeated the PA has grown. There is a widespread belief that the members of the political class are concerned primarily with serving their own particularistic interests.

5. The deepening vertical divide between haves and have-nots

For many Palestinians the most obvious manifestation of the way in which the political class sought to prioritised the pursuit of their own interests at the cost of the common good was the spread of private mansions in and around Ramallah, the seat of the PA, and the conspicuous consumption patterns displayed there.

6. Vested interest of elites in the status quo

The perception of many has been that the dominant political class and associated business/entrepreneurial class have a vested interest in 'business as usual'. They might mouth their support for popular resistance and the struggle to bring the occupation to an end, but they remain very wary of any kind of popular movement that might threaten their life-style and their privilege. As one activist explained in conversation:

> They came back here never having had experience of occupation, and they created a bubble for themselves in Ramallah where they still don't feel the occupation. Our sense is that they are nurturing different priorities of consumerism, cars etc. – not liberation. We also know about the corruption and the internal conflicts. They are frightened of popular resistance – they want to co-opt us and our methods, turn us into projects of NGOs.

7. Economic impoverishment

The economic impoverishment of large numbers of Palestinians denied the opportunity of working in Israel and with restricted access to other sources of employment and income stands in marked contrast to the privileged minority who have prospered under the 'post-Oslo occupation'. At the same time this has required significant numbers to prioritise the satisfaction of the basic needs of their family above the participation in a collective struggle to end the occupation. After all, In a situation where few substantial gains have been achieved by popular resistance, despite the costs of detention and fines borne by activists, it is not surprising that those living on the bread-line became reluctant to add to their burdens by participating in protest actions and thereby risking fines, imprisonment and physical injury for no apparent purpose.

8. The 'ngo-isation' of community-based and civil society organisations

Following the Oslo Accords there was a massive influx of international aid agencies into the occupied Palestinian territories who sought out local partners for their programmes. As a consequence organisations and institutions that had once been vehicles for politicisation and mobilisation were transformed into professional deliverers of development aid, with a consequent haemorrhaging of their links with their original grassroots base. This development was one of the causes of the erosion of the spirit of 'voluntarism' and 'social service' in Palestinian society. As Challand noted:

> … the creation of many new professional NGOs, as a result of the large amounts of money made available by donors, has contributed to the loss of the voluntary spirit that was so characteristic of the mass-movement organizations that arose around the late 1970's. Many NGOs are now guided much more by market principles than by voluntary participation in their activities.[14]

These are some of the factors that help explain the erosion of social solidarity that is a necessary precondition for any sustained civilian-based resistance movement with a resilient organisational structure. They are summarised in table 2.

On the basis of this analysis it would seem clear that Palestinian unarmed popular resistance on its own does not have the leverage power to cause Israel to consider withdrawing from the occupation of Palestinian territory. However, there has been a significant development over the years since the first Intifada which has affected the potential for Palestinian popular resistance to bring about change – the growth of international networks of solidarity.

Table 2

	1st intifada at its height	**Post-2nd intifada period**
Social solidarity & mass mobilisation	i) Mass mobilisation. ii) Mobilisation facilitated by rich network of CBOs and CSOs.	i) Pockets of resistance. ii) NGO-isation of CBOs and CSOs, loss of 'volunteerism'.
	i) Unusual degree of social solidarity. ii) Divisions subsumed beneath shared sense of identity as Palestinians in struggle against occupation.	i) Socio- economic and spatial fragmentation (vertical & horizontal fractures). ii) Significant sections of society with vested interest in status quo.
Organisational resilience	Coherent & coordinated leadership through UNC.	Fractured leadership: between Fatah & Hamas.
	Coordination with PLO leadership outside.	PA ambivalent towards popular resistance.
	Organisational resilience at grassroots through popular committee structures.	Fractured coordination networks reflecting political fractures.

The growing significance of international networks of solidarity

Reference has been made to the increased involvement of international solidarity activists in the more recent waves of popular resistance compared with the first Intifada, when often the most obvious international presence was the number of journalists and media personnel covering the Uprising. The significance of the international activists as a protective shield on the ground and as longer-term accompaniers has also been identified. But perhaps more important than their protective function has been the role of international activists as advocates for the Palestinian cause. There can be little doubt that the lived experience of international solidarity activists in Palestine strengthens their capacity for advocacy amongst their own networks in their home countries. This has been a significant factor in the expansion over recent years of a global grassroots movement of solidarity urging an end to the Israeli occupation.[15] The growth of the transnational campaign for boycott, divestment and sanctions (BDS) targeted at Israel and initiated by Palestinian civil society organisations in 2005 is perhaps the most obvious illustration of this phenomenon.

However, the international network of advocates for the Palestinian cause rely in turn on the popular resistance of the Palestinians (and their Israeli partners) to feed into their campaigns. That is, whilst Palestinian popular resistance might be relatively weak in relation to its direct impact on Israeli decision-makers and publics, their presentation of themselves as brave people struggling for their basic rights by unarmed means against an illegitimate and brutal occupation can resonate strongly through international networks of sympathisers. They, in their turn, can use the examples and the stories of resistance to shame the Israeli occupation regime in the eyes of wider constituencies around the world. In their turn such people - links in the great chain of nonviolence - can exercise pressure on their own politicians and policy-makers to take action.

Social movement analysts have likened this type of process to that of a boomerang insofar as local movements that want to increase the pressure on their targets can 'throw a boomerang' out to external actors and networks, in the expectation that the boomerang will return to smite their opponents in the form of international pressure and sanctions. As my dear friend Howard Clark once wrote, 'In its flight the boomerang might pass through NGOs and activist constituencies, media, government departments and intergovernmental institutions before returning to make a difference at the point from where it was thrown.'[16]

Combatting despair

The challenge for Palestinians is to refuse to relinquish their resistance to occupation and to hold on to their hopes for a future when their basic human rights will be achieved. However, for such hopes to be other than a pipe-dream changes are required. It is vital that ways are found to make the occupation so burdensome to the Israelis – policy-makers, politicians and publics – that the status quo is deemed to be unsustainable. For this to happen the violence on which the occupation depends must become increasingly visible to concerned people around the world such that they start to exert sufficient pressure on policy-makers to start to exercise effective international pressure on Israel. Central to such a process would be a sustained and vibrant Palestinian unarmed resistance movement, which in turn requires that all the political factions within Palestine agree to use their cadres and organisational resources to mobilise wide swathes of the Palestinian population to actively challenge the occupation through various forms of popular resistance as part of a two-pronged approach – international diplomacy and grassroots popular resistance.

---

[1] This draws on work previously published in A. Rigby, *Palestinian resistance and nonviolence,* East Jerusalem: PASSIA, 2010.

[2] A similar pattern had already been imposed in the Gaza Strip, with Jewish settlements divided into three blocs covering about one third of the territory, with the remaining two thirds cut into cantons for the 1.1 million Palestinians.

[3] The organisational infrastructure of popular committees that had directed and guided the first Intifada had been superseded by the agencies of the PA.

[4] It has been estimated that between September 1993 and October 2000 there were about 500 people-to-people projects involving over 100 organisations and a total budget of $20-30 million. S. Herzon & A Hai, 'What do people mean when they say people-to-people?', *Palestine-Israel Journal*, v.12-13, no. 4, 2005-6. Accessible at *http://www.pij.org/details.php?id=395* (January 30, 2014)

[5] S. Roy, *Failing peace: Gaza and the Palestinian-Israeli conflict*, London: Pluto Press , 2007, p. 245.

[6] Quoted in L. Bucaille, *Growing up Palestinian: Israeli occupation and the Intifada generation*, Princeton: Princeton University Press, 2004, p. 125.

[7] See K. Kern, *As resident aliens: Christian Peacemaker Teams in the West Bank*, 1995-2005, Eugene, OR: Cascade Books, 2010.

[8] https://www.eappi.org/en/about (Accessed January 27 2015)

[9] Operation Cast Lead (December 2008), Operation Pillar of Defence (November 2012), and Operation Protective Edge (July 2014).

[10] For an overview of some of the maritime-based initiatives, see A. Rigby, 'Sea-dogs for peace: An exploration of nonviolent maritime interventions for peace and justice', *Peace and Change*, v. 39, n. 2, April 2014, pp. 242 - 269.

[11] For full text see http://tinyurl.com/oad2wvm (Accessed January 27 2015).

[12] J. Semelin, *Unarmed against Hitler: Civilian resistance in Europe, 1939 - 1943*, Westport, CT: Praeger, 1993, p. 3.

[13] It should also be noted that different attempts to coordinate popular unarmed resistance have been undermined by political rivalries. At one point in 2014 there were four different 'coordinating committees' for popular resistance in the West Bank.

[14] B. Challand, 'Looking beyond the pale: International donors and civil society promotion in Palestine', *Palestine-Israel Journal*, v. 12, n. 1, 2005.

[15] One small example – since the start of the Ecumenical Accompaniment Programme in Palestine and Israel over 1500 volunteers have spent periods of three months living and working alongside Palestinians in the 'front-line' of Israeli oppression. As part of their commitment as volunteers they are expected to devote time on their return to addressing public meetings and other gatherings in their home communities.

[16] See H. Clark, *People power: Unarmed resistance and global solidarity*, London: Pluto Press, 2009, p. 15.

OTHER RELEVANT BOOKS FROM IRENE PUBLISHING:

Whistleblowing: A Practical Guide
by Brian Martin

Humorous Political Stunts : Nonviolent Public Challenges to Power
by Majken Jul Sørensen

Backfire Manual
by Brian Martin

Tackling Trident
Edited by Stellan Vinthagen, Justin Kenrick and Kelvin Mason

Repertoire of Responses: Beyond Repression and Support in Reactions to Nonviolent Campaigns
by Majken Jul Sørensen

And we are publishing the **Journal of Resistance Studies** www.resistance-journal.org

www.ingramcontent.com/pod-product-compliance
Lightning Source LLC
Chambersburg PA
CBHW071832270326
41929CB00013B/1972

* 9 7 8 9 1 8 8 0 6 1 0 5 8 *